a gift from

Grace Christian Church
50 Barnes Street
Winnipeg
MB R3T 4Z7

Pastor Alan Redmond

40 Days of Discipleship
A Self-Paced Doctrinal Instruction Plan
Volume 1

Edited by Michael D. Morrison

Published by Grace Communion International

3120 Whitehall Park Dr.

Charlotte, NC 28273

www.gci.org

First edition

Copyright © 2016 Grace Communion International

Minor edits, 2018

All rights reserved.

ISBN 10: 978-1534964815

ISBN 13: 1534964819

Contents

Introduction

A self-paced doctrinal instruction plan

We recommend that church leaders pursue formal education that gives both breadth and depth.[1] However, formal education is not practical for everyone. We recommend here a plan by which a person might use free resources from the GCI website to guide them in their education.

There are two important components of this list: 1) prioritization and 2) breadth.

1) Prioritization: Our website has more than a thousand articles, and it can be difficult to know where to start. Of these articles, which are the most important? We try to provide some guidance on that by putting them into three groups. This book is the first of three groups. These are not necessarily levels of difficulty (most of our articles are from publications aimed at a lay audience), but this organization provides some guidance about how to spread the reading out.

   Since most of the articles on our website were previously published in our denominational magazines, you may have read these articles before. Nevertheless, do not assume that you know what is in them! Almost all our website articles have been edited to remove phrasings we now realize to be erroneous, and in some cases, to add insights we've had more recently. (Some of the articles were originally published 20 years ago, and some have been extensively revised to bring them up to date with our current theological understanding.)

2) Breadth: Do not study only the topics that already interest you. You (and the members of your church) need exposure to other important topics. Try to read all articles in group 1, in all subject areas, before you proceed to group 2. We have attempted to give breadth in each sequence, with about the same amount of reading in each area. We have grouped the articles into 2000-3000 words for each day. If you read about 15 minutes per day, you'll be done in 40 days. Some people might want to go faster, others slower. Since you set your own pace, you will need some self-discipline to continue the journey.

---

[1] Ambassador College of Christian Ministry provides instruction at an undergraduate level; Grace Communion Seminary provides accredited instruction at a graduate level (although people without a bachelor's degree may be admitted – see the *GCS Academic Catalog* for details). Both ACCM and GCS charge tuition.

Why Bother With Theology?

Many people find theology to be complicated, confusing and even irrelevant. They wonder why they should bother with it at all. "Surely," they exclaim, "the Bible isn't that difficult! Why read the works of head-in-the-clouds theologians with their long sentences and fancy terms?"

Sadly, it is common to ridicule things we don't understand. But doing so is a formula for continuing in ignorance and possibly falling into heresy.

I acknowledge that some academic theologians are hard to understand. In fact, it is unusual to find a genuine scholar who is also a gifted communicator. People in academic circles often deal in lofty ideas, and speak and write mainly with their peer group in mind. They leave it to others to bring those ideas down to earth. The situation is not unlike the difference between the practices of science and technology. The experimental scientist in his laboratory discovers a new process or material, and leaves it mostly to others to harness the idea into something practical for the ordinary person.

Theology has been called "faith seeking understanding," and we should not despise it. As Christians we trust God, but God has made us to want to understand the one we trust and why we trust him. Our God apparently wants us to grow in our knowledge and trust in him, having our minds more and more transformed. But knowledge about God is not something that we humans can just come up with on our own by thinking it out. The only way we can know anything true about God is to listen to what he tells us about himself.

God has chosen to preserve the revelation of himself to us in the Bible, a collection of inspired writings compiled over many centuries under the supervision of the Holy Spirit. However, even the most diligent study of the Bible does not automatically convey to us a right or full understanding of who God is. Most heresies come from wrong understandings of who God is, often promoted by one or a few individuals who fail to grasp how God has revealed himself in the Bible and ultimately in Jesus Christ, and who have given little or no attention to the biblically based teaching of the church down through the ages.

What then do we need? First, we need the Holy Spirit to enable our minds to understand what God reveals in the Bible about himself and give us the humility to receive it. The Bible and the work of the Spirit together are sufficient to bring the humble reader (or hearer) with a mustard seed's worth of faith to an initial trust that repents of unbelief and acknowledges that Jesus is Lord and that he alone brings us God's gracious salvation. Second, growth in our knowledge of who God is calls for a comprehensive grasp of the whole of Scripture with Jesus Christ standing at the center of it all. No one can do that for themselves in even a lifetime. We need the wisdom of others. Third, we may misunderstand some or much of what we read in the Bible due to assumptions we bring with us into our study of the Bible. We need help to remove these obstacles to spiritual growth. Fourth, we will not instantly know how best to communicate our understanding to those around us. Some are specifically called to help sort all these things out. And this is where theology comes in.

The word *theology* comes from a combination of two Greek words, *theos*, meaning God, and *logia*, meaning knowledge or study — *study of God*. Theologians are those members of the body of Christ who are called to synthesize and sum up the biblical witness to the nature, character, mind, purposes and will of God. In doing this they survey the results of others in the history of the church who attempted to do the same. They also analyze our contemporary context to discern the best words, concepts, stories, analogies or illustrations that most faithfully convey the truth and reality of who God is. The result is theology. While not all theologies are equally faithful, the church is wise to make use of those results that do help it keep its proclamation of the Gospel resting on the firm foundation of God's own revelation of himself in Jesus Christ according to Scripture.

The church as a whole has an ongoing responsibility to examine its beliefs and practices critically, in the light of God's revelation. Theology, therefore, represents the Christian community's continuous quest for faithful doctrine as it humbly seeks God's wisdom and follows the Holy Spirit's lead into all truth. The church ought to make use of those members of the Body who are specially called to help it do just that. Until Christ returns in glory, the church cannot assume that it has reached its goal. That is why theology should be a never-ending process of critical self-examination. Theology can thus serve the church by combating heresies, or false teachings, and helping us find the most faithful ways we can speak the truth in love today in our current context.

My point is that theology — good theology based in a profound respect for the biblical revelation and a sound understanding of its intent, background, context and comprehensive meaning for today — is a vital ingredient to a growing Christian faith. The 21st century is posing unprecedented challenges that are not addressed directly in the inspired Scriptures. Times change, but "Jesus Christ is the same yesterday and today and forever" (Hebrews 13:8). At the Last Supper, Jesus told his disciples, "I have much more to say to you, more than you can now bear. But when he, the Spirit of truth, comes, he will guide you into all the truth. He will not speak on his own; he will speak only what he hears, and he will tell you what is yet to come. He will glorify me because it is from me that he will receive what he will make known to you. All that belongs to the Father is mine. That is why I said the Spirit will receive from me what he will make known to you" (John 16:12-15).

So let's not despise the understanding that comes from good theology, even though it sometimes comes wrapped in difficult language. As the "resident theologian" to the people you serve, strive to understand it and then serve it up to your people in a way they can also understand.

Joseph Tkach

Strong Theology vs. Weak Theology

One of the best definitions of theology is the one ascribed to Anselm of Canterbury (1033-1109), who called it "faith seeking understanding." The converse of this — "understanding seeking faith" is known as apologetics. Pursued properly, both disciplines can lead us to dig deeper and deeper, coming to appreciate more and more the simple,

yet profound statement that "God is love."

But just digging deeper does not guarantee that our conclusions will be good. We need to dig in the right direction. As we are reminded in 2 Timothy 3:7, it is possible to be "always learning but never able to come to a knowledge of the truth."

Theology has been described as being weak or

strong based upon its arrangement and understanding of various doctrines and/or a specific understanding of the attributes of God. When I first heard this, I thought of it in terms of correct and incorrect doctrine. However, the more I think about it, I realize it is more than that. Doctrine is only one ingredient of authentic Christianity. It is important, to be sure — it is essential that the church teach right doctrines. However, doctrine is not all that we must include in our worship of our Creator, Savior and Sanctifier. Doctrine does not save us. No matter how much we know, Paul reminds us that it doesn't do us any good if we don't have love (1 Corinthians 13:2).

I first realized a distinction when, with Dr. Mike Feazell, I attended a large evangelistic conference several years ago. In one session it was noted that there was a tremendous evangelical opportunity to be had in the wake of the attacks we now refer to as *9/11*. The presenter suggested that we celebrate the firefighters, police officers and other heroes who saved the lives of others, sometimes losing their own in the process — a powerful analogy of what Jesus has done for humanity.

During a later talk, a serious contradiction became apparent, although most seemed oblivious to it. Another presenter, in order to motivate us to evangelism, emphasized that unless someone had made a conscious decision for Christ, God would send them to hell forever. Mike, putting the two presentations together, elbowed me and said, "So, how do you celebrate a hero who gave his life to save others but who had been sent to hell forever because he had not accepted Jesus as his Savior? What is there to celebrate about a hero who is now burning in hell?"

"That's the problem with a weak theology," I replied.

Our theology defines how we understand God's nature, character, heart, mind and purpose. It fills out for us how God views us and others and what kind of relationship he wants with us.

Strong theology has a clear and coherent grasp of who God is and what God wants for us: God is

exactly like Jesus all the way down. He is the fullness of deity, bearing the stamp of the character of God. He is the visible image of the Father and the Spirit. In Jesus, what you see is what you get.

Weak theology, however, presents God in bits and pieces, often leaving us with a view of a God who is of two minds, or who has two different wills, or even two different sides to his character. Sometimes Jesus is presented as one "side" of God who wants to save us by grace and the Father as the other "side" who wants to condemn us under the Law. This God has two wills, two purposes, two attitudes towards his creation and so has two kinds of relationship with us. This God is *for* some of us, but *against* others.

Weak theology leaves us with two minds toward others. We're supposed to love others, even our enemies, and present the Gospel to them and encourage them to surrender their lives to Christ who died for them. But if we believe God only loves some and will only call some to himself but is against others and just as happy to send them to hell, it's hard, if not impossible, to have the same attitude and hope for all. We are left with the sense that we're not being totally truthful when we present the Gospel as if it's for everyone.

While it is true that some may somehow reject the Gospel of grace no matter what we or even God does for them, perhaps for all eternity, God's revelation to us of his single mind, will and purpose for all is made clear by Paul:

> For God was pleased to have all his fullness dwell in him, and through him to reconcile to himself all things, whether things on earth or things in heaven, by making peace through his blood, shed on the cross. (Colossians 1:19-20)

Weak theology undermines this vital truth leaving us with the impression that Jesus only shows us one side of God, not the fullness of God and that God is interested only in reconciling some things, not everything. Weak theology can lead to an "us vs. them" elitist mentality where, after the evangelistic meeting is over, we minister to those on the "inside" far differently from those on the "outside."

While weak theology leads us down this dark and conflicted path of exclusivism, strong theology affirms that God loves everyone profoundly and places love above all other gifts from God:

> If I have the gift of prophecy and can fathom all mysteries and all knowledge, and if I have a faith that can move mountains, but do not have love, I am nothing. (1 Corinthians 13:2)

While weak theology leads us to erect barriers between people, strong theology understands that God, who is no respecter of persons, *"wants all men to be saved and to come to a knowledge of the truth"* (1 Timothy 2:3-4). Led by this truth, we are encouraged to join with Paul in tearing down barriers that divide people from God and one another:

> Though I am free and belong to no one, I have made myself a slave to everyone, to win as many as possible. To the Jews I became like a Jew, to win the Jews. To those under the law I became like one under the law (though I myself am not under the law), so as to win those under the law. To those not having the law I became like one not having the law (though I am not free from God's law but am under Christ's law), so as to win those not having the law. To the weak I became weak, to win the weak. I have become all things to all people so that by all possible means I

might save some. I do all this for the sake of the gospel, that I may share in its blessings. (1 Corinthians 9:19-23)

While weak theology includes or excludes people from coming under God's reconciling work based upon their performance, strong theology recognizes that Jesus' atonement has pre-qualified everyone for salvation. Note Paul's words to the Christians in Colossae:

> Giving thanks to the Father, who has qualified us to share in the inheritance of the saints in light. For He rescued us from the domain of darkness, and transferred us to the kingdom of his beloved Son, in whom we have redemption, the forgiveness of sins. (Colossians 1:12-14, NAS)

To sum it up, whereas weak theology begins with bad news, hoping to convince (or frighten) people into hoping there is good news, strong theology starts and ends with the Good News for all:

> God so loved the world that he gave his one and only Son, that whoever believes in him shall not perish but have eternal life. For God did not send his Son into the world to condemn the world, but to save the world through him. (John 3:16-17)

Strong theology is profoundly and consistently evangelical, while weak theology is a pretender. As we dig deep into theology, it is important that we dig in the proper direction.

Joseph Tkach

Theology Affects the Way We Live

Ideas have consequences. The way we think about God affects the way we respond to him. In other words, our *theology* affects the way we live. Some people think theology is dull and irrelevant, but perhaps that is because they think God is dull and irrelevant; they would rather get on with their life without dragging God into the discussion.

Everyone has a theology, whether they know it or not. They have some concepts of what God is like. They may think he is distant and unconcerned, or harsh and angry, or even that he doesn't exist. All these ideas affect the way we live. If we believe God is distant and unconcerned, we may be angry because we are suffering from the sins of other people, and God doesn't seem to care. We may need help, but God doesn't seem to answer our cries for help. Or we may indulge our baser desires or take advantage of others, thinking God doesn't care one way or the other.

Living by faith

My point is that the way we *think* about God affects the way we live. This is implied throughout the Bible, which repeatedly connects doctrine and behavior.

God cares about us, Jesus said, so we should not worry. Worry comes from a lack of faith that God is good, powerful, merciful and will not cease to love us and do what is good and right for us. If we don't trust God, we may think that he doesn't care, or that he doesn't have the power to take care of us, or that he is harsh, unforgiving or unpredictable toward us.

But when we trust in God, we do not worry even when bad things happen to us. We are confident that God is faithful to us, suffering with us, holding us, and that he will use even our pain to make us stronger and bless us. He works all things,

even bad things, for good. He brings light out of our darkness. Our belief about God's power and love affects the way we react to the situations we face.

Paul uses a similar kind of logic in his letters. He explains that we are saved by grace through the work of Jesus our Savior, and then he writes, Therefore we should be living sacrifices, set apart to do God's will, putting off the old self and putting on the new, acting like the new people that God has declared us to be. In other words, our theology should affect the way we live.

The book of Hebrews uses similar logic at several points. After explaining a concept, the author says, Therefore let us hold fast to our confession, therefore let us approach the throne with confidence, therefore let us encourage one another. He sees a close connection between ideas and consequences, between doctrine and practice.

Need for an accurate view

Since the way we think about God affects the way we live, we want to have the best understanding of God we can. If we think of God as a powerful physical being, then we will tend to focus on physical life, on external behavior, on a future based on physical things. We will tend to neglect spiritual qualities such as grace and love, and give little attention to concepts such as the heavenly and the eternal.

On the other hand, when we think of God as eternal and triune, then we see a God for whom relationships are essential to his very being, for whom love is essential, a God who gives himself when he gives his Son, a God who lives within us when his Spirit is in us.

The triune God is a God who has fellowship with us directly, not through intermediaries. In contrast, a God who is only Father, but not Father, Son and Holy Spirit, unity in trinity, is more likely to be seen as aloof, distant, legalistic, stressing law rather than mercy. This is how many people view God. If such a God sent his Son to die on the cross, he would be sending another being to appease his angry judgment, rather than (as actually happened) taking humanity into his own being and redeeming it through union with his own sinless Son, with whom he, with the Spirit, is One God.

It is not my intention here to discuss the nature of God in detail. We have already published quite a bit of material on that, and it is on our website (https://www.gci.org/article-categories/god-jesus-holy-spirit/). We have an article summarizing it and listing a number of books for further study ("Introduction to God"). It highlights two qualities of God — his greatness and his goodness. God always uses his enormous power to further his covenant of love and grace toward his people. He is gentle, loving, slow to anger and full of mercy.

Trust

Here, I want to focus on the "so what" question. How is this relevant to us? What difference does it make in our lives? How do we respond to a God who is simultaneously powerful and gentle? When we realize that God has all power to do anything he wants, and that he always uses it for the good of humanity, then we can have absolute confidence that we are in good hands.

He has both the ability and the covenanted purpose to work all things, including all our rebellion, hatred and betrayal against him and one another, toward our redemption and glorification in Jesus Christ. He is completely trustworthy — worthy of our trust.

When we are in the midst of trials, sickness, suffering and even dying, we can be confident that God is still with us, that he cares for us, that he has everything under control. It may not look like it, and we certainly do not feel in control, but we can be confident that God isn't caught off guard. He can and does redeem any situation, any misfortune, for our good.

We need never doubt God's love for us. "God demonstrates his own love for us in this: While we were still sinners, Christ died for us" (Romans 5:8). "This is how we know what love is: Jesus Christ laid down his life for us" (1 John 3:16). The God who did not spare his own Son can be counted on to give us through his Son everything we need for eternal happiness.

God did not send somebody else: The Son of God, essential to the Godhead, became human so that he could die for us and rise again for us (Hebrews 2:14). We were redeemed not by the blood of animals, not by the blood of a very good man, but by the blood of the God who became human.

We can be confident that he loves us. Every time we take communion, we are reminded of the extent of his love for us — both of his death wherein we are forgiven, and his resurrection wherein we are given union with him and presented holy and blameless to God. He has earned our trust.

"God is faithful," Paul tells us. "He will not let you be tempted beyond what you can bear" (1 Corinthians 10:13). "The Lord is faithful, and he will strengthen and protect you from the evil one" (2 Thessalonians 3:3). Even "if we are faithless, he will remain faithful" (2 Timothy 2:13). He is not going to change his mind about wanting us, about calling us, about being merciful to us. "Let us hold unswervingly to the hope we profess, for he who promised is faithful" (Hebrews 10:23).

He has made a commitment to us, a covenant with us, to redeem us, to give us eternal life, to love us forever. He will not be without us. He is trustworthy, but how do we respond to him? Do we worry? Do we struggle to be worthy of his love? Or do we trust him?

We need never doubt God's power, either. This is shown in the resurrection of Jesus from death. This is the God who has power over death itself, power over all the beings he created, power over all other powers (Colossians 2:15). He triumphed over all things through the cross, and this is demonstrated through his resurrection. Death could not hold him, for he is the author of life (Acts 3:15).

The same power that raised Jesus from death will also give immortal life to us (Romans 8:11). We can trust that he has the power, and the desire, to fulfill all his promises toward us. We can trust him with everything — and that's a good thing, since it is foolish to trust in anything else.

Of ourselves, we will fail. Left to itself, even the sun will fail. Our only hope is in a God who has power greater than the sun, greater than the universe, more faithful than time and space, full of love and faithfulness toward us. We have that sure hope in Jesus our Savior.

Joseph Tkach

Theology in Perspective

Sound theology is important, for unsound theology distorts our understanding of God and our relationship with him. However, it's important to note that we are not saved by theology. And so we need to keep it in perspective.

Christianity has never been theologically or doctrinally perfect. We often hear preachers urging people to "get back to the faith once delivered." By this, they usually mean the early apostolic church, which they assume had a complete and uncorrupted understanding of the faith. However, those apostolic churches were not perfect. They too had to grow in their understanding of what was "sound doctrine."

In fact, much of the New Testament is polemic — meaning that it was written to correct various wrong ideas. In Corinth, for example, some Christians were tolerating incest, suing one another in court, offending each other by their understanding of what they were permitted to eat and becoming drunk at the Lord's Supper. Some thought they should be celibate even if married and others thought they should divorce their non-Christian spouses. Paul had to correct these ideas, and history tells us that he had only limited success. But the people were Christian despite their lack of complete doctrinal understanding.

There are many examples of the disciples failing to understand Jesus, even when he was with them.

For example, after Jesus miraculously fed thousands of people, he and the disciples got into a boat and Jesus warned them, "Watch out for the yeast of the Pharisees and that of Herod" (Mark 8:14). The disciples concluded that Jesus meant that, since they hadn't brought any bread they would have to buy some on the other shore; moreover, they shouldn't buy any bread from a Pharisee or Herodian because something was incorrect about the yeast they used.

Why didn't they just ask Jesus what he meant? Perhaps because they were afraid of looking foolish (that happens today, too!). Jesus chided them for not understanding something that they should have been able to grasp. The disciples didn't need to worry about bread or yeast. Jesus had just shown that he could make bread miraculously. They could remember facts (verses 19-20), but they didn't always draw right conclusions from those facts. The miracle of the loaves was not just a way to save money — it also had a much deeper meaning that the disciples had failed to understand (Mark 6:52). It figuratively symbolized the fact that Jesus is our source of life.

I am encouraged to know that Jesus' own disciples frequently didn't fully comprehend what he was doing. Nevertheless, Jesus still co-ministered with them, as he does with us. It demonstrates that any "success" we have is the result of God's guidance, not our human ability to figure things out exactly.

Those first disciples were thrown into confusion by Jesus' death even though he explained it to them more than once. But, like us, they could only absorb so much at a time. If you follow the flow of the conversation at the Last Supper, you can see by their questions and frequent attempts to change the subject that the disciples did not understand what was going on. So Jesus told them, "I have much more to say to you, more than you can now bear. But when he, the Spirit of truth, comes, he will guide you into all the truth" (John 16:12-13).

After his resurrection, Jesus appeared to his disciples and instructed them for 40 days, after which he ascended to heaven. While with them, he said, "Do not leave Jerusalem, but wait for the gift my Father promised, which you have heard me speak about. For John baptized with water, but in a few days you will be baptized with the Holy Spirit" (Acts 1:4-5).

Jesus' words were fulfilled on the day of Pentecost. And as we read in Acts 2:4, the disciples were filled with the Holy Spirit and through his guidance, what had been isolated facts and an unsound theology came together in a new and exciting way. The apostle Peter preached his first public sermon, urging his audience to repent, to believe in Jesus Christ as their Messiah and to receive the gift of the Holy Spirit (verse 38). On that day, some 3,000 people were baptized and became the people of God (verse 41). The church had been born.

From that day on, the Holy Spirit has continued to guide the church into "all the truth," helping her to "prove the world to be in the wrong about sin and righteousness and judgment" (John 16:9). The New Testament writers, led by the Holy Spirit, showed those first Christians how to live godly lives in the turbulent environment of the first century. He is doing the same with us today, as we struggle to "get it right" while facing the complex and controversial challenges of our time.

We need to remember then, that the ultimate object of our faith and the only object of our worship is our Triune God, not our theological statements. We want to tune our theological understandings as best we can to do nothing less and nothing more than serve our faith in and worship of the Father, Son and Spirit. By the Spirit and the Word our theological understandings can be continually sanctified. This coming week on Pentecost Sunday we celebrate the descent of the Spirit that gave birth to the church. While not yet perfect, the children of God have been given the good and perfect gift of the Spirit, who will in the end enable all of us to share in Jesus' own perfection!

Joseph Tkach

Theology: What Difference Does It Make?

"Don't talk to me about theology. Just teach me the Bible."

To the average Christian, theology might sound like something hopelessly complicated, frustratingly confusing and thoroughly irrelevant. Anybody can read the Bible. So why do we need head-in-the-clouds theologians with their long sentences and fancy terms?

Faith seeking understanding

Theology has been called "faith seeking understanding." In other words, as Christians we trust God, but God has made us to want to understand who we are trusting and why we trust him. That's where theology comes in. The word *theology* comes from a combination of two Greek words, *theos*, meaning God, and *logia*, meaning knowledge or study—study of God.

When properly used, theology can serve the church by combating heresies, or false teachings. That is because most heresies come from wrong understandings of who God is, understandings that don't square with the way God has revealed himself in the Bible. The church's proclamation of the gospel needs to rest on the firm foundation of God's own revelation of himself.

Revelation

Knowledge about God is not something that we humans can just come up with on our own by thinking it out. The only way we can know anything true about God is to listen to what God tells us about himself. The main way God has chosen to reveal himself to us is through the Bible, a collection of inspired writings compiled over many centuries under the supervision of the Holy Spirit. But even diligent study of the Bible, in itself, cannot convey to us right understanding of who God is.

We need more than mere study—we need the Holy Spirit to enable our minds to understand what God reveals in the Bible about himself. The bottom line is that true knowledge of God comes only from God, not merely by human study, reasoning or experience.

The church has an ongoing responsibility to critically examine its beliefs and practices in the light of God's revelation. Theology is the Christian community's continuous quest for truth as it humbly seeks God's wisdom and follows the Holy Spirit's lead into all truth. Until Christ returns in glory, the church cannot assume that it has reached its goal.

That is why theology should never become a mere restatement of the church's creeds and doctrines, but should rather be a never-ending process of critical self-examination. It is only as we stand in the divine Light of God's mystery that we find true knowledge of God.

Paul called that divine mystery "Christ in you, the hope of glory" (Colossians 1:27), the mystery that through Christ it pleased God "to reconcile to himself all things, whether things on earth or things in heaven, by making peace through his blood, shed on the cross" (verse 20).

The Christian church's proclamation and practice are always in need of examination and fine-tuning, sometimes even major reform, as it continues to grow in the grace and knowledge of the Lord Jesus Christ.

Dynamic theology

The word *dynamic* is a good word to describe this constant effort of the Christian church to look at itself and the world in the light of God's self-revelation and then to let the Holy Spirit conform it accordingly to be a people who reflect and proclaim God as God truly is. We see this *dynamic* quality in theology throughout church history. The apostles reinterpreted the Scriptures when they proclaimed Jesus as the Messiah.

God's new act of self-revelation in Jesus Christ brought new light to the Bible, light that the Holy Spirit opened the eyes of the apostles to see. In the fourth century, Athanasius, bishop of Alexandria, used descriptive words in the creeds that were not in the Bible in order to help Gentiles understand the meaning of the biblical revelation of God. In the 16th century, John Calvin and Martin Luther contended for the renewal of the church in light of the demand of the biblical truth that salvation comes only by grace through faith in Jesus Christ.

In the 1800s, John McLeod Campbell attempted to broaden the Church of Scotland's narrow view on the nature of Jesus' atonement for humanity, and was thrown out for his efforts.

In modern times, no one has been more effective in calling the church to a dynamic theology rooted in active faith than Karl Barth, who "gave the Bible back to Europe" after liberal Protestant theology had nearly swallowed up the church by embracing Enlightenment humanism and the "natural theology" of the German church, and ended up supporting Hitler.

Listening to God

Whenever the church fails to hear the voice of God and instead gives in to its own assumptions and presuppositions, it becomes weak and ineffective. It loses relevance in the eyes of those it is trying to reach with the gospel message. The same is true of any part of the Body of Christ when it wraps itself up in its own preconceived ideas and traditions. It becomes bogged down, stuck or *static,* the opposite of *dynamic,* and loses its effectiveness in spreading the gospel.

When that happens, the church begins to fragment or break up, Christians become alienated from one another, and Jesus' command that we love one another fades into the background. Then,

gospel proclamation becomes merely a set of words, a proposition that people unthinkingly agree with. The power behind it to offer healing to sinful minds loses its force. Relationships become external, only surface contacts that miss the deep union and communion with Jesus and one another where genuine healing, peace and joy become real possibilities. Static religion is a barrier that can prevent believers from becoming the real people God intends them to be in Jesus Christ.

'Double predestination'

The doctrine of election or double predestination has long been a distinctive, or identifying doctrine, in the Reformed theological tradition (the tradition that stands in the shadow of John Calvin). This doctrine has frequently been misunderstood, distorted and the cause of endless controversy and distress. Calvin himself struggled with this issue, and his teaching on it has been interpreted by many as saying, "From eternity God has decreed some to salvation and others to damnation."

This latter interpretation of the doctrine of election is usually described as hyper-Calvinistic. It fosters a fatalistic view of God as an arbitrary tyrant and an enemy of human freedom. Such an approach to the doctrine makes it anything but good news as proclaimed in God's self-revelation in Jesus Christ. The biblical witness describes the electing grace of God as astonishing, but not dreadful! God, who loves in freedom, offers his grace freely to all who will receive it.

Karl Barth

In correcting this hyper-Calvinism, the preeminent Reformed theologian of the modern church, Karl Barth, recast the Reformed doctrine of election by centering rejection and election in Jesus Christ. He carefully laid out the full biblical doctrine of election in Volume II of his *Church Dogmatics* in a way that is consistent with the whole of God's revelation.

Barth forcefully demonstrated that within a Trinitarian context, the doctrine of election has one central purpose: it declares that God's works in creation, reconciliation and redemption are fully realized in the free grace of God made known in Jesus Christ.

It affirms that the triune God who lives eternally in loving communion graciously wills to include others in that communion. The Creator Redeemer deeply desires a relationship with his creation. And relationships by nature are dynamic, not static. Relationships penetrate the abyss of our existence and turn it into real life.

In the *Dogmatics*, where Barth rethought the doctrine of election in a Trinitarian, Creator Redeemer context, he called it "the sum of the gospel." In Christ God elected *all* of humanity in covenant partnership to share in his life of communion by freely and graciously choosing to be God for humanity.

Jesus Christ is both the Elected and the Rejected for our sakes, and individual election and rejection can be understood as real only in him. In other words, the Son of God is the Elect on our behalf. As the universal elected man, his vicarious, or substitutionary, election is at the same time both to the condemnation of death (the cross) in our place and to eternal life (the resurrection) in our place. This atoning and reconciling work of Jesus Christ in the incarnation was complete in the redeeming of fallen humanity.

We must therefore say yes to God's yes for us in Christ Jesus and embrace and begin to live in the joy and light of what he has already secured for us—union, communion and participation with him in a new creation.

New creation

In his important contribution to the doctrine of election, Barth writes: "For in God's union with this one man, Jesus Christ, he has shown his love to all and his solidarity with all. In this One he has taken upon himself the sin and guilt of all, and therefore rescued them all by higher right from the judgment which they had rightly incurred, so that he is really the true consolation of all." Everything changed at the cross. The entire creation, whether it knows it or not, has been, is being and will be redeemed, transformed and made new in Jesus Christ. We are becoming a new creation in him.

Thomas F. Torrance, premier student and interpreter of Karl Barth, served as editor when Barth's *Church Dogmatics* was translated into English. Torrance believed that Volume II was some of the finest theology ever written. He agreed with Barth that all of humanity has been redeemed and elected in Christ. Professor Torrance, in his book *The Mediation of Christ,* lays out the biblical revelation that Jesus is not only our atoning reconciler through his vicarious life, death and resurrection, but serves as our perfect response to God's grace.

Jesus took our fallenness and judgment on himself, assuming sin, death and evil in order to redeem the creation at all levels and transform everything that stood against us into a new creation. We have been freed from our depraved and rebellious natures for an internal relationship with the One who both justifies and sanctifies us.

Torrance goes on to explain that "the unassumed is the unhealed." What Christ has not taken upon himself has not been saved. Jesus took our alienated mind on himself, becoming what we are in order to reconcile us to God. He thereby cleansed, healed and sanctified sinful humanity in the depths of its being in his vicarious loving act of incarnation for us.

Instead of sinning like all other human beings, he condemned sin in our flesh by living a life of perfect holiness within our flesh, and through his obedient Sonship he transformed our hostile and disobedient humanity into a true, loving relationship with the Father.

In the Son, the triune God took up our human nature into his Being, and he thereby transformed our nature. He redeemed us and reconciled us. By making our sinful nature his own and healing it, Jesus Christ became the Mediator between God and a fallen humanity.

Our election in the one man Jesus Christ fulfills God's purpose for the creation and defines God as the God who loves in freedom. Torrance explains that "all of grace" does not mean "nothing of humanity," but *all of grace means all of humanity.* That is, we cannot hold onto even one percent of ourselves.

By grace through faith, we participate in God's love for the creation in a relational way that was not possible before. That means that we love others as God loves us because by grace Jesus Christ is in us and we are in him. This can happen only within the miracle of a new creation. God's revelation to humanity comes from the Father through the Son in the Spirit, and a redeemed humanity now responds by faith in the Spirit through the Son to the Father.

We have been called to holiness in Christ. We enjoy freedom in him from the sin, death, evil, misery and judgment that stood against us. We reciprocate, or return, God's love for us through thanksgiving, worship and service in the community of faith. In all his healing and saving relations with us, Jesus Christ is engaged in personalizing and humanizing us—that is, in making us real people in him. In all our relations with him, he makes us more truly and fully human in our personal response of faith. This takes place in us through the creative power of the Holy Spirit as he unites us to the perfect humanity of the Lord Jesus Christ.

All of grace really does mean all of humanity. The grace of Jesus Christ who was crucified and resurrected for us does not depreciate the humanity he came to save. God's unconditional grace brings into the light all that we are and do. *Even in our repenting and believing we cannot rely on our own response, but in faith we rely only on the response that Christ has offered to the Father in our place and on our behalf!* In his humanity, Jesus, the new Adam, became our vicarious response to God in all things, including faith, conversion, worship, celebration of the sacraments and evangelism.

Ignored

Unfortunately, Karl Barth has generally been ignored or misinterpreted by American evangelicalism, and Thomas Torrance is often presented as too hard to understand. But to fail to appreciate the dynamic nature of theology displayed in Barth's reworking of the doctrine of election causes many evangelicals and Reformed Christians alike to remain caught in the behavioralism trap, struggling to understand where God draws the line between human behavior and salvation.

The great Reformation principle of ongoing reformation should free us from old worldviews and behavior-based theologies that inhibit growth, promote stagnation and prevent ecumenical cooperation within the Body of Christ. Yet today doesn't the church often find itself robbed of the joy of grace as it shadowboxes with all its various forms of legalism? For this reason the church is not uncommonly characterized as a bastion of judgmentalism and exclusivism rather than as a testament to grace.

We all have a theology—a way that we think about and understand God—whether we know it or not. And our theology affects how we think about and understand God's grace and salvation.

If our theology is dynamic and relational, we will be open to hear God's ever-present word of salvation, which he freely gives us by his grace though Jesus Christ alone. On the other hand, if our theology is static, we will shrivel into a religion of legalism, judgmentalism and spiritual stagnation.

Instead of knowing Jesus as he is in a way that seasons all our relationships with mercy, patience, kindness and peace, we will know judgment, exclusivity and condemnation of those who fail to meet our carefully defined standards of godliness.

New creation in freedom

Theology does make a difference. How we understand God affects the way we understand salvation and how we live the Christian life. God is not the prisoner of some static, humanly reasoned idea about what he must and should be.

Humans are not capable of reasoning out who God is and what he must be like. God tells us who he is and what he is like, and he is free to be exactly how he chooses to be, and he has revealed himself in Jesus Christ as being the God who loves us, is for us and who chooses to make humanity's cause— including your cause and my cause—his own.

In Jesus Christ, we are freed from our sinful minds, from our boasting and despair, and graciously renewed to experience God's *shalom* peace in his loving faith community.

Recommended reading

Michael Jinkins, *Invitation to Theology*

Thomas Torrance, *The Mediation of Christ*

Karl Barth, *Dogmatics in Outline*

James Torrance, *Worship, Community and the Triune God of Grace*

Thomas Torrance, *The Christian Doctrine of God, One Being Three Persons*

Thomas Torrance, *The Trinitarian Faith*

Ray Anderson, *Theology, Death and Dying*

C. Baxter Kruger, *The Great Dance*

Robert Farrar Capon, *Parables of Judgment*

Donald Bloesch, The Christian Foundations series (seven books)

Terry Akers and J. Michael Feazell

Answering Questions About Our Theology

The label, "Incarnational Trinitarian Theology" should be understood as descriptive rather than as prescriptive of our doctrinal statements. Our critics sometimes want to regard this label as being prescriptive, but that is not the case. Also, it is not the case that our theological perspective is Barthian or Torrancian or whatever. At best, such labels are only partially descriptive. Any similarities are definitely not prescriptive.

What is prescriptive for us is the reality of who God has revealed himself to be in Jesus Christ according to Scripture. Our theological formulations are derived from and meant to point faithfully to that reality, which exceeds what can be contained in our theological understandings.

When we quote any theologians positively, or even when the historic Christian Creeds are referenced, they are being used as illustrative of our own theological position, not as a source or final norm of it. They show that other members of the Body of Christ at other times and places grasped the biblical revelation in a way similar to how we have come to understand it. It demonstrates that we are concerned not to be esoteric or eccentric in our teaching and that we believe that other members of the Body of Christ can be helpful to us, saying at least as well, if not better than ourselves, how we also understand God's Word.

Given what is noted above, the label "Incarnational Trinitarian Theology" is not meant to indicate that we hold to a special (or superior) form of Christianity. It indicates that the center and heart of our faith and worship corresponds to the center and heart of the revelation of the gospel itself—just as the whole of the historic, orthodox church has done down to this day. This label reminds us of the core reality of who God is and has revealed himself to be in and through Jesus Christ, according to Scripture. It also represents the nature of our renewal and restoration to true Christian faith which we have come to share with all the Christian church. If others have been pushed or pulled off-center we hold out to them these foundational truths, from which flow all other Christian doctrines, that they too might be renewed and restored in their faith and worship.

Some critics say we don't make distinctions between believers and non-believers because of the way we speak of God having a oneness of mind, heart and purpose towards all. Though it is not true, they say we affirm universalism. Why do they come to this wrong conclusion? Because they make inferences from our statements about God to our views about his creatures. "If God regards all the same way, then all must regard God the same way." But we do not come to our understanding through logical inferences made from one single affirmation about God. That would amount to both bad theology and bad logic. No simple logical inference is ever *necessarily* true, most especially when moving from God to talking about creatures.

It seems that their critique of our theology is a mirror-image of how their own theology works. Seeing a difference between believers and non-believers, they then imagine a corresponding difference in God. Again, they make a simple logical inference, but this time in the reverse direction: from a description of the differences among humans to what God then must prescribe for that difference among human persons. We do not reason in that way. Doing so would, in our view, constitute mythological projection, which is idolatry. Doing so would mean concluding something about what God prescribes from a description of individual creatures or a class of them. John Calvin made this mistake in reasoning in his polemical writings about predestination. Thankfully, he did not succumb to that faulty reasoning in most of his writings on theology (in his *Institutes* and elsewhere).

Typically, the difference between our viewpoint and that of those who criticize it, is that we start with God's self-revelation as the criterion for our statements about God ("only God reveals God"). We do not start with our own, or even the Bible's descriptions of how humans respond differently to God and then logically infer something about who God is and what God wants for his human creatures. Descriptions of human creatures and even of their potential eternal ends, either by means of our own observations or by reference to isolated biblical passages interpreted out of context, do not prescribe for us a definitive revelation of who God is and what he wants. Jesus Christ alone, according to divine revelation (Scripture) alone, prescribes for us our trust in and understanding of God's heart, mind, purposes and character. On that basis, we conclude that God is a redeemer who has a redemptive nature and heart, does not want any to perish, but wants all to repent and receive eternal life. That is, God is identical in character to Jesus Christ who is Lord and Savior.

Some condemn or dismiss our theological stance, typically labeling it as Universalism, Aminianism or Calvinism. However, we have no need to be aligned with a particular school of theology. Though each school has understandings deserving our consideration, each also has significant weaknesses that obscure important, even crucial elements of the biblical revelation. Those weaknesses have not only been identified by us but have been brought to light in the ongoing discussions and debates down through the history of the church. While we share faith in the same realities as do all Christians, our theological understanding and articulation does not fall neatly along the lines drawn in the typical Universalist-Arminian-Calvinist debates.

Those who are satisfied with one of these primary theological traditions and insist that these are the only options, likely will not be able to properly hear our theological testimony or grasp its source and norm the way we do. Their critiques likely will assume that we have bought into the one or two theological options which they have rejected — ones that might include being "incarnational" or "Trinitarian." While we can offer our reasons for why and how we understand the Christian faith the way we do, we don't have to accept any labels nor defend the one we use. We are simply trying to be as faithful as we can in understanding and explaining the biblical revelation. We hold out our convictions first to our own members for their benefit and second to others in trust — hoping that others might be renewed and blessed as we have been as the Lord has corrected and restored us.

It was not a particular theology or theologian who transformed Grace Communion International. Rather it was Jesus Christ speaking through his Holy Word who revealed to us the true nature and character of God. Grace Communion International was grasped by the gospel of Jesus Christ, as our Lord placed himself at the center of our worship and faith. If the label, "Incarnational Trinitarian Theology" properly *describes* that transformation, then we accept it. However, we have no need to defend a label, for it *prescribes* nothing.

Gary Deddo

Beware Theological Labels

As our understanding of who God is (our theology) developed, we began using the term "Incarnational Trinitarian Theology" to identify and summarize our understanding. However, use of that term (and others like it) might cause some problems. First, it might confuse some who are not trained in theology. Second, it might be used by some who do not understand it well. Third, it might be overused and thus become cliché. Last, it might become a denominational label that could lead some to misunderstand what we actually believe and teach.

It is helpful to think of Incarnational Trinitarian Theology as describing *how* we believe rather than merely *what* we believe. Of course, all orthodox Christians accept the doctrines of the Trinity and the Incarnation. But for us, they are more than two doctrines on a list of many — they are the heart of our faith and worship.

Why is that not so for all Christians? Partly because these truths are deep mysteries beyond our fallen human imaginations. Also, these doctrines at times are poorly taught or not taught at all. Thus it is easy to drift away from this defining core and begin to emphasize secondary (even tertiary) issues. When that happens, everything becomes distorted.

This was seen clearly in the way Jewish religious leaders resisted Jesus. Those leaders looked to Scripture as a source of truth, but disagreed about its details. Nevertheless, they were united against Jesus. And so Jesus told them, "You have your heads in your Bibles constantly because you think you'll find eternal life there. But you miss the forest for the trees. These Scriptures are all about me! And here I am, standing right before you, and you aren't willing to receive from me the life you

say you want" (John 5:39-40, *The Message*). Note how Jesus placed himself at the center as the living key to interpreting Scripture. He himself was the source of their life. If they would accept and understand that, they would put their petty disagreements in perspective and come together in acknowledging him as Messiah. Instead, they saw him as a heretic and plotted to kill him.

As Christians today, we can make the same mistake. Even if we accept Jesus as Lord and Savior, we can sideline the fundamental truths that define who he is. The result is the fragmenting of Christianity into competing "schools" of thought with their own doctrinal distinctives. This leads to a "my Christianity is better than yours" mentality. Though the distinctives may be accurate, they emphasize peripheral matters. The result is that the reality of who God is and what he has done for us in his Son is diminished, if not lost. Division within the Body of Christ results.

That is why we need to avoid using labels in ways that imply that we are setting ourselves apart as having a Christianity that is superior in comparison to others. The reason we use a label at all is to remind ourselves (and others, if they are interested) of the focus of our renewal — the reality of what is revealed in Jesus Christ according to Scripture.

Also, in using a label, we must avoid implying that we are slavishly beholden to some systematic theology or to certain theologians — even those identified as Incarnational or Trinitarian. There are approximately 50 systematic theologies extant today. However, there is no single concrete, uniform, particular school of thought called "Trinitarian Theology."

For example, Barth, the Torrance brothers and

Thomas Oden drew on many other theologians throughout the ages and on the writings of the early church councils. Rather than seeking to establish a new theology, they were seeking to serve Jesus Christ and to build up his church through their teaching and research. Yes, they might be described as "Incarnational Trinitarian Theologians" because they saw that these particular elements of Christian faith were being neglected or even forgotten. They discerned that the church needed to get back on the central path of Christian faith.

When we use the term, "Incarnational Trinitarian Theology," we are referring to the fact that Jesus is the lens through which we read and interpret the Bible and how we have come to know God. Consequently, any other doctrinal points should flow from and fit with the Trinitarian nature of God. Our role in the administration of our denomination is to pass on the best formulations of Christian theology that we can find—especially on the major issues. We are blessed to incorporate the ideas of the great theologians of Christian history and we can learn from those alive today. But we do not do so slavishly and biblical revelation always has the controlling authority.

So, when we say that we believe and teach Incarnational Trinitarian Theology, we are describing how we understand and believe Scripture based upon Jesus as the centerpiece of God's plan for humanity. It is perhaps more like your computer's operating system rather than one of many programs you load into it. Individual doctrines are like the software applications, which must be able to interface with the operating system if they are to work properly. But it's the operating system that orders, organizes, prioritizes and produces all other useful results.

The focus of our renewal as a denomination has been the very theological issues that have been central to historical, orthodox Christianity. We are not the only branch of the church that neglected or even misunderstood the doctrines of the Trinity and the Incarnation. We hope that we might benefit other parts of the Body of Christ with what we have learned. It is in this spirit that we offer our *Speaking of Life* and *You're Included* videos. If you have not viewed them, I urge you to do so. They will help us all keep the Center in the center, feed our continuing renewal in the Spirit, and enable us to join with all Christians down through the ages in giving witness to the glory of our triune God: Father, Son and Holy Spirit.

Joseph Tkach

An Introduction to God

As Christians, our most basic religious belief is that God exists. By the capitalized word "God," we mean the God described in the Bible: a good and powerful spirit being who created all things, who cares about us, who cares about what we do, who is involved in our lives, and who offers us an eternity with his goodness.

Humans cannot understand God in totality, but we can have a solid beginning point for understanding who God is and what God is doing in our lives. Let's focus on the qualities of God that a new believer, for example, might find most helpful.

His existence

Many people, even long-time believers, want proof of God's existence. But there is no way to "prove" God's existence so that everyone is convinced. It is probably better to talk in terms of evidence, rather than proof. The evidence gives us confidence that God exists and is the sort of being the Bible describes.

God "has not left himself without testimony," Paul told the pagans in Lystra (Acts 14:17). Well then, what is the evidence?

Creation. Psalm 19:1 tells us, "The heavens declare the glory of God." Romans 1:20 tells us, "Since the creation of the world God's invisible qualities—his eternal power and divine nature—have been clearly seen, being understood from what has been made." Creation itself tells us something about God.

It is reasonable for us to believe that something caused the earth, sun and stars to be the way they are. Scientists say the universe began with a big bang, and it is reasonable for us to believe that something caused the bang. That something, we believe, was God.

Design. Creation shows signs of order, of laws of physics. If various properties of matter were different, then earth would not exist, or humans could not exist. If the size or orbit of earth were different, then conditions on this planet would not permit human life. Some people believe that this is a cosmic accident; others believe that the more reasonable explanation is that the solar system was designed by an intelligent Creator.

Life. Life is based on incredibly complex chemicals and reactions. Some people believe that life had an intelligent cause; others believe that it happened by chance. Some have faith that scientists will eventually demonstrate a non-god origin for life. But for many people, the existence of life is evidence of a Creator God.[1]

Humans. Humans are self-conscious creatures who explore the universe, who ponder the meaning of life, who seek significance. Physical hunger suggests the existence of food; thirst suggests that there is something that can quench our thirst. Does our intellectual yearning for purpose suggest that there is in fact a meaning to be found? Many people claim to have found meaning in relationship with God.

Morality. Is right and wrong a matter of opinion, of majority rule, or is there some supra-human authority that defines good and evil? If there is no God, then humans have no basis for proclaiming anything evil, no reason to condemn racism, genocide, torture or any atrocity. The existence of evil is therefore evidence that God exists. If there is no God, then there is no basis for authority except power. It is reasonable to believe in God.

Greatness

What sort of being is God? Bigger than we can imagine! If he created the universe, then he is bigger than the universe—and not limited by time, space or energy, for he existed before time, space, matter and energy did.

2 Timothy 1:9 mentions something God did "before the beginning of time." Time had a beginning, and God existed before that. He has a timeless existence that cannot be measured by years. He is eternal, of infinite age—and infinity plus several billion is still infinity. Mathematics is too limited to describe God's existence.

Since God created matter, he existed before matter, and he is not made of matter. He is spirit—but he is not "made of spirit." God is not made at all; he simply *is,* and he exists as spirit. He defines existence—he defines spirit and he defines matter.

God existed before matter did, and the dimensions and properties of matter do not apply to him. He cannot be measured in miles or kilowatts. Solomon acknowledged that even the highest heavens could not contain God (1 Kings 8:27). He fills heaven and earth (Jeremiah 23:23); he is everywhere, or omnipresent. There is no place in the universe where he does not exist.

How powerful is God? If God can cause a big bang, design solar systems, create the codes in DNA and manage all these levels of power, then he must be unlimited in power, or omnipotent. "With God all things are possible," Luke 1:37 tells us. God can do whatever he wants to do.

God's creativity demonstrates an intelligence greater than we can understand. He controls the universe, constantly causing its continued existence (Hebrews 1:3). That means he must know what is happening throughout the universe; he is unlimited in intelligence—he is omniscient. He knows whatever he wants to know.

God defines right and wrong, and is by definition right, and he has the power to always do right. "God cannot be tempted with evil" (James 1:13). He is consistently and perfectly righteous (Psalm 11:7). His standards are right, his decisions are right, and he judges the world in righteousness, for he is, in his very nature, good and right.

From our *Statement of Beliefs:*

God, by the testimony of Scripture, is one divine Being in three eternal, co-essential, yet distinct Persons—Father, Son, and Holy Spirit. The One God may be known only in the Three and the Three may be known only as the one true God, good, omnipotent, omniscient and omnipresent, and immutable in his covenant love for humanity. He is Creator of heaven and earth, Sustainer of the universe, and Author of human salvation. Though transcendent, God freely and in divine love, grace and goodness involves himself with humanity directly and personally in Jesus Christ, that humanity, by the Spirit, might share in his eternal life as his children.

(Mark 12:29; Matthew 28:19; John 14:9; 1 John 4:8; Romans 5:8; Titus 2:11; Hebrews 1:2-3; 1 Peter 1:2; Galatians 3:26)

In all these ways, God is so different from us that we have special words that we use only for God. Only God is omniscient, omnipresent, omnipotent, eternal. We are matter; he is spirit. We are mortal; he is eternal. This great difference between us and God, this otherness, is called his *transcendence.* It means that he transcends us, is beyond us, is not like us.

Other ancient cultures believed in gods and goddesses who fought with one another, who acted selfishly, who could not be trusted. But the Bible reveals a God who is in complete control, who needs nothing from anyone, who therefore acts only to help others. He is perfectly consistent, his behavior is perfectly righteous and completely trustworthy. This is what the Bible means when it says that God is holy: morally perfect.

This makes life much simpler. People do not have to try to please 10 or 20 different gods; there is only one. The Creator of all is still the Ruler of all, and he will be the Judge of all. Our past, our present and our future are all determined by the one God, the All-knowing, All-powerful, Eternal One.

Goodness

If all we knew about God is that he had incredible power over us, we might obey him out of fear, with bent knee and resentful heart. But God has revealed to us another aspect of his nature: The incredibly great God is also incredibly gentle and good.

One of Jesus' disciples asked him, "Show us the Father" (John 14:8). He wanted to know what God was like. He knew the stories of the burning bush, the pillar of cloud and fire at Mt. Sinai, the science-fiction throne that Ezekiel saw, and the whisper that Elijah heard (Exodus 3:4; 13:21; 1 Kings 19:12; Ezekiel 1). God can appear in all these ways, but what is he really like? Where should we look?

Jesus said, "Anyone who has seen me has seen the Father" (John 14:9). If we want to know what God is like, we need to look at Jesus. We can learn a bit about God from nature; we can learn more from the way he revealed himself in the Old Testament, but we learn the most from the way that God has revealed himself in Jesus.

Jesus shows us what God is like. Jesus is called Immanuel, which means God with us (Matthew 1:23). He lived without sin, without selfishness. He is a person of compassion. He has feelings of love and joy, disappointment and anger. He cares about individuals. He calls for righteousness, and he forgives sin. He served others, even in his suffering and death.

God is like that. He described himself to Moses in this way: "The Lord, the compassionate and gracious God, slow to anger, abounding in love and faithfulness, maintaining love to thousands, and forgiving wickedness, rebellion and sin. Yet he does not leave the guilty unpunished" (Exodus 34:6-7).

The God who is above all creation is also free to work within creation. This is his *immanence*, his being with us. Although God is larger than the universe and everywhere within the universe, he is with believers in a way that he is not with unbelievers. The enormous God is always close to us. He is near and far at the same time (Jeremiah 23:23).

In Jesus, he entered human history, space and time. He worked in human flesh, showing us what life ought to be like in the flesh, and showing us that God wants more for our lives than merely flesh. We are offered eternal life, life beyond the physical limits we know now. We are offered spirit life, as the Spirit of God himself comes into us to live in us and make us children of God (Romans 8:11; 1 John 3:2). God continues to be with us, working in space and time to help us.

The great and powerful God is also the gentle and gracious God; the perfectly righteous Judge is also the merciful and patient Savior. The God who is angry at sin also provides salvation from sin. He is mighty in mercy, great in gentleness. This is what we should expect from a Being who can create the codes in DNA, the colors in a rainbow and the delicate wisps on dandelion seeds. We would not exist at all, except for the fact that God is kind and gentle.

God describes his relationship to us in several ways. In one analogy, he is a father and we are his children. In another, he is the husband and all believers together are his wife. Or he is a king and we are his subjects. He is a shepherd and we are the sheep. In all these analogies, God puts himself in a situation of responsibility to protect and provide for the needs of his people.

God knows how tiny we are. He knows he could obliterate us in the snap of a finger, in the slightest miscalculation of cosmic forces. But in Jesus, God shows us how much he loves us, how much he cares for us. Jesus was humble, willing even to suffer, if it would help us. He knows the kind of pain we go through, because he has felt it. He knows the pain that evil causes, and he accepted it, showing us that we can trust God.

God has plans for us, for he has made us to be like himself (Genesis 1:27). He invites us to become more like himself — in goodness, not in power. In Jesus, God gives us an example to follow: an example of humility, selfless service, love and compassion, faith and hope.

"God is love," John wrote (1 John 4:8). God demonstrated his love by sending Jesus to die for our sins, so barriers between us and God might be removed, so we might live with him in eternal joy. God's love is not wishful thinking — it is action that helps us in our deepest need.

We learn more about God from the crucifixion of Jesus than from his resurrection. Jesus shows us that God is willing to suffer pain, even pain caused by the people who are being helped. His love invites us, encourages us. He does not force us to do his will.

God's love for us, shown most clearly in Jesus Christ, is our example: "This is love: not that we loved God, but that he loved us and sent his Son as an atoning sacrifice for our sins. Dear friends, since God so loved us, we also ought to love one another" (1 John 4:10-11). If we live in love, then eternal life will be a joy not only for us but also for those who live with us.

If we follow Jesus in life, we will also follow him in death, and then in resurrection. The same God who raised Jesus from the dead will also raise us and give us life eternal (Romans 8:11). But if we do not learn to love, then we will not enjoy everlasting life. So God is teaching us to love, at a pace we can follow, giving us a perfect example, changing our hearts by the Holy Spirit working in us. The Power who controls the nuclear furnaces of the sun is working gently in our hearts, wooing us, winning our affection, winning our allegiance.

God gives us meaning in life, direction for life, hope for life eternal. We can trust him, even when we suffer for doing good. God's goodness is backed up by his power; his love is guided by his wisdom. He has all the forces of the universe at his control, and he is using them for our benefit. "In all things God works for the good of those who love him" (Romans 8:28).

Response

How do we respond to a God so great and gentle, so terrible and tender? We respond with worship: awe at his glory, praise for his works, reverence for his holiness, respect for his power, repentance in the presence of his perfection, obedience in the authority found in his truth and wisdom.

To his mercy, we respond with thankfulness; to his grace, with our allegiance; to his goodness, with our love. We admire him, we adore him, we give ourselves to him even as we wish we had more to give. Just as he has shown his love for us, we let him change us so that we love the people around us. We use all that we have, all that we are, all that he gives us, to serve others, just as Jesus did.

This is the God we pray to, knowing that he hears every word, that he knows every thought, that he knows what we need, that he cares about our feelings, that he wants to live with us forever, that he has the power to fulfill every request, and that he has the wisdom not to.

God has proven himself faithful in Jesus Christ. God exists to serve, not to be selfish. His power is always used in love. Our God is supreme in power, and supreme in love. We can trust him in absolutely everything.

Things to think about

- Do the evils in this world weaken our faith in God, or strengthen it?
- If God is good, why did he make humans fallible, able to choose wrong?
- What does God say about the way we use his creation?
- How can God be distant to one person, but near to another?
- Can we trust a God who has all power but isn't always good? Can we trust one who is always good but is limited in power?
- In what way is God like Jesus, and in what way is he different?
- Does God's mercy cause you to admire him, or to ignore him?

Five facts to know about God

1. God is omnipotent — able to do whatever he wants. He is the Almighty.
2. God is immortal, constant in character, always reliable. He is the Eternal.
3. God is omnipresent — unlimited by space and time. He is always near.
4. God is omniscient — knowing all truth and all wisdom. Father knows best.

5. God is consistently good, never selfish. God is love.

For further reading

Now that you've had an introduction to God, wouldn't you like to know him better? We get to know God in several ways: through nature, through our experience with the Holy Spirit, through the Scriptures, through spiritual disciplines and through the words of other believers.

To learn more about God, read the Bible, especially the New Testament. For evidence of God's existence, we recommend the following (easiest listed first):

Paul Little, *Know Why You Believe*

C.S. Lewis, *Mere Christianity*

Lee Strobel, *The Case for a Creator*

Peter Kreeft and Ronald Tacelli, *Handbook of Christian Apologetics*

C. Stephen Evans, *Why Believe?*

James Sire, *Why Should Anyone Believe Anything at All?*

William Lane Craig, *Reasonable Faith*

C.S. Lewis, *Miracles*

Alister McGrath, *Intellectuals Don't Need God and Other Modern Myths*

For discussions of the attributes of God:

Max Anders, *God: Knowing Our Creator*

Paul Little, *Know What You Believe,* chapter 2

Gilbert Bilezekian, *Christianity 101,* chapter 2

J.I. Packer, *Knowing God*

Millard Erickson, *Introducing Christian Doctrine,* chapters 8-15

Donald G. Bloesch, *God the Almighty*

[1]Footnote on creation: The diversity of life is a separate question. Some people accept the theory of evolution; others reject it. Some people believe that the evolutionary theory describes the way that God produced biological diversity; others believe that God worked in some other way. The controversies about evolution are too complex to be resolved here; we simply note that they do not affect the question of how life originated in the first place. We should also note that few people have studied evolution well enough to make their own conclusions about it; for the most part, they simply accept the word of "experts." That includes opponents as well as supporters of evolution. For further study, see *Three Views on Creation and Evolution,* edited by J.P. Moreland and John Mark Reynolds (Zondervan, 1999).

Michael Morrison

The God Revealed in Jesus Christ

An Introduction to Trinitarian Faith

If we want the most accurate picture of God, we don't need to look any further than Jesus Christ. In Jesus we meet God as God really is. "Anyone who has seen me," Jesus said, "has seen the Father" (John 14:9).

Jesus Christ is the perfect revelation of the Father. "No one has ever seen God, but the one and only Son [Jesus]…has made him known" (John 1:18).

Through Jesus' words and actions, we hear and see what matters most to every human being — that God the Father loves us unconditionally. "God so loved the world that he gave his one and only Son, that whoever believes in him shall not perish but have eternal life" (John 3:16).

Even at our worst, God loves us. John continues, "For God did not send his Son into the world to condemn the world, but in order that the world might be saved through him" (verse 17). The Father sent Jesus out of his love and his commitment to save us.

Trinitarian-based

Jesus is God's self-revelation to the world. God has broken through to us by sending his eternal Son into our world. Jesus upheld the understanding that the one God is the object of our love and worship (Mark 12:29-31).

Jesus emphasized that God (Father, Son and Holy Spirit) was reconciling humanity to himself. That is why he instructed his followers to welcome people into right relationship with God by baptizing them in the name of the Father, and of the Son and of the Holy Spirit (Matthew 28:19).

The God we worship through Jesus Christ is the Triune God. The doctrine of the Trinity is central to how we understand the Bible and all points of theology[2] that flow from it. That theology begins with an essential "who" question: "Who is the God made known in Jesus Christ, and who are we in relation to him?"

Trinitarian faith is based on a belief in the doctrine of the Trinity (the biblical teaching that there is one God, who is eternally Father, Son and Holy Spirit). Furthermore, it refers to a Christ-centered understanding of who God is.

Christ-centered

Christians recognize Jesus as the center of our faith and our devotion to God. Jesus reveals to us what God is like (John 6:37). "No one knows the Father except the Son and those to whom the Son chooses to reveal him" (Matthew 11:27). Trinitarian theology is first and foremost Christ-centered. Jesus is the unique Word of God to humanity and the unique Word of humanity to God (John 1:1-14). As the representative of all humanity, Jesus responded to God perfectly.

Jesus indicates that he is the key to understanding Scripture. He said to a group of Jewish religious leaders in John 5:39-40: "You diligently study the Scriptures because you think that by them you possess eternal life. These are the Scriptures that testify about me, yet you refuse to come to me to have life." Jesus, who is the focus of Scripture, is our source of salvation.

---

[2] Theology explains, as faithfully as we can, the understanding we have of the truth and reality of God and our relationship to God.

So we seek to understand the Bible through the lens of who Jesus is. He is the basis and logic of our faith—for he alone is the self-revelation of God.

Relationship-focused

Trinitarian faith is relational. Even before creation, there was a relationship of love between the Father and the Son (John 17:24). And in Jesus, that relationship of love is extended to all humanity. Jesus Christ, the only Son of God, has become one with us in our humanity to represent us as his brothers and sisters in the very presence of the Father (see John 1:14; Ephesians 1:9-10, 20-23; Hebrews 2:11, 14).

Human beings have turned away from God and broken the bonds of communion with God. But because of Jesus, God has reconciled us and renewed our relationship with him!

Not only that, as we respond to his call to us to share in that restored relationship, he comes to live in us by the Holy Spirit (Romans 8:9-11). In Jesus and through the Holy Spirit, we become God's treasured children, adopted by grace (Romans 8:15-16).

This means that Christian life and faith are primarily about four kinds of personal relationship:

- the relationship of perfect love shared by the Father, the Son and the Holy Spirit from all eternity,
- the relationship of the eternal Son with humanity, established when the Son became human in the person of Jesus,
- the relationship of humanity with the Father through the Son and by the Spirit, and,
- the relationship of humans with one another, in the Spirit, as children of the Father.

Who is Jesus?

"Who are you, Lord?" was Paul's anguished question on the Damascus Road, where he was confronted by the resurrected Jesus (Acts 9:5). He spent the rest of his life answering this question and then sharing the answer with all who would listen. The answer, revealed to us in his writings and elsewhere in Scripture, is the heart of the gospel and the focus of Trinitarian theology.

The Son of God, who is united from eternity to the Father and the Spirit, is now also joined to humanity because of his incarnation—his becoming a real flesh-and-blood human being (John 1:14). We summarize this by saying that Jesus is both fully God and fully human. That fact will never change, because he remains, in his divine nature and his human nature, the one mediator between God and humanity for all time (1 Timothy 2:5). His Incarnation did not end with his death or with his ascension. It continues forever. He was resurrected bodily and he ascended bodily. He will return bodily, the same as he departed. So when we say Jesus Christ, we are referring to God, and we are also referring to humanity.

As the One who is uniquely God (Creator and Sustainer of all) and also fully human, Jesus is the unique meeting place of God and humanity. Through the life, death, resurrection and ascension of Jesus, God and humanity were reconciled and human nature was regenerated—made new (2 Corinthians 5:17-18). In Jesus Christ all humans are reconciled to God. As the Lord and Savior of all humanity he has opened up the way for all to enter into an eternal union and communion with God.

Incarnation for salvation

The miracle of the Incarnation is not something that happened "once upon a time," now long past and simply affecting one person, Jesus. What he accomplished changed human nature itself, changed history, changed how the entire cosmos is "wired"—it is a new creation (2 Corinthians 5:17). The spiritual reality is, for now, hidden in Christ, and we still experience the effects of evil that still occur in this world. The Incarnation of the eternal Son of God, entering time and space and taking on our human nature to change everything forever, reaching back through all human history, and reaching forward to encompass all time. He has now become our Lord and Savior, not as an external agent, but from the inside, in his humanity.

As Paul teaches, God was, in Christ, reconciling the world to himself (2 Corinthians 5:19). Paul speaks of this transformation in Romans 7:4, where he says that even while we are alive, we are already dead to the law by the body of Christ. Jesus' death in human flesh for us, though a historical event, is a present reality that applies to all humanity (past, present and future). "You died," Paul says to the Colossians, "and your life is now hidden with Christ in God" (Colossians 3:3). Even before we die physically, we are given new life—made alive with Jesus in his resurrection.

Christ's incarnation and atoning work accomplished the renewal of our human nature. In him, God has reconciled to himself every human being, even those who lived before Jesus came.

In Ephesians 2:5-6 we read that those who trust in Christ share in his life, death, resurrection and ascension. Here Paul asserts that just as we are dead already in Jesus' substitutionary death, we have also already been "made alive together with him" and we are "raised up together with him" and "seated together with him in the heavenly realms." All this comes from God's grace and is experienced through faith—the faith of Jesus that he shares with us by the Spirit.

Jesus, the second Adam

In Romans 5, Paul addresses believers, but he also explains what Christ accomplished on behalf of all humanity even before anyone came to faith in God through Christ. Jesus Christ died for people who were still:

- "powerless" and "ungodly" (verse 6).
- "sinners" (verse 8).
- "God's enemies" (verse 10).

God accomplished his great work for us out of his "love for us" even while "we were still sinners" (verse 8). The result was that even "while we were God's enemies, we were reconciled to him through the death of his Son" (verse 10).

Paul goes on to explain that what Jesus Christ accomplished as the second Adam counteracts what the first Adam did. Through Christ, as the new head of all humanity, "God's grace and the gift that came by the grace of that one man Jesus Christ abounded for the many" (verse 15). Paul continues:

- The gift "brought justification" rather than condemnation (verse 16).
- "Those who receive God's abundant provision of grace and of the gift of righteousness reign in life through the one man, Jesus Christ" (verse 17).
- "One righteous act resulted in justification and life for all people" (verse 18).
- "Through the obedience of the one man the many will be made righteous" (verse 19).
- "Grace increased all the more" so that "grace might reign through righteousness to bring eternal life through Jesus Christ our Lord" (verses 20-21).

God did all this for us before we were even born. The benefit of what Jesus did so long ago extends to the past, to the present and into the future. Paul says, "how much more, having been reconciled, shall we be saved through his life!" (verse 10). This shows that salvation is not a one-time event, but an enduring relationship that God has with all humanity—a relationship formed within the person of Jesus Christ, who has brought God and humanity together in peace.

Jesus has not simply done something for us, he has done something *with* us by including us in his life, death, resurrection and ascension. Paul explains this in Ephesians 2:4-6:

- When Jesus died, we, in our sinful human nature, died with him.
- When Jesus rose, we, in our reconciled human nature, rose with him.
- When Jesus ascended, we, in our redeemed human nature, ascended and became seated with him at the Father's side.

Everything God has done in Christ shows us the mind, heart and character of the Father, the Son and the Holy Spirit. God is on the side of his people and all his creation. God is for us, even before we respond to him (verse 5). He has provided reconciliation and eternal life in communion with himself for every human being.

For all humanity

As Jesus made his way into Jerusalem for his final Passover with his disciples, the crowds shouted: "Hosanna! Blessed is he who comes in the name of the Lord! Blessed is the king of Israel!" (John 12:13).

Shortly thereafter, he proclaimed his impending death to those who went up to the Temple to worship. Jesus called to the Father: "Father, glorify your name!" A voice then thundered to the crowd: "I have glorified it, and will glorify it again" (verse 29).

Jesus told them the voice was for their benefit and that God's judgment on evil had come so that the prince of this world would be driven out (verses 30-31). He also said, "And I, when I am lifted up from the earth, will draw all people to myself" (verse 32). Jesus conquered evil in order to attract all people to himself. The apostles believed that Jesus died to redeem us all:

- 2 Corinthians 5:14: "Christ's love compels us, because we are convinced that one died for all, and therefore all died."
- Colossians 1:19-20: "God was pleased to have all his fullness dwell in him, and through him to reconcile to himself all things, whether things on earth or things in heaven, by making peace through his blood, shed on the cross."
- 1 Timothy 2:3-6: "This is good, and pleases God our Savior, who wants all people to be saved and to come to a knowledge of the truth. For there is one God and one mediator between God and mankind, the man Christ Jesus, who gave himself as a ransom for all people."
- 1 Timothy 4:9-10: "This is a trustworthy saying that deserves full acceptance… we have put our hope in the living God, who is the Savior of all people, and especially of those who believe."
- Hebrews 2:9: "We do see Jesus, who…suffered death, so that by the grace of God he might taste death for everyone."
- 1 John 2:2: "[Jesus is] the atoning sacrifice for our sins, and not only for ours but also for the sins of the whole world."

These passages show that Jesus died for all humanity, that is, in their place and on their behalf. Jesus did for us, as one of us, what we could never do for ourselves. This is what is meant by the vicarious humanity of Jesus (the word *vicarious* refers to a representative substitute).

The God Revealed in Jesus Christ

An Introduction to Trinitarian Faith

Part 2

In our place and on our behalf

Throughout the book of Hebrews, Jesus is depicted as our great High Priest, representing all humanity, providing on our behalf a perfect response to God. He is presented as the one who stands among us, in the midst of the congregation, and who leads us in worship (Hebrews 2:12-13). He represents us as our older brother. He has become one of us, sharing our very nature, learning obedience, being tempted as we are, but overcoming that temptation perfectly (Hebrews 2:14-18; 4:15).

Theologian Thomas Torrance explained it this way:

> Jesus steps into the actual situation where we are summoned to have faith in God, to believe and trust in him, and he acts in our place and in our stead from within the depths of our unfaithfulness and provides us freely with a faithfulness in which we may share…. That is to say, if we think of belief, trust or faith as forms of human activity before God, then we must think of Jesus Christ as believing, trusting, or having faith in God the Father on our behalf and in our place. (*The Mediation of Christ*, p. 82)

Jesus is the one who, as we respond, perfects our faith and makes us holy (Hebrews 12:2;2:11; 10:10, 14). He acted as one of us "in our place" or "on our behalf" (Hebrews 2:9; 5:1;6:20; 7:25, 27; 9:7).

The response of faith

So how do we personally share in all that Christ has graciously done for us? How can we personally participate and be in communion with God who has, already, reconciled us to himself? We do so by trusting in him—by having faith that he, by grace, has accomplished for us all that is needed for our salvation. In short, we say we are saved by grace through faith (Ephesians 2:8).

Does this mean that we are saved by a faith that we work up? Does our salvation depend upon how great and sincere our repentance or our faith is? No, for salvation would then be dependent on something we do rather than dependent upon grace alone.

The good news is that our salvation does not depend on what we do—it does not depend on the strength of our faith or our repentance. It depends on the strength of our Savior, it depends on his faithfulness. He died for us. The gift has been given; our repentance and faith are simply responses to what God has given us. They are the way we accept and receive the free gift. Jesus has done everything necessary for our salvation from start to finish, so even our responses of repentance and faith are gifts of sharing in Jesus' perfect responses for us as our faithful mediator.

As Thomas Torrance explained, "if we want to think of faith as a human activity, then we must think of Jesus as having done that for us as well. Just as he died for us, he lived righteously for us." As our representative, he presents to God a perfect response on behalf of all humanity. We are saved by his obedience (Romans 5:19)—and that includes his faith. Our salvation rests on Jesus—the perfect foundation.

As our High Priest, Jesus takes our responses, perfects them and gives them to the Father, all in the Spirit. As our mediator (1 Timothy 2:5), he ministers both from God to us and represents us in our relationship to God. So we join him in his response.

The role of human choice

What God has done in Christ to reconcile us to himself calls for a response. We are urged to accept him, to welcome and receive him. We do so by trusting in him and what he has accomplished for us. The Holy Spirit enables us to freely welcome the truth and walk in it. But God does not force us to accept the truth of his love for us. A love that forced a responding love would not be loving. God's love then calls for our decision to freely receive and freely love God in return.

Our choice is to either affirm or deny the reality that God loves us and has made every provision for us to be his children. Denial of this truth has consequences, but it will not change the reality of what God has done for us in Christ and thus who we are in Christ. Human beings choose to accept who Christ is or attempt to live in denial of who he is.

Real freedom is found in God, as theologian Karl Barth reminds us:

> The real freedom of man is decided by the fact that God is his God. In freedom he can only choose to be the man of God, i.e., to be thankful to God. With any other choice he would simply be groping in the void, betraying and destroying his true humanity. Instead of choosing freedom, he would be choosing enslavement. (*Church Dogmatics* IV.1, p. 43)

So what is our place in all of this? We choose to accept Jesus and all he has to offer or to reject him. Through the Spirit, God the Father is calling all people to place their trust in Jesus with a thankful and hopeful heart, and to share with other believers in the Body of Christ, which is the church. As we celebrate together in communities of faith and worship, our lives are transformed.

Personal response

Jesus called people to repent and believe (Mark 1:15). The early church continued this message, calling people to repent and be baptized (Acts 2:38) and to be changed (3:19).

Our response is important. The apostle Paul writes in Romans 5:17 that "those who *receive* God's abundant provision of grace and of the free gift of righteousness [will] reign in life." Abundant and freely given grace calls for us to *receive* it in faith. In Romans 5 Paul weaves together 1) elements of the reality accomplished by Christ on behalf of all humanity and 2) our response and participation in that relationship and reality. We must take care not to confuse what is true in Jesus for all humanity with each person's response to that truth.

God's gift is offered to all in order to be received by all. It is received by having faith in what God in Christ through the Holy Spirit has done for us. It is by faith in the grace of God that we begin participating in the relationship Jesus has restored, and start receiving the benefits included in that relationship.

We do not "decide for Christ" in the sense that our personal decision causes our salvation. Rather, we accept what is ours already in Christ, placing our trust in Jesus, who has already perfectly trusted for us in our place. When we accept the grace of Jesus Christ, we begin to participate in God's love for us. We begin to live according to who we really are, as the new creation that God, prior to our ever believing, made us to be in Christ.

Some people find it helpful to explain this using the terms *objective* and *subjective.* An objective truth is a reality, whereas our understanding of and response to that reality is subjective. There is a universal, or objective, truth about all humanity in Jesus, based on the fact that he has joined himself to our human nature and turned it around. But there is also the personal, or subjective, experience of this truth that comes as we surrender to the promptings of the Holy Spirit and join with Jesus Christ.

These categories of objective (universal) and subjective (personal) truth are found in Scripture.

For one example, in 2 Corinthians, Paul starts with the objective nature of salvation: "All this is from God, who reconciled [past tense] us to himself through Christ and gave us the ministry of reconciliation: that God was reconciling the world to himself in Christ, not counting people's sins against them. And he has committed to us the message of reconciliation" (verses 18-19).

Here we find an objective truth that applies to all—God has already reconciled all to himself through Jesus, the incarnate Son of God. Paul then goes on in verses 20-21 to address the subjective truth: "We are therefore Christ's ambassadors, as though God were making his appeal through us. We implore you on Christ's behalf: Be reconciled to God."

How can all be "reconciled" already and yet some need to "be reconciled"? The answer is that both are true. All are already reconciled in Christ—this is the universal/objective truth—but yet not all embrace and therefore personally experience their reconciliation with God—that is the personal/subjective truth. God has a gracious attitude toward all people, but not everyone has responded to his grace. No one benefits even from a freely given gift if that gift is refused, especially the gift of coming under the grace of God in Jesus Christ in the power of the Spirit.

A second example of objective/subjective truth is found in the book of Hebrews where the author states in a straightforward manner, "For good news came to us just as to them, but the message they heard did not benefit them, because they were not united by faith with those who listened" (Hebrews 4:2) The benefits of a relational reality such as salvation can only be subjectively (personally) experienced when received by faith.

So while Christ is Lord and Savior of all, has died for all, and has reconciled all to God, not all will necessarily be saved. Not all will necessarily receive Christ who is their salvation. Not all will necessarily enter into their salvation, which is eternal union and communion with God as his beloved children. Some may somehow "deny the Savior who bought them" (2 Peter 2:1). While Scripture teaches the unlimited scope of Christ's atoning work, taking away the sins of the whole cosmos, it does not offer us a guarantee that all will necessarily receive the free gift of grace.

No explanation is given as to why or how this rejection of grace could happen. But rejection is presented as a real possibility, one that God has done everything needed to prevent. If there are those who reject Christ and their salvation, it will not be due to any lack or limit of God's grace. So we, sharing in the very heart of God, can also be those "not wanting any to perish, but all to come to repentance" (2 Peter 3:9).

What is our Christian mission?

Jesus' life and ministry provides the motivation for every aspect of our life, including our participation in mission and ministry with Jesus. The love of Christ compels us to take part in what Jesus is doing in the world through the Spirit. Out of love we declare the gospel and invite all people to receive and embrace it. In doing so, we hope what is true of them already in Christ will be experienced by them personally in faith. Like Jesus, we desire all to participate and receive all the benefits of Christ now. Then they, too, can join in Jesus' ongoing mission to draw others into a living relationship with their Lord and Savior. What greater joy and privilege could there be?

Our participation now in Jesus' love and life bears good fruit and personal joy that stretch into eternity. As we welcome the truth of the gospel, we can't help but worship our Lord and Savior!

Key Points of Trinitarian Theology

Following are some basic precepts of the theology presented in this booklet.

- The Triune God created all people through the Son of God, who also is known as the Word of God.
- We were created so that we could participate in the love relationship enjoyed by the Father, the Son and the Holy Spirit.
- We are enabled and qualified to participate in this relationship of love through Jesus Christ.

- The Son became human, the man Jesus Christ, taking on our human nature.
- He did this to reconcile all humanity to God through his birth, life, death, resurrection and ascension.
- The crucified, resurrected and glorified Jesus is the representative and the substitute for all humanity.
- As Savior and Lord of all humanity, Jesus now sits at the right hand of the Father, and he draws all people to himself by the power of the Holy Spirit.
- In Christ, humanity is loved and accepted by the Father.
- Jesus Christ paid for all our sins—past, present and future—and there is no longer any debt to pay.
- The Father has in Christ forgiven all our sins, and he eagerly desires that we receive his forgiveness.
- We can enjoy his love only as we believe/trust that he loves us. We can enjoy his forgiveness only when we believe/trust he has forgiven us.
- When we respond to the Spirit by turning to God, believing the good news and picking up our cross and following Jesus, the Spirit leads us into the transformed life of the kingdom of God.

Recommended Resources for Further Study

To study Trinitarian theology in greater depth, we recommend the following resources:

GCI articles

Grace Communion International has hundreds of helpful articles that address Christian belief and practice. Following is a list of articles (with web addresses noted) that unpack key aspects of GCI's Trinitarian, Christ-centered theology.

- "Getting a Grip on Repentance" https://www.gci.org/articles/getting-a-grip-on-repentance/
- "Introduction to Trinitarian Theology" https://www.gci.org/articles/an-introduction-to-trinitarian-theology/
- "The Gospel Really Is Good News" https://www.gci.org/articles/the-gospel-really-is-good-news/
- "The Trinity: Just a Doctrine?" https://www.gci.org/articles/the-trinity-just-a-doctrine/
- "Theology: What Difference Does It Make?" https://www.gci.org/articles/theology-what-difference-does-it-make/

GCI video programs

Speaking of Life. This online program presents short messages by Dr. Joseph Tkach, GCI president, on biblical topics from a Trinitarian perspective. View or download these programs at www.speakingoflife.org.

You're Included. This online program presents interviews with Trinitarian theologians and authors. View or download these interviews at www.youreincluded.org.

Books

Michael Jinkins, *Invitation to Theology* (InterVarsity, 2001; 278 pages)

Darrell Johnson, *Experiencing the Trinity* (Regent College, 2002; 112 pages)

C. S. Lewis, *Mere Christianity* (HarperCollins, often reprinted; 225 pages)

Fred Sanders, *The Deep Things of God: How the Trinity Changes Everything* (Crossway, 2010; 256 pages)

James B. Torrance, *Worship, Community and the Triune God of Grace* (InterVarsity, 1996; 130 pages)

Thomas F. Torrance, *The Mediation of Christ* (Helmers & Howard, 1992; 144 pages)

We Were Always on His Mind

The doctrine of the Trinity has been with us for more than 1,600 years. Most Christians consider it to be one of the "givens" of their faith, and don't give it much thought. Theologian J.I. Packer noted that the Trinity is usually considered a little-thought-about piece of "theological lumber" that no one pays much attention to.[1]

But whatever your level of understanding of the doctrine of the Trinity, one thing you can know for sure: The Triune God is unchangeably committed to including you in the wonderful fellowship of the life of the Father, the Son and Holy Spirit.

Communion

The doctrine of the Trinity teaches that there are not three Gods, only one, and that God, the only true God, the God of the Bible, is Father, Son and Holy Spirit. This has always been a concept that is difficult to put into words. But let's try. The Father, Son and Spirit, we might say, mutually indwell one another, that is, the life they share is perfectly interpenetrating. In other words, there is no such thing as the Father apart from the Son and the Spirit. There is no such thing as the Son apart from the Father and the Spirit. And there is no Holy Spirit apart from the Father and the Son.

That means that when you are in Christ, you are included in the fellowship and joy of the life of the Triune God. It means the Father receives you and has fellowship with you as he does with Jesus. It means that the love that God once and for all demonstrated in the Incarnation of Jesus Christ is no less than the love the Father has always had for you even before you were a believer and always will have for you.

It means that God has declared in Christ that you belong to him that you are included, that you matter. That's why the Christian life is all about love God's love for you and God's love in you.

God did not make us to be alone. To be created in God's image, as the Bible says humanity is (Genesis 1:27), is to be created for loving relationships, for communion with God and with one another. The late systematic theologian Colin Gunton put it this way: "God is already 'in advance' of creation, a communion of persons existing in loving relations."[2]

Mutual indwelling

This union/communion of Father, Son and Spirit was referred to as *perichoresis* by the early Greek fathers of the church. They used the word in the sense of *mutual indwelling*.[3]

Why does this matter? Because it is that very inner life of love in the Triune God that God shares with *us* in Jesus Christ.

Michael Jinkins describes it this way:

> Through the self-giving of Jesus Christ, through God's self-emptying assumption of our humanity, God shares God's own inner life and being in communion with us, uniting us to himself by the Word through the power of the Holy Spirit. Thus the God who is Love brings us into a real participation in the eternal life of God.[4]

Too "theological" sounding? Let's make it simpler. Just as Paul told the pagans at Athens, in God we all "live and move and have our being" (Acts 17:28). The God in whom we live and move and have our being is the Father, the Son and the Holy Spirit, each existing in the other in perfect communion and love. The Son became human so that we humans can join him in that perfect communion of love that he shares with the Father and the Spirit. All this we learn from God's own perfect revelation of himself in Jesus Christ attested in the Scriptures.

- "I am the way and the truth and the life. No one comes to the Father except through me. If you really knew me, you would know my Father as well" (John 14:6-7).
- "Don't you believe that I am in the Father, and that the Father is in me?... Believe me when I say that I am in the Father and the Father is in me" (John 14:10-11).
- "On that day you will realize that I am in my Father, and you are in me, and I am in you" (John 14:20).
- "I pray also for those who will believe in me through their message, that all of them may be one, Father, just as you are in me and I am in you" (John 17:20-21).
- "For God was pleased to have all his fullness dwell in him [Jesus Christ], and through him to reconcile to himself all things, whether things on earth or things in heaven, by making peace through his blood, shed on the cross" (Colossians 1:19-20).

Salvation flows from God's absolute love for and faithfulness to humanity, not from a desperate attempt to repair the damages of sin. God's gracious purpose for humanity existed *before* sin ever entered the picture (Ephesians 1:4). God has assured our future — he has, as Jesus said, "been pleased to give you the kingdom" (Luke 12:32). Jesus has taken us with him where he is (Ephesians 2:6).

God has purposed to never be without us. *All* of us, for "God was pleased to have all his fullness dwell in him, and through him to reconcile to himself all things, whether things on earth or things in heaven, by making peace through his blood, shed on the cross" (Colossians 1:19-20). We often forget that. But God never does.

In his embrace

In Jesus Christ through the Holy Spirit by the will of the Father, we mortal, sinning human beings, in spite of ourselves, are graciously and lovingly held in the divine embrace of the triune God. That is exactly what the Father intended for us from the beginning. "In love he predestined us to

be adopted as his sons through Jesus Christ, in accordance with his pleasure and will — to the praise of his glorious grace, which he has freely given us in the One he loves" (Ephesians 1:5-6).

Redemption starts with God's nature, his absolute and unquenchable love for humanity, not with human sin. Through the incarnation of the Son, his becoming one of us and making us one with him, God includes us humans in the all-embracing love of the Father for the Son and the Son for the Father. God made us for this very reason—so that in Christ we can be his beloved children.

This has been God's will for us from before creation. "For he chose us in him before the creation of the world to be holy and blameless in his sight. In love he predestined us to be adopted as his sons through Jesus Christ, in accordance with his pleasure and will — to the praise of his glorious grace, which he has freely given us in the One he loves…. And he made known to us the mystery of his will according to his good pleasure, which he purposed in Christ…to bring all things in heaven and earth together under one head, even Christ" (Ephesians 1:4-6, 9-10).

Through the atoning Incarnation of the Son, Jesus Christ, humans are already forgiven, reconciled and saved in him. Divine amnesty has been proclaimed for all humanity in Christ. The sin that entered the human experience through Adam cannot hold a candle to the overwhelming flood of God's grace through Jesus Christ. "Consequently," the apostle Paul wrote, "just as the result of one trespass was condemnation for all men, so also the result of one act of righteousness was justification that brings life for all men" (Romans 5:18).

Universal salvation?

So will everyone automatically—perhaps even against their will, enter into the joy of knowing and loving God? Such a thing is actually an oxymoron. That is, it is impossible for you to love someone against your will. God draws all humanity to himself (John 12:32), but he does not force anyone to come. God wants everyone to come to faith (1 Timothy 2:4), but he does not force anyone. God loves every person (John 3:16), but he doesn't force anyone to love him — love has to be voluntary, freely given, or it is not love.

Contrary to the idea of universal salvation, only those who trust Jesus are able to love him and experience the joy of his salvation. Those who don't trust him, who refuse his forgiveness or the salvation he has already won for them, whether because they don't want it or simply because they don't care, can't love him and enjoy fellowship with him. For those who consider God their enemy, God's constant love for them is a grossly aggravating intrusion. The more they are confronted with his love, the more they hate him. For those who hate God, life in God's world is hell.

As C.S. Lewis put it, "The damned are, in one sense, successful, rebels to the end; that the doors of hell are locked on the inside."[5] Or as Robert Capon explained: "There is no sin you can commit that God in Jesus hasn't forgiven already. The only way you can get yourself into permanent Dutch [trouble] is to refuse forgiveness. *That's* hell."[6]

Always on his mind

The doctrine of the Trinity is far more than just a creed to be recited or words printed on a statement of faith. The central biblical truth that God is Father, Son and Holy Spirit actually shapes our faith and our lives as Christians. The wonderful and beautiful fellowship shared by the Father, Son, and Spirit is the very fellowship of love into which our Savior Jesus places us through his life, death, resurrection and ascension as God in the flesh (John 16:27; 1 John 1:2-3).

From before all time the Triune God determined to bring humanity into the indescribable life and fellowship and joy that Father, Son and Holy Spirit share together as the one true God (Ephesians 1:4-10). In Jesus Christ, the Son of God incarnate, we have been made right with the Father, and in Jesus we are included in the fellowship and joy of the shared life of the Trinity (Ephesians 2:4-6). The church is made up of those who have already come to faith in Christ. But redemption applies to all (1 John 2:1-2). The gap has been bridged. The price has been paid. The way is open for the human race

— like the prodigal son in the parable - to come home.

Jesus' life, death, resurrection and ascension are proof of the total and unwavering devotion of the Father to his loving purpose of including humanity in the joy and fellowship of the life of the Trinity. Jesus is the proof that the Father will never abandon us. In Jesus, the Father has adopted us and made us his beloved children, and he will never forsake his plans for us.

When we trust Jesus to be our all in all, it is not an empty trust. He *is* our all in all. In him, our sins are forgiven, our hearts are made new, and we are included in the life he shares with the Father and the Spirit.

Salvation is the direct result of the Father's ever-faithful love and power, proven incontrovertibly through Jesus Christ and ministered to us by the Holy Spirit. It's not our faith that saves us. It's God alone — Father, Son and Spirit — who saves us. And God gives us faith as a gift to open our eyes to the truth of who he is — and who we are, as his beloved children.

God's eternal and almighty word of love and inclusion for you will never be silenced (Romans 8:32, 38-39). You belong to him, and nothing in heaven or Earth can ever change that.

Endnotes

[1] James Packer, *God's Words* (Baker, 1998), 44.

[2] Colin Gunton, *The Triune Creator: A Historical and Systematic Study* (Eerdmans 1998), 9.

[3] Other theological terms that describe this inner communion of the Father, Son and Spirit are *coinherence,* each existing within the other) and *circumincessio* (the Latin equivalent of *perichoresis).*

[4] Michael Jinkins, *Invitation to Theology* (Inter-Varsity, 2001), 92.

[5] C.S. Lewis, *The Problem of Pain* (Collier, 1962), chapter 8, page 127).

[6] Robert Farrar Capon, *The Mystery of Christ* (Eerdmans, 1993), 10.

Joseph Tkach

Who Is This Man?

Jesus asked his disciples, "Who do people say that I am?" The question confronts us, too: Who is this man? What authority does he have? Why should we trust him?

The Christian faith centers on Jesus Christ. We need to understand what kind of person he is.

Fully human—and then some

Jesus was born in the normal way, grew in the normal way, got hungry and thirsty and tired, ate and drank and slept. He looked normal, talked in ordinary language, and walked in the normal way. He had emotions such as compassion, surprise, sorrow and apprehension (Matthew 9:36; Luke 7:9; John 11:38; Matthew 26:37). He prayed to God, as humans need to. He called himself a man and other people called him a man. He was a human being.

But Jesus was such an extraordinary human that after he ascended to heaven, some people claimed he was not human after all (2 John 7). They thought that Jesus was so holy that surely he would have nothing to do with flesh, with its dirt, sweat, digestive functions and imperfections. Perhaps he merely *appeared* to be human, in the way that angels sometimes appeared as humans, without actually becoming human.

So the New Testament makes it clear that Jesus was really a human. John tells us, "The Word became flesh" (John 1:14). He didn't just appear as flesh, or clothe himself in flesh. He *became* flesh. "Jesus Christ has come in the flesh" (1 John 4:2). We know, says John, because we saw him and touched him (1 John 1:1-2).

Paul said that Jesus was "made in human likeness" (Philippians 2:7), "born under the law" (Galatians 4:4), "in the likeness of sinful man" (Romans 8:3). Since he came to save humans, the author of Hebrews reasons, it was necessary that he

"shared in their humanity" (Hebrews 2:14-17).

Our salvation depends on the reality of Jesus' humanity. His role as our intercessor, our high priest, depends on his experience as a human (Hebrews 4:15). Even after his resurrection, Jesus had flesh and bones (John 20:27; Luke 24:39). Even in heavenly glory, he continues to be a human (1 Timothy 2:5).

Acting like God

"Who is this fellow?" asked the Pharisees when they heard Jesus forgive sins. "Who can forgive sins but God alone?" (Luke 5:21). Sin is an offense against God, so how could a human speak for God and say the offense is removed from the record? It was blasphemy, they said.

Jesus knew what they thought about it, but he forgave sins anyway. He even implied that he had no sins of his own (John 8:46). He made some astonishing claims:

- He said he would sit at God's right hand in heaven—another claim the Jewish leaders thought blasphemous (Matthew 26:63-65).
- He claimed to be the Son of God—another blasphemy, they said, since in that culture it implied equality with God (John 5:18; 19:7).
- Jesus claimed to be in such perfect communication with God that he did only what God wanted (John 5:19).
- He claimed to be one with the Father (John 10:30), which the Jewish leaders again said was blasphemous (v. 33).
- He claimed to be so much like God that people should look at him to see the Father (John 14:9; 1:18).

- He claimed to be able to send God's Spirit (John 16:7).
- He claimed that he had angels he could send (Matthew 13:41).
- He knew that God was the judge of the world, but he also claimed to be the judge (John 5:22).
- He said he could raise the dead, even himself (John 5:21; 6:40; 10:18).
- He said that everyone's eternal life depends on their relationship with him (Matthew 7:23).
- He said that the words of Moses were not enough (Matthew 5:21-48).
- He claimed to be the Lord of the Sabbath — the Lord of a God-given law! (Matthew 12:8).

If he were merely a human, his teaching was arrogant and sinful. But Jesus backed up his words with some amazing actions. "Believe me when I say that I am in the Father and the Father is in me; or at least believe on the evidence of the miracles" (John 14:11). Miracles can't force anyone to believe, but they can provide powerful supporting evidence.

To show that he had the authority to forgive sins, Jesus healed a paralyzed man (Luke 5:23-25). His miracles give evidence that what he said about himself is true. He has more-than-human power, because he is more than a human. The claims that would have been blasphemous in anyone else were true for Jesus. He could speak like God and act like God because he was God in the flesh.

Who did he think he was?

Jesus had a clear sense of self-identity. Even at age 12, he had a special relationship with his Father in heaven (Luke 2:49). At his baptism, he heard a voice from heaven say that he was God's Son (Luke 3:22). He knew he had a mission to perform (Luke 4:43; 9:22; 13:33; 22:37).

When Peter said, "You are the Christ, the Son of the living God," Jesus answered, "Blessed are you, Simon son of Jonah, for this was not revealed to you by man, but by my Father in heaven" (Matthew 16:16-17). Jesus was the Son of God. He was the Christ, the Messiah — the person uniquely anointed by God for a special mission.

When Jesus called 12 disciples, one for each tribe of Israel, he did not count himself among the 12. He was above them, for he was above all Israel. He was the maker and builder of the new Israel. At the last Supper, he proclaimed himself to be the basis of the new covenant, a new relationship with God. He saw himself as the focal point of what God was doing in the world.

Jesus spoke boldly against traditions, against laws, against the temple, against religious leaders. He demanded that his followers abandon everything to follow him, to put him first in their lives, to give him complete allegiance. He spoke with the authority of God — but he spoke on his own authority. He had authority equal to God.

Jesus believed that he was the fulfillment of Old Testament prophecies. He was the suffering servant who would die to ransom the people from their sins (Isaiah 53:4-5, 12; Matthew 26:24; Mark 9:12; Luke 22:37; 24:46). He was the king of peace who would ride into Jerusalem on a donkey (Zechariah 9:9-10; Matthew 21:1-9). He was the son of man who would be given all power and authority (Daniel 7:13-14; Matthew 26:64).

Previous life

Jesus claimed to be alive before Abraham was born: "I tell you the truth," he said, "before Abraham was born, I am!" (John 8:58). The Jewish leaders thought that Jesus was claiming something divine, and they wanted to kill him (v. 59). The phrase "I AM" is an echo of Exodus 3:14, where God revealed his name to Moses: "This is what you are to say to the Israelites: 'I AM has sent me to you.'" Jesus used this name for himself.

Jesus said he shared glory with God before the world began (John 17:5). John tells us that he existed even in the beginning of time, as the Word (John 1:1). John tells us that the universe was made through the Word (John 1:3). The Father was the Designer, and the Word was the Creator who carried out the design. "All things were created by him and for him" (Colossians 1:16; 1 Corinthians 8:6). Hebrews 1:2 says that God made the universe through the Son.

Both Hebrews and Colossians tell us that the Son sustains the universe (Hebrews 1:3; Colossians 1:17). Both tell us that he is "the image of the invisible God" (Colossians 1:15), "the exact representation of his being" (Hebrews 1:3).

Who is Jesus? He is a divine being who became flesh. He was in the beginning with God; he was the Creator of all, the Author of life (Acts 3:15). He is exactly like God, has glory like God, and has powers that only God has. Little wonder that the disciples concluded that he *was* God, even in the flesh.

Worthy of worship

Jesus was conceived in a supernatural way (Matthew 1:20; Luke 1:35). He lived without ever sinning (Hebrews 4:15). He was blameless, without impurity (Hebrews 7:26; 9:14). He committed no sin (1 Peter 2:22); in him there was no sin (1 John 3:5); he knew no sin (2 Corinthians 5:21). No matter how tempting the sin was, Jesus always had a greater desire to obey God. His mission was to do God's will (Hebrews 10:7).

On several occasions, people worshiped Jesus (Matthew 14:33; 28:9,17; John 9:38). Angels refuse worship (Revelation 19:10), but Jesus did not. Indeed, the angels worship Jesus, the Son of God (Hebrews 1:6). Some prayers are addressed to Jesus (Acts 7:59-60; 2 Corinthians 12:8; Revelation 22:20). He is worthy of worship.

The New Testament gives elaborate praises to Jesus Christ, with doxologies that are normally reserved for God: "To him be glory for ever and ever. Amen" (2 Timothy 4:18; 2 Pet 3:18;Revelation 1:6). He has the highest title that can ever be given (Ephesians 1:20-21). Even if we call him God, that title is not too high.

In Revelation, equal praise is given to God and to the Lamb, implying equality: "To him who sits on the throne and to the Lamb be praise and honor and glory and power, for ever and ever!" (Revelation 5:13). The Son must be given equal honor with the Father (John 5:23). Both God and Jesus are called the Alpha and the Omega, the beginning and end of everything (Revelation 1:8, 17; 21:6; 22:13).

The New Testament often uses Old Testament passages about God and applies them to Jesus Christ. One of the most striking is this passage about worship: "God exalted him to the highest place and gave him the name that is above every name, that at the name of Jesus every knee should bow, in heaven and on earth and under the earth, and every tongue confess that Jesus Christ is Lord, to the glory of God the Father" (Philippians 2:9-11, quoting Isaiah 45:23). Jesus will get the honor and respect that Isaiah said would be given to God.

Isaiah says there is only one Savior — God (Isaiah 43:11; 45:21). Paul just as clearly says that God is Savior and Jesus is Savior (Titus 1:3-4; 2:10, 13). So, is there one Savior, or two? Early Christians concluded that the Father is God and Jesus is God, even though there is only one God, only one Savior. The Father and Son are the same in essence (God), but different in person.

Several other New Testament verses also call Jesus God. John 1:1 says, "the Word was God." Verse 18 says, "No one has ever seen God, but God the One and Only, who is at the Father's side, has made him known." Jesus is the God who made the Father known. After the resurrection, Thomas recognized Jesus as God: "Thomas said to him, 'My Lord and my God!'" (John 20:28).

Paul says that the patriarchs are great because "from them is traced the human ancestry of Christ, who is God over all, forever praised! Amen" (Romans 9:5). In Hebrews, God himself is said to call Jesus God: "About the Son he says, 'Your throne, O God, will last for ever and ever'" (Hebrews 1:8).

"In Christ," Paul said, "all the fullness of the Deity lives in bodily form" (Colossians 2:9). Jesus Christ is fully divine, and even now has bodily form. He is the exact representation of God — God made flesh. If Jesus were only a human, it would be wrong to put our trust in him. But because he is divine, we are *commanded* to trust in him. He is utterly trustworthy, because he is God.

The divinity of Jesus is crucial for us, for he could reveal God to us accurately only if he is divine (John 1:18; 14:9). Only a divine person could forgive our sins, redeem us, and reconcile us to God. Only a divine person could be the object of our faith, the Lord to whom we give complete allegiance, the Savior we worship in song and prayer.

Truly human, truly God

As you can see from the scripture references above, the biblical information about Jesus is scattered throughout the New Testament. The picture is consistent, but it is not all drawn together in one place. The early church had to put the facts together. They drew these conclusions from the biblical revelation:

- Jesus, the Son of God, is divine.
- The Son of God became genuinely human, but the Father did not.
- The Son of God and the Father are distinct, not the same.
- There is only one God.
- The Son and the Father are persons in that one God.

The Council of Nicea (A.D. 325) declared that Jesus, the Son of God, was divine, of the same essence as the Father. The council of Chalcedon (A.D. 451) explained that he was also human:

> Our Lord Jesus Christ is one and the same Son; the same perfect in Godhead and the same perfect in manhood, truly God and truly man... begotten of the Father before all ages as regards his Godhead and... begotten of the Virgin Mary the Theotokos [the "God-Bearer"] as regards his manhood; one and the same Christ, Son, Lord, only-begotten, made known in two natures... the difference of the natures being by no means removed because of the union but the property of each nature being preserved and coalescing in one person.

The last part was included because some people said that the divine nature so overpowered Jesus' human nature that he wasn't really human. Others

From our *Statement of Beliefs:*

The Son of God is the second Person of the triune God, eternally begotten of the Father. He is the Word and the express image of the Father. The Father created all things through the Son, and the Son sustains all things by his word. He was sent by the Father to be God revealed in the flesh for our salvation, Jesus Christ. Jesus was conceived by the power of the Holy Spirit and born of the virgin Mary, fully God and fully human, two natures in one Person. He is the Son of God and Lord of all, worthy of worship, honor and reverence.

As the prophesied Savior of humanity, he suffered and died for all human sin, was raised bodily from the dead, and ascended to heaven. Taking on our broken and alienated humanity, he has included the entire human race in his right relationship with the Father, so that in his regeneration of our humanity we share in his sonship, being adopted as God's own children in the power of the Spirit. As our representative and substitute, he stands in for all humanity before the Father, providing the perfect human response to God on our behalf and reconciling humanity to the Father. He will come again in glory as King of kings over all nations.

(John 1:1, 10, 14; Colossians 1:15-17;Hebrews 1:3; John 3:16; Titus 2:13; Matthew 1:20; Acts 10:36; 1 Corinthians 15:3-4; Titus 3:4-5; Hebrews 2:9; 7:25; Galatians 4:5; 2 Corinthians 5:14; Ephesians 1: 9-10;Colossians 1:20; 1 Timothy 2:5; Hebrews 1:8;Revelation 19:16)

said that the two natures combined to form a third nature, so that Jesus was neither human nor divine. No, the biblical data says that he was truly human, and truly divine, and this is what the church must say, too.

How can this be?

Our salvation depends on Jesus being both human and divine. But how can this be? How can someone infinite become finite? How can the holy Son of God become a human, in the likeness of sinful flesh?

Our question comes mainly because the only humanity that we can see now is woefully corrupt. But this is not the way God made it. Jesus shows us what true humanity is. For one thing, he shows us a person who is completely dependent on the Father. This is the way humanity ought to be.

Jesus also shows us what God is capable of doing. He is able to become part of his creation. He can bridge the gap between the uncreated and the created, between the holy and the sinful. What we might think is impossible, is possible with God. Jesus also shows us what humanity will be in the new creation. When he returns and we are resurrected, we will look like him (1 John 3:2). We will have bodies like his glorious body (1 Corinthians 15:42-49).

Jesus is our trailblazer, showing us that the way to God is through Jesus. Because he is human, he sympathizes with our weaknesses, and because he is divine, he effectively intercedes for us at God's right hand (Hebrews 4:15). With Jesus as our Savior, we can be confident that our salvation is secure.

Questions for discussion

- Is it easier to think of Jesus as a human, or as a God? Are you troubled by his divine characteristics, or by his humanity?
- Which of Jesus' words or actions best shows that he was divine?

- Do we slight the Father when we worship Jesus? Do we slight Jesus when we worship only the Father?
- What does Jesus reveal to us about God? About humanity?

Five facts about Jesus

- Jesus was a physical, mortal human.
- Jesus has the authority of God.
- Jesus had shared in God's glory.
- It is appropriate for people to worship Jesus.
- Jesus is truly human and truly divine, showing us what God is like and what humanity should be.

For further reading

(in order of difficulty)

Michael Green, *Who Is This Jesus?* Nelson, 1992.

Murray Harris, *Three Crucial Questions About Jesus.* Baker, 1994.

Lee Strobel, *The Case for Christ.* Zondervan, 1998.

Alister McGrath, *Understanding Jesus.* Zondervan, 1987.

Millard Erickson, *Introducing Christian Doctrine.* Baker, 1992. Chapters 23-25.

I. Howard Marshall, *The Origins of New Testament Christology.* InterVarsity, 1990.

Donald Bloesch. *Jesus Christ: Lord and Savior.* InterVarsity, 1997.

Michael Morrison

Is Jesus Really God?

A Look at the Arian Controversy

Few Christians are aware that two of the most fundamental doctrines of the Christian faith — the divinity of Jesus Christ and the Trinity — were not finally decided until some 350 years after the death of Jesus.

Both doctrines were forged in the fourth century out of the religious and political firestorm sparked by Arius, a popular presbyter of the church in Alexandria, Egypt. Arius had a simple formula for explaining how Jesus Christ could be divine — and therefore worthy of worship along with God the Father — even though there is only one God.

The simple formula taught by Arius was well received by the common believers in Alexandria, but not by Arius' supervisor, bishop Alexander. Each man lined up supporters and the battle lines were drawn for what history would call the Arian Controversy. This bitter ordeal for the Christian churches of the eastern and western Roman Empire began in A.D. 318, led to the Creed of Nicea in 325 and finally ended with the Nicene Creed established at the Council of Constantinople in 381.

Monarchianism

Church Fathers from as early as the late 100s had been writing that the Word of God, the *Logos* of John 1:1-2, was co-eternal with the Father — and therefore uncreated and without beginning. The presbyter Arius was not the first to dispute this. Similar challenges had already arisen by the late second and early third centuries in the form of Monarchianism.

Monarchians fell into two broad categories. The Adoptionist or Dynamic Monarchians held that Jesus was only a man in whom dwelled the power of the supreme God.[1] The Modalist Monarchians taught that God revealed himself in three modes — as Father, Son and Spirit — but never at the same time. This preserved the idea of the full divinity of the Son, but at the expense of any real distinction between the Son and the Father. Some Modalists believed that Jesus Christ was actually the Father in the flesh. All forms of Monarchianism were eventually branded as heresy and rejected by the Christian churches across the empire.

Arius

In one sense, Arius was simply the latest thinker to try to reconcile monotheism (belief in one God) with the Christian belief that Jesus Christ was divine. But there was a great difference between Arius' attempt and all previous efforts. No longer was Christianity an officially unsanctioned, often underground and persecuted religion. Now the Roman emperor Constantine had granted Christianity unprecedented legitimate status in the Empire, so that the question of who Jesus is could finally come before the whole Church to be settled.

Arius was a popular senior presbyter in charge of Baucalis, one of the twelve "parishes" of Alexandria in the early fourth century.[2] By A.D. 318, Arius had begun teaching his followers that the Son of God (who is also the *Logos* or Word of John 1:1-2) did not exist until the Father brought him into existence. To Arius, the Father first created the Word, and then the Word, as the Father's unique and supreme agent, created everything else.

Arius' idea seemed to preserve monotheism as well as uphold the divinity of the Son, even if it was a bestowed divinity as distinct from the inherent and eternal divinity of the Father. With the help of catchy rhymes and tunes, Arius' ideas quickly caught on among the common converts of Alexandria.

Alexander

Alexander, the bishop of Alexandria, and his assistant, a presbyter named Athanasius, saw great danger in Arius' teaching and took action to arrest it. Contrary to Arius' teaching that God was once without the Word, Alexander asserted that God *cannot* be without the Word, and that the Word is therefore without beginning and eternally generated by the Father.

Alexander sent letters to neighboring bishops requesting support and convened a council at Alexandria that excommunicated Arius and a dozen other clergy.[3] Arius also sought backing, however, and obtained the support of several leaders, including Eusebius, the bishop of Nicomedia. Eusebius enjoyed a close relationship with Emperor Constantine, which would play a major role in the unfolding of the controversy. Another supporter of Arius was the historian, Eusebius of Caesarea, whose history of the early Christian church is still available today.

Constantine steps in

The Emperor Constantine became aware of the developing problem, and saw a need to resolve it. As Emperor, Constantine's concern was not so much for the unity of the Church as for the unity of the empire itself. Theologically, he viewed it as a "trifle."[4] Constantine's first move was to send his religious advisor, Bishop Hosius of Cordova, Spain, to sort out the differences. Hosius was unsuccessful in bringing Arius and Alexander to peace, but he presided over a council in Antioch in early 325 that condemned Arianism and censured Eusebius of Caesarea.[5] But the division continued, so Constantine called a universal council of the Church to settle the dispute.

Ancyra had been the original choice of venue, but Constantine changed the location to Nicaea, a city closer to his Nicomedia headquarters. The emperor personally opened the council in June of 325 with about 300 bishops present (most from the east). Constantine was looking for mutual tolerance and compromise. Many of the bishops present were also apparently prepared to find compromise.

As the proceedings unfolded, however, thoughts of compromise quickly eroded. Once the tenets of the Arian position became clear, it did not take long for them to be rejected and condemned. The ideas that the Son of God is God only as a "courtesy title" and that the Son is of created status were vehemently denounced. Those who held such views were anathematized. The divinity of the Logos was upheld, and the Son was declared to be "true God" and co-eternal with the Father. The key phrase from the Creed established at Nicaea in 325 was "of the essence of the Father, God of God and Light of Light, very God of very God, begotten, not made, being of one substance with the Father."

Homoousios (of the same essence) was the key Greek word. It was intended to convey, against the Arians, that the Son is equally divine with the Father. This it did, but it also left unanswered the question of how the Son and the Father, if they are of the same essence, are in fact distinct. Consequently, though Arianism was condemned and Arius banished, the Council of Nicaea did not see an end to the controversy.

A little letter makes a big difference

Athanasius and most other eastern bishops said that the Son was *homoousias* with the Father, meaning "of the same essence." The Arian theologians disagreed, but suggested a compromise: they could accept the word with the addition of only one letter, the smallest Greek letter, the iota. They said that the Son was *homoiousias* with the Father — a Greek word meaning "similar essence."

But similarity is in the "i" of the beholder, and the Arians actually meant that Jesus was not the same kind of being as the Father. It would be like saying that he was "almost" divine. The orthodox theologians could not accept that, and would not accept a word that allowed such an unorthodox interpretation.

Imperial reversals

Eusebius of Nicomedia, who presented the Arian cause to the Council and was deposed and banished for it, enjoyed a close personal relationship with Emperor Constantine. In time, he was able to convince Constantine to ease the punishment on the Arians, and to order Arius himself recalled from exile. Eventually, after a council at Jerusalem formally acquitted him of the charge of heresy in 335, Arius was to have been received back into the fellowship of the church in Constantinople. Philip Schaff wrote:

> But on the evening before the intended procession from the imperial palace to the church of the Apostles, he suddenly died (A.D. 336), at the age of over eighty years, of an attack like cholera, while attending to a call of nature. This death was regarded by many as a divine judgment; by others, it was attributed to poisoning by enemies; by others, to the excessive joy of Arius in his triumph.[6]

Athanasius, meanwhile, had succeeded Alexander as bishop of Alexandria in 328 only to be condemned and deposed by two Arian councils, one at Tyre under the presidency of Eusebius of Caesarea, and the other at Constantinople in about 335. He was then banished by Constantine to Treves in Gaul in 336 as a disturber of the peace of the church.[7]

This turn of events was followed by the death of Constantine in 337 (who received the sacrament of baptism on his deathbed from the Arian Eusebius of Nicomedia). Constantine's three sons, Constantine II, Constans, and Constantius succeeded him. Constantine II, who ruled Gaul, Great Britain, Spain, and Morocco, recalled Athanasius from banishment in 338. In the east, however, matters were quite different. Constantius, who ruled the east, was firmly Arian. Eusebius of Nicomedia, the leader of the Arian party, was appointed Bishop of Constantinople in 338. Before long, war in the west between Constantine II and Constans gave Constantius a free hand to again exile Athanasius in 340.

When Constantine II died, however, and the western empire was united under Constans, Constantius had to follow a more moderate line with the Nicene party. The two emperors called a general council in Sardica in 343, presided over by Hosius, at which the Nicene doctrine was confirmed. Constans also compelled Constantius to restore Athanasius to his office in 346.[8]

Semi-Arianism

When Constans died in 350, the pendulum swung again. Constantius, now the sole emperor and still Arian, held councils supporting Arianism and banished bishops who opposed their edicts, including Hosius and Athanasius. By now, Arianism had itself become divided into two factions. One party had slightly modified its position to affirm *homoiousios*, or similarity of essence, rather than the original *heteroousios*, or difference of essence, still held by the strictest Arians.

This "compromise," sometimes called "semi-Arianism," still represented an unbridgeable chasm from the orthodox *homoousios*, or same essence. It only served to pit the Arians against one another. For Nicenes who still had difficulty with the apparent lack of distinction between the Father and the Son represented by *homoousios*, though, the semi-Arian *homoiousios* did, for a time, afford a reasonable compromise. In any case, by the time of the death of Constantius, the Church had become Arian, at least on the surface.

Imperial reversals

It was the death of Constantius in 361 that set the stage for the permanent triumph of Nicene faith. Julian the Apostate became emperor and implemented a policy of toleration for all the Christian parties. Though Julian's policy, at first glance, seems positive toward Christianity, his real hope was that the opposing factions would destroy one another. He recalled the exiled bishops, including Athanasius (though Athanasius was soon banished again as an "enemy of the gods" but was again recalled by Julian's successor Jovian).[9]

It was through the efforts of Athanasius that the

concerns of the Nicenes and the semi-Arians about blurring the distinction between the Father and the Son were assuaged. Athanasius argued that *homoousios* could be interpreted in such a way as to affirm the same essence as long as the distinction between the Father and Son were not destroyed. In other words, he made it plain that "same essence" must retain the unity but never be allowed to destroy the distinctions in the Godhead. With this understanding, along with the compelling work of the Cappadocian bishops, Basil, Gregory of Nazianzus, and Gregory of Nyssa, the Nicene faith again began to gain ascendancy.

Julian died in 363, and was followed by Jovian, who was favorable toward Athanasius and the Nicene faith. His reign was short, though, ending in 364. He was succeeded by Valens, a fanatical Arian, whose intensity against both semi-Arians and Nicenes tended to bring those two parties together. In 375, he was followed by Gratian, who was of Nicene faith, and who recalled all the exiled orthodox bishops.

By the end of Gratian's reign, Arianism was greatly waning in intellectual defense and in morale. At last, it was the long reign of Theodosius I, who was educated in the Nicene faith, that finally ended the long controversy. He required all his subjects to confess the orthodox faith. He appointed a champion of Nicene faith, Gregory of Nazianzus, as patriarch of Constantinople in 380. In 381, Gregory presided over the Council of Constantinople.

The Council of Constantinople

The Council of Constantinople affirmed the Creed of Nicaea, altering it only slightly and in non-essential ways. It is the form of the Creed adopted at Constantinople that today bears the name Nicene Creed. The controversy was at last ended in the empire. However, Arianism would continue to impact the Church for the next two centuries in the form of the various peoples outside the empire who had become Christians according to the Arian faith (most of whom scarcely even knew the difference).

Athanasius, who had so diligently and unswervingly opposed the Arian heresy, did not live to see the conflict ended. He died in 373 in his native Alexandria. In the end, the unyielding Athanasius is a fair representation of the unyielding truth of the orthodox Christian faith. Fundamental to the validity of Christianity is the reality of redemption, made possible only by the work of no being less than true God, the Lord Jesus Christ.

Arius believed that a Christ designated as divine by virtue of his special creation could serve as true Redeemer and true Mediator between God and humanity. It took the dogged, relentless, unwavering faith of an Athanasius to hold fast to the truth that no being less than true God could in fact reconcile humanity to God.

The apostle Paul wrote to the church in Corinth: "No doubt there have to be differences among you to show which of you have God's approval" (1 Corinthians 11:19). Likewise, the Arian controversy became an essential waypoint on the journey of the church, for despite the trial and pain of controversy, the truth of the nature of the divine One who had come to redeem humanity had to be made plain.

Who was who?

Arius (c. 250-336): Theologian in Alexandria, Egypt, a presbyter (an elder) of the church. He taught his followers that the Son of God did not exist until he was brought into existence by the Father.

Alexander of Alexandria (d. 326): Bishop of Alexandria and Arius' supervisor. He strongly opposed Arianism.

Athanasius (293-373): A presbyter of the church in Alexandria and assistant to Bishop Alexander. He later succeeded Alexander as Bishop of Alexandria and spearheaded the effort to oppose Arianism and establish the Nicene faith.

Eusebius of Caesarea (c. 263-339): Bishop of Caesarea and author of several works chronicling the history of early Christianity, including *Ecclesiastical History.* He hoped for a compromise in the Arian controversy, and as a historian he recorded the proceedings at the Council of Nicea.

Eusebius of Nicomedia (d. 341): Bishop of Nicomedia. He supported Arius' ideas and presented the Arian side of the controversy at the Council of Nicea.

Constantine the Great (272-337): Emperor of the Roman Empire who legalized Christianity in the Empire. He called the Council of Nicea in an effort to bring an end to the dispute among the churches that was threatening the security of the Empire.

Hosius of Cordova (c. 256-358): Bishop of Cordova, Spain. He was sent to Alexandria by Constantine to mediate the Arian controversy.

Endnotes

1 Clyde Manschreck, "Monarchianism," in *Dictionary of Bible and Religion* (Nashville: Abingdon, 1986), 704.

2 David Wright, "Councils and Creeds," *The History of Christianity* (Herts, England: Lion Publishing, 1977), 156.

3 Wright, 157.

4 Wright, 159.

5 William Rusch, *The Trinitarian Controversy* (Philadelphia: Fortress, 1980), 19.

6 Philip Schaff, *History of the Christian Church* (Charles Scribner's Sons, 1910; reprinted by Eerdmans, 1987), vol. III, 663.

7 Schaff, 663.

8 Schaff, 635.

9 Schaff, 638.

J. Michael Feazell

What Jesus' Incarnation Shows Us About What It Means to Be a Human

The Word became flesh and made his dwelling among us. We have seen his glory, the glory of the One and Only, who came from the Father, full of grace and truth (John 1:14).

"The Word became flesh and made his dwelling among us," is arguably the most profound and exciting statement in the Bible. Jesus came to seek and save the lost, but the good news goes much farther than that. Salvation is not merely the removal of our sins—it is a new creation, a radical transformation of what it means to be human.

You might even say that Christmas is not only about Jesus; it's ultimately about you!

True humanity

When John wrote in John 1:14 that Jesus became flesh and lived among us, he used an image the Jews were familiar with. The word that is translated "dwelled" literally means "to pitch one's tent." It referred to God's dwelling among the Israelites in the tabernacle, a special tent that was the precursor to the temple of Solomon (see Exodus 40:34-38). The difference is that the Word—Jesus—didn't just dwell *among* humanity, he *became* human.

As the perfect human, Jesus is the definition of everything it means to be human. Whatever Jesus is, that is what he has made humanity to be in him. This tells you at least three things about yourself.

It tells you that God is on your side. Jesus is God's beloved Son in whom he is well pleased (Matthew 17:5). Because your life is in Jesus, and he is your life (Colossians 3:4), you share in his personal relationship with the Father. With him and in him, you are God's beloved child.

It tells you that your sins have been removed.

Isaiah 59:2 declares that sin separates people from God. When Jesus came, he took that sin upon himself so that we could be reconciled to God. In other words, Jesus became sin (2 Corinthians 5:21) so that we could be completely reconciled to God.

It tells you that nothing stands between you and God. John 1:14 says that Jesus "came from the Father, full of grace and truth." Jesus restored us to God through grace, without our input or help. We were reconciled even when we were still sinners, Paul wrote in Romans 5:10. It's a gift.

Jesus restored us to God by taking our broken human condition on himself. He became the representative and the substitute for all of humanity. Paul sums this up in 2 Corinthians 8:9: "For you know the grace of our Lord Jesus Christ, that though he was rich, yet for your sakes he became poor, so that you through his poverty might become rich." As a human, Jesus brings humanity into perfect relationship with God and as God, he brings God into perfect relationship with humanity.

Paul wrote in Ephesians 2:4-5, "Because of his great love for us, God, who is rich in mercy, made us alive with Christ even when we were dead in transgressions—it is by grace you have been saved." This is reconciliation at its finest. Paul went one step further in verse 6, saying, "God raised us up with Christ and seated us with him in the heavenly realms in Christ Jesus." We are not waiting for God to accept us. Because of Christ, he already has accepted us, and this never depended on us.

In the Parable of the Prodigal Son, Jesus illustrates God's unconditional love for wayward humanity. In this parable the betrayed father represents God and the prodigal son represents all of us.

The Father never rejected us—we rejected the Father. He eagerly awaits our repentance (turning our hearts back to him) and is watching for the first sign of our return. As soon as he sees us, he runs down the road to embrace us, honor us, and declare us his beloved child.

To be fully human is to know God

Jesus is the perfect revelation of the Father. As Ray Anderson put it in his book, *The Shape of Practical Theology*, "To know Jesus is to be confronted with the reality of God himself." There is no difference between the heart of Jesus and the heart of the Father. Jesus said he was one with the Father (John 10:30). To know Jesus is to know God.

In coming to be with us, Jesus showed us the Father's love and compassion toward us. He "pitched his tent" among us because he *wants* to be with us and to identify with us. God didn't turn his back on sinners—he came to live among them, to love them and to heal them.

God created us to be in relationship with him. This was the plan from the foundation of the earth. Paul wrote in Ephesians 1:4-10, "In love he predestined us to be adopted as his sons through Jesus Christ… And he made known to us the mystery of his will…to bring all things in heaven and on earth together under one head, even Christ."

Jesus was never "plan B." It was always God's plan and purpose to be in loving communion with those he created in his image.

When "the Word became flesh and made his dwelling among us," he didn't come to live in a tent or a temple. He came to live in *us*. He bound himself to us, taking up our cause, bearing and vanquishing our sinfulness. He called us his friends and made us his brothers and sisters, bringing us with him into the Father's embrace.

As Anderson said: Jesus confronts us with the reality of God. The Spirit leads us to Jesus, and when we know Jesus, we know the Father. When we are in communion with Jesus, we are in communion with the Father and with the Spirit.

To be fully human is to know God — to know he loves us, wants us, and will never let us go. Jesus heals and restores our full humanity, becoming for us the image of God into which we were created.

Jesus shows us what life is all about. It's about walking in communion with God—being in relationship with the One who created us, loves us, dwells among and in us, and adopts us as his own precious children.

Jesus shows us what it means to be truly human. He became a human for us, for our benefit. The story of his birth is about you.

A Fresh Look at Nothing

"[Jesus], being in very nature God, did not consider equality with God something to be grasped, but made himself nothing, taking the very nature of a servant, being made in human likeness" (Philippians 2:6-7).

When Paul says that the Son of God made himself "nothing," he is not implying that humans are nothing. Paul is using a figure of speech to express that Jesus humbled himself in love in order to serve us. We should follow his example by humbling ourselves in order to love and serve one another.

Theologian Gordon Fee summarizes it this way:

In Christ Jesus God has shown his true nature; this is what it means for Christ to be "equal with God" — to pour himself out for the sake of others and to do so by taking the role of a slave. Hereby he not only reveals the character of God but also reveals what it means for us to be created in God's image. To bear his likeness and have his "mindset." It means taking the role of the slave for the sake of others. (Gordon Fee, *Philippians*, InterVarsity Press, 1999)

Rick Shallenberger

Jesus: The Unexpected Messiah

Why didn't Jesus go down in history as a failure?

In fact, why did he go down in history at all?

He lived on earth at a time when his people were expecting a Messiah to deliver them from the Roman occupation. It seems there were many zealots and fanatics eager to appoint themselves to that position. Some even gained a following, but their efforts came to nothing. Most died unknown, and even those we know about are just footnotes in history. However, Jesus is not a footnote in history. He remains considered one of the most influential, if not the most influential, human being who has ever lived.

When he was crucified 2,000 years ago, his followers were left in confusion. Most were expecting the Messiah to be a royal military leader who would overthrow the enemies of Israel and be honored by the Jewish religious leaders as king. This would be the proof of his Messiahship and this is what they expected Jesus would do.

Just a few days earlier, he had entered Jerusalem to the acclaim of the crowds. At last, it seemed, he was going to make his move and lead them in a war of liberation against the Romans. Then he would establish his kingdom, restoring the fortunes of his people. Those who had followed him would be given key positions. But before the week was over he was dead — executed like a common criminal, rejected by the religious leaders and his followers went into hiding.

No one (except for Jesus) expected this to happen. Although there were different ideas among the Jews about what the Messiah would do, there were some common themes. Being crucified was not one of them. In fact, coming to such an end would have been high on the list of events proving someone was *not* the Messiah. So why did his followers continue to believe in a Messiah who, instead of leading them to victory, only seemed to have brought ignominy and suffering on himself?

Let's look at it from the disciples' point of view. Clearly, Jesus did not fulfill any of those common expectations for the Jews of his day. Instead of routing the Romans, he came as the Prince of Peace, not even carrying a weapon. He was born in a borrowed stable and buried in a borrowed tomb. He was executed in mid-life by a method reserved for slaves and common criminals. So, why would his followers maintain that he was the Messiah? Why would they not just cut their losses after his death and move on? Why would they even be willing to be killed themselves for this Messiah?

New Testament scholar N.T. Wright explains it well:

> There were, to be sure, ways of coping with the death of a teacher, or even a leader. The picture of Socrates was available, in the wider world, as a model of unjust death nobly borne. The category of "martyr" was available, within Judaism, for someone who stood up to pagans... The category of failed but still revered Messiah, however, did not exist. A Messiah who died at the hands of the pagans, instead of winning [God's] battle against them, was a deceiver... Why then did people go on talking about Jesus of Nazareth, except as a remarkable but tragic memory? The obvious answer is that...Jesus was raised from the dead. (N.T. Wright, *Jesus and the Victory of God*, Minneapolis, Fortress Press, 1996, p. 658)

Suffering would not have been necessary for the

kind of Messiah the people of his time were expecting. He could have lived to a ripe old age, and then have been enshrined in legend and history like David, Joshua, or Gideon. Even if he had lost his life in a struggle against the Romans, he could have had a place of honor. But to live in relative obscurity and then die in disgrace — what kind of a Messiah is that?

But Jesus was so much more than a military hero. He had come, not just to deliver Israel from the Romans, but to rescue all humanity from captivity to evil and death, and reconcile humanity to God. And to do that, he had to suffer and die. On the very day that Jesus rose from the dead, he spoke of himself, saying, "Was it not necessary for the Christ to suffer these things and enter into his glory?" (Luke 24:26 NASB).

The full glory of the Messiah is seen on the cross. This was an important point that Jesus' disciples had missed until after his resurrection. Many still miss this point today. The glory of Jesus as our Savior was not shown only through his power and resurrection, though it could have been. His glory certainly was not shown through any status or position he had on earth. Rather, his glory was also shown in the incredible suffering he willingly endured as an expression of his immeasurable love for those he came to save.

As Paul wrote to the church at Philippi:

[Jesus] being in very nature God, did not consider equality with God something to be used to his own advantage; rather, he made himself nothing by taking the very nature of a servant, being made in human likeness. And being found in appearance as a man, he humbled himself by becoming obedient to death — even death on a cross! (Philippians 2:6-8).

After his resurrection, the full realization of who Jesus was, and what he had come to do began to sink in. As his followers absorbed the wonder, grace and glory of both his crucifixion and his resurrection, they were transformed. Led by the Holy Spirit, only then did they began to fulfill his "Great Commission," taking his message of forgiveness of sin, victory over evil and death, and of salvation to the whole world. Convinced of the truth and reality of who Jesus was and what he had accomplished, not even the suffering of hardships, persecution and, for some, execution could stop their proclamation reaching "to the uttermost parts of the earth." And we today are the beneficiaries of their mission and ministry that was handed on to others who were also faithful channels of God's own reconciling and renewing work down through the generations.

As Paul put it in 2 Corinthians 5:14-15:

For Christ's love compels us, because we are convinced that one died for all, and therefore all died. And he died for all, that those who live should no longer live for themselves but for him who died for them and was raised again.

Let's take time to renew our own sense of wonder and commitment, as we each do our part in carrying on the Great Commission. It is a message this world needs. It has been well said, "He may not have been the Messiah all had hoped for, but he is indeed the Messiah of great hope for all."

Joseph Tkach

Why Did Jesus Have to Die?

Jesus had an amazingly productive ministry, teaching and healing thousands. He attracted large crowds and had potential for much more. He could have healed thousands more by traveling to the Jews and Gentiles who lived in other areas.

But Jesus allowed this work to come to a sudden end. He could have avoided arrest, but he chose to die instead of expanding his ministry. Although his teachings were important, he had come not just to teach, but also to die. Death was an important part of Jesus' ministry. This is the way we remember him, through the cross as a symbol of Christianity or through the bread and wine of the Lord's Supper. Our Savior is a Savior who died.

The Old Testament tells us that God appeared on earth on several occasions. If Jesus wanted only to heal and teach, he could have simply appeared. But he did more: he became a human. Why? So he could die. To understand Jesus, we need to understand his death. His death is part of the gospel message and something all Christians should know about.

Born to die

Jesus said, "The Son of Man did not come to be served, but to serve, and to give his life as a ransom for many" (Matthew 20:28). He came to give his life, to die, and his death would result in salvation for others. This was the reason he came to earth. His blood was poured out for others (Matthew 26:28).

Jesus warned his disciples that he would suffer and die, but they did not seem to believe it. "Jesus began to explain to his disciples that he must go to Jerusalem and suffer many things at the hands of the elders, chief priests and teachers of the law, and that he must be killed and on the third day be raised to life. Peter took him aside and began to rebuke him. 'Never, Lord!' he said. 'This shall never happen to you!'" (Matthew 16:21-22).

Jesus knew that he must die, because the Scriptures said so. "Why then is it written that the Son of Man must suffer much and be rejected?" (Mark 9:12; 9:31; 10:33-34). "Beginning with Moses and all the Prophets, he explained to them what was said in all the Scriptures concerning himself…. 'This is what is written: The Christ will suffer and rise from the dead on the third day'" (Luke 24:26-27, 46).

It all happened according to God's plan: Herod and Pilate did only what God "had decided beforehand should happen" (Acts 4:28). In the Garden of Gethsemane, when Jesus knew that he would soon be crucified, Jesus asked his Father if there might be some other way, but there was none (Luke 22:42). His death was necessary for our salvation.

The suffering servant

It was written in the Old Testament, Jesus had said. Where was it written? Isaiah 53 is one of the prophecies. Jesus quoted Isaiah 53:12 when he said: "It is written: 'And he was numbered with the transgressors'; and I tell you that this must be fulfilled in me. Yes, what is written about me is reaching its fulfillment" (Luke 22:37). Jesus, although without sin, was to be counted among sinners. Notice what else is written in Isaiah 53:

> Surely he took up our infirmities and carried our sorrows, yet we considered him stricken by God, smitten by him, and afflicted. But he was pierced for our transgressions, he was crushed for our iniquities; the punishment that brought us peace was upon him, and by his wounds we are healed. We all, like sheep, have gone astray, each of us has turned to his own way; and the Lord has

laid on him the iniquity of us all.

> For the transgression of my people he was stricken…. Though he had done no violence … it was the Lord's will to crush him and cause him to suffer … the Lord makes his life a guilt offering…. He will bear their iniquities…. He bore the sin of many, and made intercession for the transgressors. (verses 4-12)

Isaiah describes someone who suffers not for his own sins, but for the sins of others. Although this man would be "cut off from the land of the living" (verse 8), that would not be the end of the story. "He will see the light of life and be satisfied; by his knowledge my righteous servant will justify many…. He will see his offspring and prolong his days" (verses 11, 10).

What Isaiah wrote, Jesus fulfilled. He laid down his life for his sheep (John 10:15). In his death, he carried our sins and suffered for our transgressions; he was punished so that we might have peace with God. Through his suffering and death, our spiritual illness is healed; we are justified, accepted by God.

These truths are developed in more detail in the New Testament.

Dying an accursed death

"Anyone who is hung on a tree is under God's curse," says Deuteronomy 21:23. Because of this verse, Jews considered any crucified person to be condemned by God. As Isaiah wrote, people would consider him "stricken by God."

The Jewish leaders probably thought that Jesus' disciples would give up after their leader was killed. It happened just as they hoped — the crucifixion shattered the disciples' hopes. They were dejected and said, "We had hoped that he was the one who was going to redeem Israel" (Luke 24:21). But their hopes were dramatically restored when Jesus appeared to them after his resurrection, and at Pentecost, the Holy Spirit filled them with new conviction to proclaim salvation in Jesus Christ. They had unshakable faith in the least likely hero: a crucified Messiah.

Peter told the Jewish leaders, "The God of our fathers raised Jesus from the dead — whom you had killed by hanging him on a tree" (Acts 5:30). By using the word tree, Peter reminded the leaders about the curse involved in crucifixion. But the shame was not on Jesus, he said — it was on the people who crucified him. God had blessed Jesus because he did not deserve the curse he suffered. God had reversed the stigma and shame.

Paul referred to the same curse in Galatians 3:13: "Christ redeemed us from the curse of the law by becoming a curse for us, for it is written: 'Cursed is everyone who is hung on a tree.'" Jesus became a curse on our behalf so we could escape the curse of the law, which is death. He became something he was not, so that we could become something we were not. "God made him who had no sin to be sin for us, so that in him we might become the righteousness of God" (2 Corinthians 5:21).

He became sin for us, so that we might be declared righteous through him. Because he suffered what we deserved, he redeemed us from the curse of the law. "The punishment that brought us peace was upon him." Because he suffered death, we can enjoy peace with God.

Message of the cross

The disciples never forgot the shameful way that Jesus died. Indeed, sometimes that was the focus of the message: "We preach Christ crucified: a stumbling block to Jews and foolishness to Gentiles" (1 Corinthians 1:23). Paul even called the gospel "the message of the cross" (verse 18). Paul reminded the Galatians that "before your very eyes Jesus Christ was clearly portrayed as crucified" (Galatians 3:1). That was how he summarized the way that he preached the gospel.

Why is the cross good news? Because the cross is the means by which Jesus rescued us from death. Paul focused on the cross because it is the key to Jesus being good news for us. We will not be raised into glory unless in Christ we are made "the righteousness of God." Only then do we join Jesus in his glory. The crucifixion is part of the process by which we are transformed from the old creation to the new.

Paul says that Jesus died "for us" (Romans 5:6-8; 2 Corinthians 5:14; 1 Thessalonians 5:10); he also says that he died "for our sins" (1 Corinthians 15:3; Galatians 1:4). "He himself bore our sins in his body on the tree" (1 Peter 2:24; 3:18). Paul also says that we died with Christ (Romans 6:3-8). Through our union with him in faith, we participate in his death.

It is as if we were on the cross, receiving the consequences that our sins deserved. But Jesus did it for us, and because he did it, we can be justified, or proclaimed as righteous. He takes our sin and death; he gives us righteousness and life. The prince became a pauper, so that we paupers might become princes.

Although Jesus used the word *ransom* to describe our rescue, the ransom wasn't paid to anyone in particular—this is a figure of speech to indicate that it cost Jesus an enormous amount to set us free. In the same way, Paul talks about Jesus redeeming us, buying our freedom, but he didn't pay anyone.

God loves people—but he hates sin, because sin hurts people. God wants everyone to change (2 Peter 3:9), but those who don't will suffer the result of their own sins.

In the death of Jesus, our sins are set aside. But this does not mean that a loving Jesus appeased or "paid off" an angry God. The Father is just as merciful as Jesus is, and Jesus is just as angry about sin as the Father is. He is angry at sin because sin hurts the people he loves. Jesus is the Judge who condemns (Matthew 25:31-46), as well as the Judge who loves sinners so much that he dies for them.

When God forgives us, he does not simply wipe away sin and pretend it never existed. Sins have serious consequences—consequences we can see in the cross of Christ. Humanity's tendency to sin cost Jesus pain and shame and death.

The gospel reveals that God acts righteously in forgiving us (Romans 1:17); his mercy is part of his righteous character. He does not ignore our sins, but takes care of them in Jesus Christ. Metaphorically, God presented Jesus as a sacrifice for our forgiveness. Sin has consequences, and Jesus volunteered to suffer the consequences on our behalf. The cross demonstrates God's love as well as his justice (Romans 5:8).

As Isaiah says, we have peace with God because of what Christ did. We were once enemies of God, but through Christ we have been brought near (Ephesians 2:13). In other words, we have been reconciled to God through the cross (verse 16). It is a basic Christian belief that our relationship with God depends on Jesus Christ, including his death.

Christianity is not a list of things to do—it is accepting that Christ has done everything we need to be right with God—and this was done on the cross. "When we were God's enemies, we were reconciled to him through the death of his Son" (Romans 5:10). God reconciled the universe through Christ, "making peace through his blood, shed on the cross" (Colossians 1:20). He did this before we believed it, before we were even born. Since we are reconciled through him, all our sins are forgiven (verse 22)—reconciliation, forgiveness and justification all mean the same thing: peace with God.

Victory!

Paul uses an interesting image of salvation when he writes that Jesus "disarmed the powers and authorities" by making "a public spectacle of them, triumphing over them by the cross" (Colossians 2:15). He uses the word for a military parade: the winning general brings captured enemy soldiers in a victory parade at home. They are disarmed, humiliated, and put on display. Paul's point here is that on the cross, Jesus did this to our enemies.

What looked like a shameful death for Jesus was actually a glorious triumph for God's plan, because it is through the cross that Jesus won victory over enemy powers, including Satan, sin and death. Their claim on us has been fully satisfied in the death of the innocent victim. They cannot demand any more than what he has already paid. They have nothing further to threaten us with.

"By his death," we are told, Jesus was able to "destroy him who holds the power of death—that is, the devil" (Hebrews 2:14). "The reason the Son of God appeared was to destroy the devil's work" (1 John 3:8). Victory was won on the cross.

Sacrifice

Jesus' death is also described as a sacrifice. The idea of sacrifice draws on the rich imagery of Old Testament sacrifices. Isaiah 53:10 calls our Savior a "guilt offering." John the Baptist calls him the Lamb "who takes away the sin of the world" (John 1:29). Paul calls him a "sacrifice of atonement," a "sin offering," a "Passover lamb," a "fragrant offering" (Romans 3:25; 8:3; 1 Corinthians 5:7; Ephesians 5:2). Hebrews 10:12 calls him a "sacrifice for sins." John calls him "the atoning sacrifice for our sins" (1 John 2:2; 4:10).

Several terms are used to describe what Jesus accomplished on the cross. Different New Testament authors use different words or images to convey the idea. The exact terminology or mechanism is not essential. What is important is that we are saved through the death of Jesus. "By his wounds we are healed." He died to set us free, to remove our sins, to suffer our punishment, to purchase our salvation. How should we respond? "Dear friends, since God so loved us, we also ought to love one another" (1 John 4:11).

Seven Images of Salvation

The New Testament uses a wide range of images to express the richness of the work of Christ.

We may describe these images as analogies, models or metaphors. Each gives part of the picture:

- Ransom: a price paid to achieve someone's freedom. The emphasis falls on the idea of being freed, not the nature of the price.
- Redemption: "buying back," or for a slave, buying freedom.
- Justification: being put right with God, as if declared by a court to be in the right.
- Salvation: deliverance or rescue from a dangerous situation. The word can also suggest restoration to wholeness, a healing.
- Reconciliation: the repair of a broken relationship. God reconciles us to him. He acts to restore a friendship, and we respond to his initiative.
- Adoption: making us legal children of God. Faith brings about a change in our status, from outsider to family member. The phrase "born again" suggests a different way to enter the family.
- Forgiveness: This can be seen in two ways. In legal or financial terms, forgiveness is like the cancellation of a debt. In terms of personal relationship, forgiveness means the setting aside of personal hurt or injury.

(Adapted from Alister McGrath, *Understanding Jesus,* pp. 124-135).

Michael Morrison

The Holy Spirit

The Holy Spirit is God at work—creating, speaking, transforming us, living within us, working in us. Although the Holy Spirit can do this work without our knowledge, it is helpful for us to know more.

The Holy Spirit is God

The Holy Spirit has the attributes of God, is equated with God and does work that only God does. Like God, the Spirit is holy—so holy that insulting the Spirit is just as sinful as trampling the Son of God under foot (Hebrews 10:29). Blasphemy against the Holy Spirit is an unforgivable sin (Matthew 12:32).[1] This indicates that the Spirit is holy by nature rather than having an assigned holiness such as the temple had.

Like God, the Holy Spirit is eternal (Hebrews 9:14). Like God, the Holy Spirit is everywhere present (Psalm 139:7-9). Like God, the Holy Spirit knows everything (1 Corinthians 2:10-11; John 14:26). The Holy Spirit creates (Job 33:4; Psalm 104:30) and empowers miracles (Matthew 12:28; Romans 15:18-19), doing the work or ministry of God.

Several passages discuss the Father, Son, and Holy Spirit as equally divine. In a discussion of spiritual gifts, Paul puts the Spirit, the Lord, and God in parallel constructions (1 Corinthians 12:4-6). He closes a letter with a three-part prayer (2 Corinthians 13:14). Peter begins a letter with a different three-part formula (1 Peter 1:2). These are not proof of unity, but they support it.

The baptismal formula has a stronger indication of unity—"in the name [singular] of the Father and of the Son and of the Holy Spirit" (Matthew 28:19). The three have one name, suggesting one essence and being.

When the Holy Spirit does something, God is doing it. When the Holy Spirit speaks, God is speaking. When Ananias lied to the Holy Spirit, he lied to God (Acts 5:3-4). As Peter said, Ananias did not lie to God's representative, but to God himself. People do not "lie" to an impersonal power.

In one passage, Paul says that Christians are God's temple (1 Corinthians 3:16); in another he says that we are a temple of the Holy Spirit (1 Corinthians 6:19). A temple is for the worship of a divine being, not an impersonal power. When Paul writes "temple of the Holy Spirit," he implies that the Holy Spirit is God.

The Holy Spirit and God are also equated in Acts 13:2: "The Holy Spirit said, 'Set apart for *me* Barnabas and Saul for the work to which *I* have called them.'" Here, the Holy Spirit speaks with personal pronouns, speaking as God. Similarly, the Holy Spirit says that the Israelites "tested and tried *me*"; the Holy Spirit says that "*I* was angry…. They shall never enter my rest" (Hebrews 3:7-11).

But the Holy Spirit is not just another name for God. The Holy Spirit is distinct from the Father and the Son, as shown in Jesus' baptism (Matthew 3:16-17). The three are distinct, but one.

The Holy Spirit does the work of God in our lives. We are born of God (John 1:12), which is the same as being born of the Spirit (John 3:5). The Holy Spirit is the means by which God lives in us (Ephesians 2:22; 1 John 3:24; 4:13). The Holy Spirit lives in us (Romans 8:11; 1 Corinthians 3:16)—and because the Spirit lives in us, we can say that *God* lives in us.

The Spirit is personal

Scripture describes the Holy Spirit as having personal characteristics.

- The Spirit lives (Romans 8:11; 1 Corinthians 3:16).
- The Spirit speaks (Acts 8:29; 10:19; 11:12; 21:11; 1 Timothy 4:1; Hebrews 3:7; etc.).

- The Spirit sometimes uses the personal pronoun "I" (Acts 10:20; 13:2).
- The Spirit may be spoken to, tested, grieved, insulted or blasphemed (Acts 5:3, 9; Ephesians 4:30; Hebrews 10:29;Matthew 12:31).
- The Spirit guides, intercedes, calls and commissions (Romans 8:14, 26; Acts 13:2; 20:28).

Romans 8:27 refers to the "mind" of the Spirit. The Spirit makes judgments—a decision "seemed good" to the Holy Spirit (Acts 15:28). The Spirit "knows" and "determines" (1 Corinthians 2:11; 12:11). This is not an impersonal power.

Jesus called the Holy Spirit the *parakletos*—translated as the Comforter, the Advocate or the Counselor. "I will ask the Father, and he will give you *another Counselor* to be with you forever—the Spirit of truth" (John 14:16-17). The disciples' first Counselor was Jesus. Like him, the Holy Spirit teaches, testifies, convicts, guides and reveals truth (John 14:26;15:26; 16:8, 13-14). These are personal roles.

John uses the masculine form of the Greek word *parakletos;* it was not necessary to use a neuter word. In John 16:14, masculine pronouns (he) are used even after the neuter word "Spirit" is mentioned. It would have been easy to switch to neuter pronouns (it), but John does not. The Spirit may be called *he.* However, grammar is relatively unimportant; what is important is that the Holy Spirit has personal characteristics. He is not an impersonal power, but the intelligent and divine Helper who lives within us.

The Spirit in the Old Testament

The Bible does not have a section titled "The Holy Spirit." We learn about the Spirit a little here and a little there, as Scripture happens to mention what the Spirit does. The Old Testament gives us only a few glimpses.

The Spirit was involved in creating and sustaining all life (Genesis 1:2; Job 33:4; 34:14). The Spirit of God filled Bezelel with skill to build the tabernacle (Exodus 31:3-5). He filled Moses and came upon the 70 elders (Numbers 11:25). He filled Joshua with wisdom and filled leaders such as Samson with strength or ability to fight (Deuteronomy 34:9; Judges 6:34; 14:6).

God's Spirit was given to Saul and later taken away (1 Samuel 10:6; 16:14). The Spirit gave David plans for the temple (1 Chronicles 28:12). The Spirit inspired prophets to speak (Numbers 24:2; 2 Samuel 23:2; 1 Chronicles 12:18; 2 Chronicles 15:1; 20:14; Ezekiel 11:5; Zechariah 7:12; 2 Peter 1:21).

In the New Testament, too, the Spirit caused people to speak, including Elizabeth, Zechariah and Simeon (Luke 1:41, 67;2:25-32). John the Baptist was filled with the Spirit from birth (Luke 1:15). His most important work was announcing the arrival of Jesus, who would baptize people not only with water, but with "the Holy Spirit and with fire" (Luke 3:16).

The Spirit and Jesus

The Holy Spirit was involved throughout Jesus' life. The Spirit caused his conception (Matthew 1:20), descended on him at his baptism (Matthew 3:16), led him into the desert (Luke 4:1) and anointed him to preach the gospel (Luke 4:18). Jesus drove out demons by the Spirit of God (Matthew 12:28). It was through the Spirit that he offered himself as a sacrifice for sin (Hebrews 9:14) and by that same Spirit was raised from the dead (Romans 8:11).

Jesus taught that the Spirit would speak through his disciples in times of persecution (Matthew 10:19-20). He told them to baptize followers in the name of the Father, Son, and Holy Spirit (Matthew 28:19). He said that God was certain to give the Holy Spirit to those who ask (Luke 11:13).

Some of Jesus' most important teachings about the Holy Spirit come in the Gospel of John. First, people must be "born of water and the Spirit" (John 3:5). People need a spiritual renewal, and this does not come from inside themselves: it is a gift of God. Although spirit can't be seen, the Holy Spirit does make a difference in our lives (verse 8).

Jesus also taught, "If anyone is thirsty, let him come to me and drink. Whoever believes in me, as the Scripture has said, streams of living water will flow from within him" (John 7:37-38). John adds this explanation: "By this he meant the Spirit, whom those who believed in him were later to receive" (verse 39). The Holy Spirit satisfies an internal thirst. He gives us the relationship with God that we were created for. We receive the Spirit by coming to Jesus, and the Spirit can fill our lives.

John also tells us, "Up to that time the Spirit had not been given, since Jesus had not yet been glorified" (verse 39). The Spirit had filled various men and women before Jesus, but the Spirit would soon come in a new and more powerful way—on Pentecost. The Spirit is now given on a far larger scale: to all who call on the name of the Lord (Acts 2:38-39).

Jesus promised that his disciples would be given the Spirit of truth, who would live in them (John 14:16-18). This is equivalent to Jesus himself coming to his disciples (verse 18), because he is the Spirit of Christ as well as the Spirit of the Father—sent by Jesus as well as by the Father (John 15:26). The Spirit makes Jesus available to everyone and continues his work.

Jesus promised that the Spirit would teach the disciples and remind them of what Jesus had taught (John 14:26). The Spirit taught them things that they could not understand before Jesus' resurrection (John 16:12-13).

The Spirit testifies about Jesus (John 15:26; 16:14). He does not promote himself, but leads people to Jesus Christ and the Father. He does not speak on his own, but only as the Father wants (John 16:13). Since the Spirit can live in millions of people, it is for our good that Jesus left and sent the Spirit to us (John 16:7).

The Spirit works in evangelism, convicting the world of their sin, their guilt, their need for righteousness, and the certainty of judgment (verses 8-10). The Holy Spirit points people to Jesus as the solution to guilt and the source of righteousness.

The Spirit and the church

John the Baptist said that Jesus would baptize people in the Holy Spirit (Mark 1:8). This happened on the day of Pentecost after his resurrection, when the Spirit dramatically gave new power to the disciples (Acts 2). This included speaking that was understood by people from other nations (verse 6). Similar miracles happened on a few other occasions as the church grew (Acts 10:44-46; 19:1-6), but there is no indication that these miracles happened to all new believers.

Paul says that all believers are baptized in the

> From our *Statement of Beliefs*
>
> The Holy Spirit is the third Person of the triune God, eternally proceeding from the Father through the Son. He is the Comforter promised by Jesus Christ, who unites us with the Father and the Son, and transforms us into the image of Christ. The Spirit works out in us the regeneration Christ accomplished for us, and by continual renewal empowers us to share in the Son's glorious and eternal communion with the Father as his children. The Holy Spirit is the Source of inspiration and prophecy throughout the Scriptures, and the Source of unity and communion in the church. He provides spiritual gifts for the work of the gospel, and is the Christian's constant Guide into all truth.
>
> (Matthew 28:19; John 14:16; 15:26; Acts 2:38; John 14:17, 26; 1 Peter 1:2; Titus 3:5; 1 Corinthians 3:16; Romans 8:16; 2 Peter 1:21; 1 Corinthians 12:13; 2 Corinthians 13:14; 1 Corinthians 12:1-11; John 16:13)

Holy Spirit into one body—the church (1 Corinthians 12:13). Everyone who has faith is given the Holy Spirit (Galatians 3:14). Whether miracles happen to them or not, all believers have been baptized with the Holy Spirit. It is not necessary to seek any particular miracle as proof of this.

The Bible does not command any believer to seek the baptism of the Holy Spirit. Instead, every believer is encouraged to be continually filled with the Holy Spirit (Ephesians 5:18)—to be fully responsive to the Spirit's lead. This is a continuing relationship, not a one-time event.

Rather than seeking a miracle, we are to seek God, and leave it to God's decision as to whether miracles happen. Paul often describes the power of God not in terms of physical miracles, but in the transformation that comes in a person's life—hope, love, patience, serving, understanding, suffering and preaching boldly (Romans 15:13; 2 Corinthians 12:9; Ephesians 3:7, 16-18; Colossians 1:11, 28-29; 2 Timothy 1:7-8). We might call these psychological miracles—the power of God at work in human lives.

The book of Acts shows that the Spirit

empowered the church's growth. The Spirit gave the disciples power to testify about Jesus (Acts 1:8). He gave the disciples great boldness in preaching Christ (Acts 4:8, 31; 6:10). He gave instructions to Philip and later transported him (Acts 8:29, 39).

The Spirit encouraged the church and set leaders in it (Acts 9:31; 20:28). He spoke to Peter and to the church at Antioch (10:19; 11:12; 13:2). He inspired Agabus to predict a famine and Paul to pronounce a curse (11:28; 13:9-10). He led Paul and Barnabas on their journeys (13:4; 16:6-7) and helped the Jerusalem council come to a decision (15:28). He sent Paul to Jerusalem and warned him what would happen (20:22-23; 21:11). The church existed and grew only through the Spirit working in the believers.

The Spirit and believers today

God the Holy Spirit is intimately involved in the life of believers today.

- He leads us to repentance and gives us new life (John 16:8; 3:5-6).
- He lives in us, teaches us and leads us (1 Corinthians 2:10-13; John 14:16-17, 26; Romans 8:14). He leads us through Scripture, prayer and other Christians.
- He is the Spirit of wisdom, helping us look at choices with confidence, love and self-control (Ephesians 1:17; 2 Timothy 1:7).
- The Spirit circumcises our hearts, seals us and sanctifies us, setting us apart for God's purpose (Romans 2:29; Ephesians 1:14).
- He produces in us love and the fruit of righteousness (Romans 5:5; Ephesians 5:9; Galatians 5:22-23).
- He puts us into the church and helps us know that we are God's children (1 Corinthians 12:13; Romans 8:14-16).

We are to worship God "by the Spirit," with our minds set on what the Spirit wants (Philippians 3:3; 2 Corinthians 3:6; Romans 7:6; 8:4-5). We strive to please him (Galatians 6:8). If we are controlled by the Spirit, he gives us life and peace (Romans 8:6). He gives us access to the Father (Ephesians 2:18). He helps us in our weakness, interceding for us (Romans 8:26-27).

The Holy Spirit also gives spiritual gifts, including leaders for the church (Ephesians 4:11), basic functions within the church (Romans 12:6-8), and some abilities for extraordinary purposes (1 Corinthians 12:4-11). No one has every gift, nor is any gift given to everyone (verses 28-30). All gifts, whether spiritual or "natural," are to be used for the common good, to help the entire church (1 Corinthians 12:7;14:12). Every gift is important (12:22-26).

In this age, we have only the firstfruits of the Spirit, only a deposit that guarantees much more in our future (Romans 8:23; 2 Corinthians 1:22; 5:5; Ephesians 1:13-14).

In summary, the Holy Spirit is God at work in our lives. Everything God does is done through his Spirit. Paul therefore encourages us: "Let us keep in step with the Spirit.... Do not grieve the Holy Spirit of God.... Do not put out the Spirit's fire" (Galatians 5:25; Ephesians 4:30; 1 Thessalonians 5:19). Be attentive to what the Spirit says. When he speaks, God is speaking.

[1] Blasphemy against the Holy Spirit is a deliberate rejection of the agent God uses to help people understand the gospel—the people reject the message even though they know it is from God. Anyone who is worried about this unpardonable sin shows, by their worry, that they have not committed it. The fact that they *want* to do the right thing shows that they have not deliberately rejected the Holy Spirit.

For further reading

Max Anders, *What You Need to Know About the Holy Spirit.* Nelson, 1995.

Michael Green, *I Believe in the Holy Spirit.* Eerdmans, 1975.

Craig S. Keener, *Gift and Giver.* Baker, 2001.

J.I. Packer, *Keep in Step With the Spirit.* Revell, 1984.

Clark Pinnock, *Flame of Love.* InterVarsity, 1999.

Anthony Thiselton, *The Holy Spirit.* Eerdmans, 2013.

Michael Morrison

The Use and Misuse of Spiritual Gifts

We have come to a greater awareness of the spiritual gifts God gives his people. We understand from Scripture some basic points:

- Every member has at least one spiritual gift, usually two or three.
- Every member should be using his or her gifts to serve others in the church.
- No member has all the gifts, so we need each other.
- No gift is given to all members.
- God decides who receives which gift.

Every member ought to be involved in some ministry, some area of service ("ministry" refers to all types of service, not just pastoral work). Every Christian should be using his or her gifts to serve others "for the common good" (1 Cor. 12:7; 1 Pet. 4:10).

This awareness of spiritual gifts has been a great blessing for members and congregations. However, even good things can be misused, and a few problems have developed in connection with spiritual gifts. These problems are not unique to us, of course, and it is sometimes helpful to see how other Christian leaders have dealt with them.

For example, some people use the concept of spiritual gifts as an excuse to refuse to serve others. For example, they say that their gift is administration and they refuse to do anything except try to meddle in how the church is administered. Or they may claim to be a teacher and refuse to serve in any other way. I believe that this is the opposite of what Paul intended — he explained that God gifts people for service, not for refusal.

Sometimes work needs to be done whether anybody is especially gifted for it or not. Meeting halls need to be set up and cleaned up. Compassion needs to be given when tragedies strike, whether or not you happen to have the gift of compassion. All members need to be able to teach (Col. 3:16) whether or not they have the gift of teaching. All members need to be able to explain the gospel (1 Pet. 3:15) whether or not they have the gift of evangelism.

It is unrealistic to think that every member will do only those forms of service for which he or she is specially gifted. Not only do other forms of service need to be done, each member needs to experience other forms of service. Service often requires that we get out of our comfort zones, out of the area in which we feel gifted. After all, God may be wanting to develop in us a gift we did not know we had!

Each person has one to three major gifts, and it is best if the person's primary area of service uses one or more of those primary gifts. But each person should also be willing to serve in other ways, as the church has needs. One large church uses the principle that, "you choose your primary ministry based on your own gifts, and be willing to serve in a secondary ministry based on the needs of others." Such a policy helps members grow — and the secondary ministries are assigned only for limited periods of time. Those less-desirable service roles are then rotated to other members. Some experienced pastors estimate that members can expect only about 60 percent of their service to be within their primary spiritual gifts.

The most important thing is that each member serve in some way. Service is a responsibility, not a matter of "I will accept it only if I like it."

Finding your gifts

Now a few thoughts about how we determine what spiritual gifts we have. There are several approaches to this: 1) written tests, surveys and inventories, 2) self-analysis based on interests and experiences, and 3) confirmation from people who know you well. All three approaches can be helpful, and it is especially helpful if all three lead to the same answer. But none of the three is infallible.

Some of the written inventories are simply a method of analyzing yourself and others' opinions about you. The questions might go like this: What do you like to do? What have you done well? What do other people say that you do well? What kinds of needs do you see in the church? (This last question is based on the observation that people are usually most aware of the needs that they are able to help with. For example, a person with the gift of compassion will think that the church needs more compassion.)

Often, we do not know our gifts until we have put them to use and seen whether we do well in that type of activity. Not only do gifts grow through experience, they can also be discovered through experience. That is why it is helpful for members to occasionally try different areas of service. They may learn something about themselves, as well as helping others.

Those are a few comments about gifts in general. But for the rest of this article, I want to focus on a particular gift that raises the most questions.

The gift of tongues

Historically, the most controversial gift has been tongues. It was controversial on the day of Pentecost in Jerusalem; it was controversial a few years later in Caesarea; it was controversial later on in Corinth. Throughout the centuries, small groups of Christians have occasionally spoken in tongues, almost always generating controversy.

Today, millions of Christians speak in tongues. Some are found in Roman Catholic churches, some in liberal mainstream groups, some in conservative evangelical churches, and many in Pentecostal denominations. Even though tongues-speaking has such diverse participants, it is still controversial. So now, I hope to give some perspective on this practice, both to help people who are afraid of it, and those who think too highly of this gift.

The modern resurgence of tongue-speaking is generally traced to the turn of the century. In 1900, Charles Parham and a small group in Kansas began to speak in tongues after studying about this gift in the Bible. In 1906, Parham went to Los Angeles and spoke at the Azusa Street Mission Revival (no connection with Azusa Pacific University), and the movement quickly spread from there.

In the early years, most denominations rejected tongues-speaking as lunacy or demonic, and as one might expect, tongues-speakers left such hostile churches and formed churches in which they were allowed and encouraged to speak in tongues. Thus Pentecostal denominations such as the Assemblies of God were formed.

There is no question that many of these Pentecostal churches had numerous theological errors. They made many mistakes in their zeal to follow God. As time went on, they learned more and corrected many of their errors. This is a dynamic that we should well understand.

In the 1960s, another wave of tongues-speaking occurred in more traditional churches. This time, many churches did not ridicule or drive these people away; they were accepted as charismatic subgroups within the churches. Nevertheless, tongues-speaking is still controversial. Some Christians teach that God simply does not give miraculous gifts to anyone in the church today; yet others still claim that all Christians ought to seek and practice the gift of tongues.

As recounted in his Autobiography, Herbert Armstrong encountered some Pentecostal people in his early ministry, and he found them to be divisive. And after such experiences, he was strongly opposed to tongues-speaking, even though he was strongly in favor of other miraculous gifts, such as healing. We remained opposed to tongues for decades, and if anybody ever spoke in tongues, they kept pretty quiet about it.

But more recently, we have recognized that some Christians do indeed speak in tongues. We have been slower to criticize and more willing to consider the possibility that tongues-speaking may be an authentic gift of the Holy Spirit. Meanwhile, our members have visited tongues-speaking churches, and some of our members and ministers have begun to speak in tongues, usually in private.

Knowing how controversial tongues have been in other churches, and knowing our previous dogmatic rejection of tongues, it is no surprise that questions arise when some of our members and ministers begin to speak in tongues, even privately. Due to our lack of experience in this area, it is also no surprise that some excesses have occurred. New-found zeal sometimes carries people further than it should.

Information about tongues

Since Scripture is our ultimate authority for doctrine and Christian living, it is essential that we understand what the Bible says about tongues. Here I will refer you to our booklet on tongues. Although this booklet is now out of stock, it is still a good analysis of the subject.

For those who want further study on this subject, the booklet has a bibliography of helpful resources, written from several perspectives. I also refer you to the book *Are Miraculous Gifts For Today? Four Views,* edited by Wayne Grudem (Zondervan, 1996). I will not enter the detailed arguments addressed in the book, but I will simply affirm that I believe that God still performs miracles today. I see no biblical reason to think that he no longer gives anyone the ability to speak in tongues.

However, simply because someone "speaks in tongues" does not mean that he or she has this spiritual gift. As our booklet pointed out, various non-Christians, from ancient pagans to modern Buddhists, have spoken in tongues. Tongues-speaking, in itself, is no proof of anything. (Similarly, non-Christians may also have leadership, service, compassion, teaching and other abilities that are similar to spiritual gifts.)

Some tongues-speaking is also called ecstatic speech, which is a psychomotor function of the brain. In normal speech, two parts of the brain work together. In ecstatic speech, one part of the brain tells the mouth and tongue to speak, but the conscious portion of the brain does not supply any particular guidance for what words to speak, so unintelligible syllables come out. This can happen if a person is startled, for example, or if consciousness is altered in some way.

Also, some tongues-speaking may be done in imitation (perhaps subconsciously) of a respected leader. People who are seeking a particular experience are (like hypnotized people) psychologically very susceptible to suggestions like that.

However, I do not think that all tongues-speaking can be explained in these ways, and I believe that some tongues-speaking is genuinely a gift of God. I also recognize that God sometimes works through observable phenomena, and just because some tongues-speaking has a psychomotor explanation does not mean it isn't a gift.

As I have written before, the psychological state in which tongues-speaking occurs is usually pleasant. It is liberating to get rid of some of their inhibitions. It is encouraging to put oneself in a very responsive state, ready to respond to God working in their lives. Tongues-speaking is not the only way to do this, but it is one way, and it encourages people in their walk with the Lord.

One pastor observed the irony that most Christians can talk about almost any spiritual gift with nothing but praise, but as soon as tongues is mentioned, it has to be accompanied by all sorts of cautionary statements. I agree that this is an irony. All sorts of spiritual gifts can be misused, and cautions can be given for them all. But historically, and in our present experience, tongues causes the most problems and needs the most caution. But still, I affirm that it is one of God's spiritual gifts, and it is therefore good.

I respect and honor Christians who speak in tongues; I respect and honor those who do not. I do not want to quench the Spirit; I do not want to "forbid speaking in tongues" (1 Cor. 14:39).

But I also want to follow what Paul said in the very next verse: "Everything should be done in a fitting and orderly way" (v. 40). So let me address how tongues, if used, should be done in an orderly way. Again, since Scripture is our ultimate guide for doctrine and Christian living, let us examine what Scripture says about how tongues should be used.

Biblical data

First, Paul reminds the Corinthians that God divides his gifts among his people (1 Cor. 12:8-11;29-30). It is not realistic to expect everyone to speak in tongues — and yet that is what some Pentecostals unfortunately do. This is divisive today, just as it was in ancient Corinth.

When a Christian says, my gift is better than your gift, it is an insult to other Christians, and an insult to God. No one should feel superior about a spiritual gift, since no one deserves any of the gifts. The gifts are given to serve others, not to feel superior to others.

We do not need to seek the gift of tongues. We need to seek God, and let him decide which gift is best for us. Paul says we should seek the "more excellent way" — love (1 Cor. 12:31 and chapter 13) — or the gift of prophecy, which is speaking words of encouragement, comfort and edification (1 Cor. 14:1-4).

Without love, we are spiritually worthless, no matter what tongues we speak. It reminds me of the story of one person who attended a Pentecostal church for several years and became a lay leader in one of the ministries. Eventually it was learned that this leader had never spoken in tongues, and people were shocked that the leader was "deficient" in the Christian experience! Yet the person drew a different conclusion from the situation: speaking in tongues made no discernible difference in the way a person lives. Even after years of being around a person, others simply could not know whether the person had ever spoken in tongues.

My friend Jack Hayford says he speaks in tongues in his prayers every day. That does not impress me, nor does he expect it to. That is not its purpose. Tongues is not a show of spirituality. It is to edify the self, not to impress others (1 Cor. 14:4). If it edifies the self, that's wonderful. If it is done to impress others, it's being used in a wrong way, a carnal way. Paul said he spoke in tongues a lot (v. 18). He knew what it meant to pray in words he did not understand (v. 14). But he also knew that this was not proof of spiritual greatness.

I don't care how often Jack speaks in tongues. What I care about is the way he lives the rest of his time. Does he live and function in love? Does he use his other gifts to edify the body of Christ? Does he walk humbly and give all glory to God? I think he sets a good example in all these areas. His tongues-speaking neither adds to nor takes away from his character as a Christian.

To use another example, I don't care whether you eat cereal or eggs for breakfast. Neither one makes you a better person. But I do care if you exalt your particular preference into a badge of betterness. "Everybody ought to be like me because I like the way I am." Such approaches are divisive and un-Christian. They also miss Paul's point, that God has distributed his gifts among his people and he wants them to work together in their diversity.

The Use and Misuse of Spiritual Gifts

Part 2

The Corinthian Christians had a lot of problems, and apparently the way they spoke in tongues was a problem in the church. Paul told them to stop being proud and arrogant. He told them to stop being self-centered. He told them to grow up and be more sensible (1 Cor. 14:20). But he did not tell them to stop speaking in tongues.

However, he did lay down some regulations, and they were quite limiting. For example: Only one person should speak at a time (v. 27). Church services should not be a competition to see who can talk the most. The Holy Spirit does not inspire more than one person to speak at a time.

Second, people should speak in tongues only if an interpreter is present (v. 28). Incidentally, it is interesting that many people want to speak in tongues, but not many "seek" the gift of interpretation, even though interpretation is of greater value to the church. I think this shows that tongues have been overvalued. Unfortunately, in some churches, tongues are often spoken without an interpreter present. The person simply speaks whether or not an interpreter is there, contrary to the instructions Paul gave.

And what if the speaker doesn't know whether an interpreter is present? Then the speaker ought to remain silent. After all, if the gift is genuine, the speaker should be able to control it (v. 32). God does not bypass a person's willpower. Indeed, part of the fruit of God's Spirit is self-control (Gal. 5:23; 2 Tim. 1:7).

Balanced approach

One church that I know of has an interesting approach to tongues-speaking. People who want to practice this gift may do so — not during the regular church service, but in their own small group meetings. And then there must be two or more interpreters present. The interpreters write down the interpretation, and then they see whether the interpretations match. Sometimes they do, but often they do not, which means that either one or both of the interpreters are mistaken. This cautions us not to be too quick to believe any uncorroborated interpretation — and certainly not if it contradicts Scripture!

It would just be a lot easier if people sought the gift of prophecy — speaking edifying and intelligible words — rather than tongues, which might not help anybody else (v. 5). Tongues and interpretations are often misunderstood. Even prophesy can be misunderstood, which is why Paul advises us, "the others should weigh carefully what is said" (v. 29).

However, even if an interpreter is present, it is simply best not to speak in tongues in the church service. The gift of tongues is for self-edification, not for edifying anyone else (v. 4). It just doesn't make sense for one member to interrupt everyone else and say, "Hold everything. Just wait a few minutes please while I edify myself. Watch me and listen to me, even though it won't do you any good." Tongues, since they help only the speaker, are appropriate for private prayers, but not for public assemblies.

Tongues are also a distraction. Public tongues-speaking almost always focuses attention on the speaker, not on God. Non-Christians are usually put off by tongues-speaking. Some find it quite fascinating, of course, and some even consider it to be proof of divine blessing, but most do not. It is confusing, and if the person realizes that various non-

Christians also speak in tongues, it is also inconclusive. People need to be impressed by the gospel, not by unusual phenomena. If the person is convinced by emotional impressions rather than truth, the person has an unstable foundation for belief. Emotions are important, of course, but they should be a response to the gospel, not a substitute for it.

Our practice

Paul warned the Corinthians not to allow tongues to get out of control in their worship services, since it could confuse unbelievers: "If the whole church comes together and everyone speaks in tongues, and some who do not understand or some unbelievers come in, will they not say that you are out of your mind?" (v. 23). It is not surprising, then, that some Christians also consider it inappropriate.

However, Paul had nothing against tongues-speaking. After all, he spoke in tongues himself (v. 18). But he did have a lot to say against tongues-speaking in church assemblies. "In the church I would rather speak five intelligible words to instruct others than ten thousand words in a tongue" (v. 19).

That is what we prefer. We want intelligible words; we do not want unintelligible words in our meetings. That is why I say that we are not a tongues-speaking fellowship. Some people in our fellowship speak in tongues, and I defend their privilege to do so in private or in small groups where everyone agrees to accept it. Even then, it needs to be controlled according to the scriptural guidelines.

As a fellowship, when we are gathered as a congregation, we do not want tongues-speaking. This is based not on some irrational fear of things we don't understand — it is based on the guidance Paul has given us, guidance we accept as authoritative, as inspired by the Holy Spirit.

If somebody wants to speak in tongues in a worship service, there are other denominations that allow that sort of thing. If they find it to be self-edifying, that's good, but I encourage them to seek and to use some other spiritual gift that will be helpful to others.

I might also add that even some Pentecostal churches do not allow tongues-speaking in church services. Many of them also recognize that it is unscriptural to allow everybody to speak at once, to speak without an interpreter present, etc. If the pastor were giving a sermon, for example, and a person in the audience began to speak in tongues, then the pastor would tell the person, "Lady (or Sir), control your gift. The spirits of the prophets are subject to the control of prophets. If you cannot control your gift, the ushers will escort you out." Interrupting the sermon would be just as inappropriate as a person trying to sing a hymn in the middle of the sermon. It is good to sing hymns, but only at the right time and place. Similarly, we do not allow tongues-speaking in our regular worship services.

Expressing joy in Christ

I love our Pentecostal brothers and sisters a great deal. Many of you interact with them in ministerial associations, and you have also come to love them. Many of them have warmly embraced us as fellow-members in the family of God. The Four Square denomination in particular was helpful to us. I praise their love for the Lord and their love for neighbor. Many of them set an excellent example.

Pentecostal churches are now the fastest-growing segment of Christianity, especially in Latin America, but also in North America, Europe and Asia. I suspect that one reason it is growing is that Pentecostal churches encourage people to express their emotions rather than suppress them. This can be bad, of course, if people's faith is built on emotions, but it is good if those emotions are a genuine response to the good news of Jesus Christ.

If people really understand the depths of their sinful state, of how utterly disgusting it is, and of the greatness of Jesus' sacrifice for us, of how astonishing his grace toward us is, then it is natural to respond with joy and exuberance — and this emotion does not need to be suppressed, though how it is expressed may vary widely from person to person. We have something worth singing about, something to be happy about. Although we may still be in poverty, we have experienced something wonderful in the love of Jesus Christ, and we share it.

Pentecostal churches are generally freer in how they express this joy. Visitors who attend a Pentecostal church are likely to see people expressing joy and happiness because of their faith in Jesus Christ. This example is an effective aid in evangelism and church growth.

Of course, Pentecostal churches are not the only ones who effectively express their joy in worshiping their Savior, and they are not the only churches that are growing, but as a group, they seem to do it more actively than most. Although I do not agree with all their theology, and certainly not the emphasis on the public practice of tongues-speaking, I do applaud them for the things they are doing well.

Scripture is the ultimate authority for what we do. If growth alone were evidence of truth, then we might all become Muslims or Mormons. Experience may be helpful, but it is not authoritative. Experience may even be very impressive, but that alone does not make it authoritative. Even so, it is still very impressive.

Seeking experience

Consider a not-so-unusual example: people who attend a church every week, but rarely (if ever) experiencing the presence of God in their church services. They have doubts as to their own walk with the Lord. They want to have more assurance that they are making progress. They want to have tangible, observable evidence that the Lord is with them. Then they attend a church in which the preacher confidently, boldly, dogmatically says that "you can have confidence if you have a certain experience. That will give you the assurance of the presence of God in your life."

The people want this experience. It doesn't matter whether it is really proof — it is desirable. Once it comes, it is extremely self-authenticating and reinforcing. The people wanted reassurance, were told in a persuasive way that the particular experience would give them that assurance, and then they had the experience, and true enough, they gained assurance! The people become sold on the experience and sometimes even become an "evangelist" for the experience.

This has happened within our fellowship, just as it has happened in other denominations. People who were spiritually yearning, and not completely grounded doctrinally, were overwhelmed by a particular experience. I do not doubt that the experience was powerful and spiritual. It may have been an enormous spiritual boost, or the highlight of one's life. But that does not mean that it is true, or that everyone should have the same experience, or that Christians should be looked down on if they do not have the same experience. The shock treatment that helped one patient is not the right medicine for the next patient.

More unusual manifestations

For many years, speaking in tongues was the primary experience promoted in some Pentecostal circles. But in more recent years, more exotic experiences have been promoted — such things as being slain in the Spirit (fainting and remaining motionless for several hours), laughing in the Spirit (uncontrollable waves of laughter), weeping in the Spirit, barking like a dog, or other para-normal activities. These may be called the Toronto Blessing or the Pensacola Blessing or some other blessing. Several prominent speakers, including Benny Hinn, have promoted some of these exciting phenomena.

These phenomena have been controversial, even in Pentecostal churches. The Toronto Blessing, for example, began in the Vineyard church. Some Vineyard churches promoted the blessing; others resisted it, and now they have split into two denominations. But the blessing makes ripples in many other denominations, too, and has affected some members. The Pensacola Blessing has circulated primarily in the Assemblies of God, but it has also affected other denominations, including our own.

I do not doubt that these experiences are extremely powerful. They feel authentic. But they have unfortunately led some astray, away from biblical authority and into an authority that is based on personal experience. As an extreme example, a pastor who has become enamored with a particular blessing may exhort everyone in the congregation to seek this particular blessing (the blessing, it sometimes seems, gets more focus than Jesus does). He may publicly berate those who do not accept the experience. He may call out names or tell people to leave if they don't like it.

This is, to put it bluntly, legalism. (Sometimes it is easy to call things we don't like an insulting term, like "legalism," but I am confident that in this case I am using the term legalism correctly. It is teaching as a requirement something that is not in Scripture.) We've had experience with old covenant legalism. These people are experiencing a completely nonbiblical legalism. Legalism is unfortunately found in many segments of Christianity, and some of these "blessing" people have fallen into a form of legalism, in which they insist that everybody ought to be like them.

Now suppose the whole congregation got touched and remained unconscious for three hours. Would that make them better Christians, better followers of Jesus Christ? Jesus never did anything of the sort. People who are slain in the spirit do not come out any better than they went in. The experience may encourage them, reassure them, but it does not edify the body of Christ and it should not be promoted as normal or preferable. Would these people eventually yearn for something yet more exotic? At least for some, that has been the pattern. Since the experience is not grounded in any objective truth, it does not give people the solid assurance that they seek. Some eventually seek even more unusual "signs."

One of our pastors observed the results of the Pensacola revival at a nearby Pentecostal church. After an initial flurry of excitement, attendance gradually dropped in half. The same manifestations week after week simply did not build the people up. The focus was on what happened to people during church, and not on what they did the rest of the time. The "revival" has driven away half the church!

Many of the "blessing" people are Christians who love Jesus. But as we know from our own experience, it is quite possible to be Christian while also seriously wrong on major doctrinal questions. I do not want to bash and condemn. I do not attack the people, or call them agents of Satan, but I do have the responsibility, as an under-shepherd of Jesus Christ, to warn our members about false, destructive and divisive doctrines. I want to help people avoid the pain and suffering that comes from following religious errors. The truth sets people free, but errors lead people into bondage.

We do not speak in tongues in our worship services, and we do not promote the more exotic "Pentecostal" manifestations.

To use an analogy, what you eat for breakfast is your own business — but no matter how good it tastes to you, do not act like your choice is spiritually better than other people's. Do not try to get everyone to act like you do. If you have a particular gift, be thankful and rejoice, but do not be divisive. Whatever gift you have, use it to serve others, keeping Scripture as your ultimate authority for faith and practice.

Joseph Tkach

The Holy Spirit Is the Personal Presence of God Himself

Christians believe in one God whose being is the Father, the Son and the Holy Spirit. We do not worship an undifferentiated, monad God, and we do not worship three Gods or Beings. Rather, we worship the one God who is eternally triune within himself in three eternal and co-equal Persons.[1] Each of the three Persons is distinct from the other two persons of the Godhead, and each is God of God, but there are not three Gods, but only one Being called God whom Christians worship.

In respect to the Person called the Holy Spirit in the New Testament, some people believe that the Spirit is not personal in the same sense that the Father and Son are personal. In the extreme, the claim is made by a few that the Holy Spirit is no more than a power used by God that is outside of and detached from himself or his Being.

Sometimes not mentioned

One of the arguments against the Spirit's personal nature is based on some verses in the New Testament in which God and Christ are discussed together, but they contain no reference to the Spirit. It is asked, "If the Holy Spirit is divine in the same way as the Son and the Father, and is co-eternal and co-equal with them, why is the Spirit not mentioned in such cases?"

A second argument used in an attempt to deny the equal divinity of the Holy Spirit is based on the observation that the New Testament does not present a personal "face" for the Spirit in the same way that it does for the Father and Son. The conclusion is the Holy Spirit is a power outside of the being of God, a power that God uses to carry out his will.

The first argument assumes that all three Persons of the Trinity *must* be mentioned together if they are equally divine. No scriptural rationale is given for such a claim. Perhaps some people think it *ought* to be so. But let's ask, Why should the Spirit always be mentioned along with the Father and Son? The Father is often mentioned without the Son, and the Son is often mentioned without any mention of the Father or the Holy Spirit. The book of Acts often mentions the work of the Holy Spirit without reference to the Father or the Son.

In short, it is an unsubstantiated assumption and a quibbling over irrelevant details to claim that the Holy Spirit must always be mentioned wherever the Father and Son are discussed. We cannot assume that the absence of the Holy Spirit in some biblical passages tells us anything definitive about the relationship of the Spirit to the other Persons of the Godhead.

For example, in his introduction to 1 Corinthians, the apostle Paul brings the congregation grace and peace from "God our Father and the Lord Jesus Christ" (1:3), but mentions Christ four times and "God" only twice. Are we to conclude that Jesus is twice as important as the Father? In his short conclusion to the same letter, Paul refers to "Christ Jesus" and the "Lord Jesus," but makes no mention of the Father or the Holy Spirit (16:23-24). Must we then conclude that only Jesus is divine?

In the opening to 2 Corinthians, Paul mentions variants of "Jesus Christ" twice and God twice, but doesn't refer to the Holy Spirit (1:1-2). However, in his conclusion, Paul says, "May the grace of the Lord Jesus Christ, and the love of God, and the fellowship of the Holy Spirit be with you all" (13:14). Here all three divine Persons – God, Jesus and the Spirit – are mentioned together.[2] We would be hard pressed regarding what conclusion to draw about the nature of God in general and the Holy Spirit in particular from Paul's various references to God, to Jesus, to the Father and the Holy Spirit in the openings and closings of these two letters.

There are many passages in the New Testament where all three Persons of the Godhead – the Father, Son and Holy Spirit – are mentioned together. Here are the most prominent places: Matthew 28:19; 2 Corinthians 13:14; 1 Peter 1:1-2; Romans 14:17-18; 15:16; 1 Corinthians 2:2-5; 6:11; 12:4-6; 2 Corinthians 1:21-22; Galatians 4:6; Ephesians 2:18-22; 3:14-19;Ephesians 4:4-6; Colossians 1:6-8; 1 Thessalonians 1:3-5; 2 Thessalonians 2:13-14; Titus 3:4-6. We should see these Scriptures as the controlling ones in any conclusion they may imply about the nature of God, since they mention all the relevant parties.

We will now move from these superficial arguments based on formulas and isolated references to essential considerations about the work of the Holy Spirit as true God of true God. As we do so, we will occasionally refer to the important work of Thomas Torrance in understanding the doctrine of the Trinity as he discusses it in his book *The Christian Doctrine of God – One Being Three Persons*.[3]

Not prominently featured

The second objection to accepting the Holy Spirit as a divine Person and God of God is based on the observation that the Holy Spirit is not as prominently featured as the Father and Son are in the New Testament. (For example, there are no occasions in the New Testament where we are told to worship the Holy Spirit.)

This kind of distinction vis-à-vis the Spirit is explained by the fact that the three Persons of the Godhead are distinct and they have distinct roles in the plan of salvation. We conclude from the New Testament that the Holy Spirit is not sent to draw attention to himself, that is, to take center stage or to glorify himself.

When Jesus introduces the Holy Spirit – the Spirit of Truth – in John 14-16, he says of him: "When the Counselor comes, whom I will send to you from the Father, the Spirit of Truth who goes

out from the Father, he will *testify about me*" (15:26, italics ours throughout).

Later, Jesus says: "But when he, the Spirit of Truth, comes, he will guide you into all truth. He will *not speak on his own;* he will speak only what he hears… He will bring *glory to me* by taking from what is mine and making it known to you" (16:13-14).

We see here that the Spirit is another Counselor, Paraclete or Helper who is sent by Christ to be with the church. The Spirit performs his own distinctive work in redemption: he enlightens, transforms, guides and sanctifies the followers of Christ. "It is not the function of the Spirit, then, to bear witness to himself in his distinctive personal Being, but to bear witness to Christ and glorify him as Lord and Savior," writes Torrance.[4]

Torrance explains why the Holy Spirit is not presented with a personal "face," as are the Son and the Father:

The Holy Spirit is God himself speaking although he is not himself the Word of God. It was not of course the Spirit but the Word who became incarnate, and so the Spirit does not bring us any revelation other than or independent of the Word who became incarnate in Jesus Christ. The Holy Spirit has no "Face", but it is through the Spirit that we see the Face of Christ and in the Face of Christ we see the Face of the Father. The Holy Spirit does not manifest himself or focus attention upon himself, for it is his mission from the Father to declare the Son and focus attention upon him. It is through the speaking of the Spirit that the Word of God incarnate in Christ is communicated to us in words that are Spirit and Life and not flesh.[5]

And again, Torrance writes about the presence of the Holy Spirit as true God of true God:

While God the Father and God the Son are revealed to us in their distinctive personal subsistences…God the Holy Spirit is not directly known in his own Person…for he remains hidden behind the very revelation of the Father and the Son which he mediates *through* himself. He is the invisible Spirit of Truth who is sent from the Father in the name of the Son, but not in his personal name as the Holy Spirit, and thus does not speak of himself, but declares of the Father and the Son what he receives from them, while effacing himself before them.... He is the invisible Light in whose shining we see the uncreated Light of God manifest in Jesus Christ, but he is known himself only in that he lights up for us the Face of God in the Face of Jesus Christ.[6]

The Paraclete

It has not been given for us to know directly the "face" of the Holy Spirit in a personal sense. Yet, in one place Jesus does give us something of a personal "face" for the Holy Spirit. When Jesus introduced the Holy Spirit to the disciples on the night he was betrayed, he used the Greek word *parakletos* to refer to him (John 14:16, 26; 15:26; 16:7). As a title for the Holy Spirit, *parakletos* is found exclusively in the above four passages, in the so-called "Paraclete sayings" of Jesus' farewell discourse. *Parakletos* has been translated by such words as "Comforter," "Advocate," "Helper" and "Counselor." Some versions simply transliterate the Greek word into "Paraclete."

In Greek and Roman society, a paraclete could refer to a person called on for assistance as a legal advisor, advocate or helper in a court of law. But the technical meaning "attorney" or "lawyer" is rare. A Greek lexicon explains: "In the few places where the word is found in pre-Christian and extra-Christian literature as well it has for the most part a more general sense: one who appears in another's behalf, *mediator, intercessor, helper.*"[7]

Thus, Jesus is telling his disciples that his physical presence will be replaced by "another Helper," the Holy Spirit. Since the Spirit is "another" helper, we understand that Jesus himself was a helper for the disciples. In that the Holy Spirit can "replace" Jesus, we can only take this to mean that the Spirit is to be thought of as equal to Christ. Otherwise,

how could the Spirit be able to come in the place of Jesus and perform saving work?

For those who insist on having a personal "face" for the Holy Spirit, Jesus has given it to us in his choice of metaphor in his reference to the Spirit as "Paraclete." He doesn't say, "I'm going to send a non-personal abstract power to you in my place."

On the other hand, we have been given in the New Testament the anthropomorphic analogy of "Father" and "Son" for the other two Persons of the Godhead, through which their personal "faces" are given. But even here we should avoid any gender-like thinking in our visioning. We "must think of 'Father' and 'Son' when used of God as *imageless relations*" and "we may not read the creaturely content of our human expressions of 'father' and 'son' analogically into what God discloses of his own inner divine relations," cautions Torrance.[8]

We must use human language when we speak of the Persons of the triune God, because we have no other language to use. But we should never lose sight of the fact that our language is inadequate and can only approximate in an approximate way the reality of God to which our words point.

Only a force?

Finally, let us take up the question of whether the Holy Spirit could be simply a force detached from the Being of God. An analogy would be that of electricity. Human beings use the power of electricity to achieve their will and work in countless ways. Electricity is not internal to our human selves, but is an external power we use.

Let's begin with an obvious point: There is no place in either the Old or New Testaments where the Holy Spirit is said to be or is regarded as an "appendage" to God rather than the presence of God himself. On that basis alone, we have no evidence to back up the assertion that the Spirit is not the presence of God, and therefore, not God of God.

To help us understand that the Holy Spirit *is* true God of true God, we begin by looking at the salvific work of Jesus, something that Thomas Torrance has explained. That is, Jesus as the Son must be God of God for his work to be effective in our salvation. Only God himself is our Savior. "This is to say, unless God himself were directly involved in the saving work of Christ in the depths of our human existence and in the heights of his eternal Being, what took place on the Cross would have been in vain," says Torrance.[9]

Jesus could not have been simply a special human being to whom God gave a mission, in the way he did to the Old Testament prophets such as Moses or David. Our Savior had to be very God with us, though as a human being, in order to perform his saving work.

Salvation is the gift of eternal life given to creatures who do not possess such spirit life within themselves. As creatures, we are spiritually fallen and mortal beings who ultimately die. How can mortal creatures be given eternal life – something that mortal creatures by definition do not have and cannot obtain on their own? They must somehow be taken up into God so that the eternal life that only God has may be something that adheres to them as well.

John 14:5-27 explains how the life of God can adhere to us, if we are careful to see the implications of what Jesus says in the passage. His explanation demands that the Holy Spirit be true God of true God. Jesus, having finished the redemptive work through which we are reconciled to God, will send the Holy Spirit. The Spirit will be "in" the believers, and through him, the Father and Jesus will make their "home" with them (verses 17, 23). Through the Spirit, the disciples can be in Jesus and he in them (verse 21). The passage shows the unity and salvific work of the Father, of the Son as Jesus Christ, and of the Holy Spirit. All three Persons bring about the salvation of believers, and all must be true God of true God in order to do so – including the Holy Spirit.

As 1 Peter 1:3 states, we have a "new birth into a living hope" through the Holy Spirit. We are joined to God through the Spirit, and the eternal life of God becomes ours in that union. Those who are God's "have been born again, not of perishable seed, but of imperishable, through the living and enduring word of God" (1 Peter 1:23).

The apostle Paul explains that the completion of our salvation results in the "putting on" of immortality (1 Corinthians 15:50-54). In another place, he says: "If the Spirit of him who raised Jesus is living in you, he who raised Christ from the dead will also give life to your mortal bodies *through his Spirit, who lives in you*" (Romans 8:11).

It is not some "power" separate from God that accomplishes this miracle, but the presence of God himself in the Person of the Holy Spirit. When the Holy Spirit lives in us, God lives in us. When the Holy Spirit gives us new birth, we are children of God. We are joined by the Holy Spirit to God, and through the Holy Spirit we become God's children as this work of transformation and life-giving is accomplished (verses 15-16).

We do not become God. We are creatures, and will always remain creatures. But God in his freedom can unite himself to our creaturely state so that his eternal life can be ours in that union. God himself must be present for this union to occur, and he is present in the Person of the indwelling Holy Spirit.

In saving us, the Holy Spirit cannot be "something" outside of God himself. The Spirit must be divinity himself – God of God – working in the church and transforming human creaturely beings into the image of Christ, who is Life himself. Torrance explains this point in this way:

> If the Act which God directs towards us is other than or detached from his Being, then he does not give *himself* to us in his activity and cannot therefore be known by us as he is in himself; but if his Act and his Being instead of being separate from one another inhere in each other, then in giving us his Spirit God actively makes himself open to us and known by us.[10]

In order for us to participate in the eternal life that alone belongs to God, it is necessary that the Holy Spirit – who transforms our minds and hearts from within – must be Divinity, and true God of true God. "To *be* 'in the Spirit' is to *be* in God, for the Spirit is not external but internal to the God-head," says Torrance.[11]

Thanks be to God, who in the Person of the Father sent Jesus Christ to reconcile us to himself by the forgiveness of sin and sinfulness. Jesus as Son of Man and Son of God overcame every enemy of God – including sin and death – on our behalf. In the Person of the Holy Spirit, whom Jesus sent, we are transformed and united to God, and we partake of the eternal life that is God's alone.

Endnotes

[1] "Person" is the English word we use in place of the Greek *hypostasis*. The word "Person" shows that God in his Triune Being is personal and that we are dealing with the personal presence of God in the Father, Son and Holy Spirit. The word "Person" has its drawback in that people may wrongly apply to God, in an anthropomorphic way, our experience of persons as individual human beings.

[2] We are assuming in this verse that Paul's reference to "God" is not absolute, but that he uses the term relatively of the Person of the Father, something we cannot know for certain here.

[3] Most footnoted references in this article are to Thomas Torrance's book *The Christian Doctrine of God.*

[4] Ibid., page 66.

[5] Ibid., page 63.

[6] Ibid., page 151.

[7] *A Greek-English Lexicon of the New Testament and other Early Christian Literature,* 4th edition, revised and edited by Frederick William Danker, page 766.

[8] Torrance, pages 157-158.

[9] Ibid., page 146.

[10] Ibid., page 152.

[11] Ibid., page 153.

Paul Kroll

The Written Word of God

How do we know who Jesus is, or what he taught? How do we know when a gospel is false? Where is the authority for sound teaching and right living? The Bible is the inspired and infallible record of what God wants us to know and do.

A witness to Jesus

Perhaps you've seen newspaper reports about the "Jesus Seminar," a group of scholars who claim that Jesus didn't say most of the things the Bible says he did. Or perhaps you've heard of other scholars who say that the Bible is a collection of contradictions and myths.

Many well-educated people dismiss the Bible. Many other equally educated people believe it is a trustworthy record of what God has done and said. If we cannot trust what the Bible says about Jesus, for example, then we will know almost nothing about him.

The Jesus Seminar began with a preconceived idea of what Jesus would have taught. They accepted the sayings that fit this idea, and rejected the sayings that didn't, thereby, in effect, creating a Jesus in their own image. This is not good scholarship, and even many liberal scholars disagree with the Seminar.

Do we have good reason to trust the biblical reports about Jesus? Certainly—they were written within a few decades of Jesus' death, when eyewitnesses were still alive. Jewish disciples often memorized the words of their teachers, so it is quite possible that Jesus' disciples preserved his teachings accurately. We have no evidence that they invented sayings to deal with early church concerns, such as circumcision. This suggests that they are reliable reports of what Jesus taught.

We can also be confident that the manuscripts were well preserved. We have some copies from the fourth century, and smaller sections from the second. This is better than all other historical books. (The oldest copy of Virgil was copied 350 years after Virgil died; of Plato, 1,300 years.) The manuscripts show that the Bible was copied carefully, and we have a highly reliable text.

Jesus' witness to Scripture

Jesus was willing to argue with the Pharisees on many issues, but he did not seem to argue with their view of the Scriptures. Although Jesus disagreed on interpretations and traditions, he apparently agreed with other Jewish leaders that the Scriptures were authoritative for faith and practice.

Jesus expected every word in Scripture to be fulfilled (Matthew 5:17-18; Mark 14:49). He quoted Scripture to prove his points (Matthew 9:13; 22:31; 26:24; 26:31; John 10:34); he rebuked people for not reading Scripture carefully enough (Matthew 22:29; Luke 24:25; John 5:39). He referred to Old Testament people and events without any hint that they were not real.

Scripture had the authority of God behind it. When Jesus answered Satan's temptations, he said, "It is written" (Matthew 4:4-10). The fact that something was written in Scripture meant, for Jesus, that it was an indisputable authority. The words of David were inspired by the Holy Spirit (Mark 12:36); a prophecy was given "through" Daniel (Matthew 24:15) because its real origin was God.

Jesus said in Matthew 19:4-5 that the Creator said in Genesis 2:24: "A man will leave his father and mother and be united to his wife." However, Genesis does not describe this verse as the words of God. Jesus could say that God said it simply because it was in Scripture. The assumption is that God is the ultimate author of all of Scripture.

The evidence throughout the Gospels is that

Jesus viewed Scripture as reliable and trustworthy. As he reminded the Jewish leaders, "the Scripture cannot be broken" (John 10:35). Jesus expected it to be valid; he even upheld the validity of old covenant commands while the old covenant was still in force (Matthew 8:4; 23:23).

Witness of the apostles

The apostles, like their teacher, considered Scripture authoritative. They quoted it repeatedly, often as proof of an argument. The sayings of Scripture are treated as words of God. Scripture is even personalized as the God who spoke to Abraham and Pharaoh (Romans 9:17; Galatians 3:8). What David or Isaiah or Jeremiah wrote was actually spoken by God, and therefore certain (Acts 1:16; 4:25; 13:35; 28:25; Hebrews 1:6-10; 10:15). The law of Moses is assumed to reflect the mind of God (1 Corinthians 9:9). The real author of Scripture is God (1 Corinthians 6:16; Romans 9:25).

Paul called the Scriptures "the very words of God" (Romans 3:2). Peter says that the prophets "spoke from God as they were carried along by the Holy Spirit" (2 Peter 1:20). The prophets didn't make it up—God inspired them, and he is the real origin of their words. They often wrote, "the word of the Lord came..." or "Thus says the Lord..."

Paul also told Timothy that "all Scripture is God-breathed and is useful for teaching, rebuking, correcting and training in righteousness" (2 Timothy 3:16). It is as if God breathed his message through the biblical writers.

However, we must not read into this our modern ideas of what "God-breathed" has to mean. We must remember that Paul said this about the Greek Septuagint *translation* (the Scriptures that Timothy had known since childhood—v. 15), and this translation is in some places considerably different than the Hebrew original. Paul used this translation as the word of God without meaning that it was a perfect text.

Despite its translation discrepancies, it is God-breathed and able to make people "wise for salvation through faith in Christ Jesus" and it is still able to equip believers "for every good work" (v. 17).

Imperfect communication

The original word of God is perfect, and God is certainly able to cause people to state it accurately, to preserve it accurately and (to complete the communication) make us understand it accurately. But God has not done all this. Our copies have grammatical errors, copyist errors, and (far more significantly) humans always make errors in receiving the message. There is "noise" that prevents us from hearing perfectly the word God inspired to be written in Scripture. Nevertheless, God uses Scripture to speak to us today.

Despite the "noise" that puts human mistakes between God and us, the purpose of Scripture is accomplished: to tell us about salvation and about right behavior. God accomplishes his purpose in Scripture: he communicates his word to us with enough clarity that we can be saved and we can learn what he wants us to do.

Scripture, even in a translation, is accurate for its purpose. But we would be wrong to expect more from it than God intended. He is not teaching us astronomy or science. The numbers in Scripture are not always mathematically precise by today's standards. We must look at Scripture for its purpose, not for minor details.

For example, in Acts 21:11, Agabus was inspired to say that the Jews would bind Paul and hand him over to the Gentiles. Some people might assume that Agabus was specifying who would tie Paul up, and what they would do with him. But as it turns out, Paul was actually rescued by the Gentiles and bound by the Gentiles (21:30-33).

Is this a contradiction? Technically, yes. The prediction was true in principle, but not in the details. Of course, when Luke wrote this, he could have easily doctored the prediction to fit the result, but he was willing to let the differences be seen. He did not expect people to expect precision in such details. This should warn us about expecting precision in all the details of Scripture.

We need to focus on the main point of the message. Similarly, Paul made a mistake when he wrote 1 Corinthians 1:14 — a mistake he corrected in verse 16. The inspired Scriptures contain both the mistake and the correction.

Proof of the Bible

No one can prove that all of the Bible is true. They may show that a particular prophecy came true, but they cannot show that the entire Bible has the same validity. This is based more on faith. We see the historical evidence that Jesus and the apostles accepted the Old Testament as the word of God. The biblical Jesus is the only one we have; other ideas are based on guesswork, not new evidence. We accept the teaching of Jesus that the Holy Spirit would guide the disciples into more truth. We accept the claim of Paul that he wrote with divine authority. We accept that the Bible reveals to us who God is and how we may have fellowship with him.

We accept the testimony of church history, that Christians through the centuries have found the Bible useful for faith and practice. This book tells us who God is, what he did for us, and how we should respond. Tradition also tells us which books are in the biblical canon. We trust that God guided the process so that the end result accomplishes his purpose.

Our experience also testifies to the accuracy of Scripture. This is the book that has the honesty to tell us about our own sinfulness, and the grace to offer us a cleansed conscience. It gives us moral strength not through rules and commands, but in an unexpected way — through grace and the ignominious death of our Lord.

The Bible testifies to the love, joy and peace we may have through faith — feelings that are, just as the Bible describes, beyond our ability to put into words. This book gives us meaning and purpose in life by telling us of divine creation and redemption. These aspects of biblical authority cannot be proven to skeptics, but they help verify the Scriptures that tell us these things that we experience.

The Bible does not sugar-coat its heroes, and this also helps us accept it as honest. It tells us about the failings of Abraham, Moses, David, the nation of Israel, and the disciples. The Bible is a word that bears witness to a more authoritative Word, the Word made flesh, and the good news of God's grace.

The Bible is not simplistic; it does not take the easy way out. The New Testament claims both continuity and discontinuity with the old covenant. It would be simpler to eliminate one or the other, but it is more challenging to have both. Likewise, Jesus is presented as both human and divine, a combination that does not fit well into Hebrew, Greek or modern thought. This complexity was not created through ignorance of the philosophical problems, but in spite of them.

The Bible is a challenging book, not likely to be the result of fishermen attempting a fraud or trying to make sense of hallucinations. Jesus' resurrection gives additional weight to the book that announces such an phenomenal event. It gives additional weight to the testimony of the disciples as to who Jesus was and to the unexpected logic of conquering death through the death of the Son of God.

Repeatedly, the Bible challenges our thinking about God, ourselves, life, right and wrong. It commands respect by conveying truths to us we do not obtain elsewhere. Just as the proof of the pudding is in the eating, the proof of the Bible is in its application to our lives.

The testimony of Scripture, of tradition, of personal experience and reason all support the authority of the Bible. The fact that it is able to speak across cultures, to address situations that never existed when it was written, is also a testimony to its abiding authority. The proof of the Bible is conveyed to believers as the Holy Spirit uses it to change their hearts and lives.

Inerrancy and Infallibility

Some evangelical Christians believe that Christians should call the Bible inerrant; others prefer to call the Bible infallible. Although in normal usage these words mean practically the same thing, in theology they are used for different concepts.

Inerrant generally means without error in theology, history or science. *Infallible* (sometimes called limited inerrancy) refers to doctrine; it does not insist on scientific and historical accuracy, since those are outside of the Bible's purpose.

Some believe the Bible is inerrant; others prefer the term infallible. We use the less-specific word, *infallible*. On that we can all agree, since people who believe in inerrancy also believe that the Bible does not fail in its purpose: to teach us about salvation.

John Stott, who accepts inerrancy, nevertheless lists "five reasons why the word *inerrancy* makes me uncomfortable. First, God's self-revelation in Scripture is so rich—both in content and in form—that it cannot be reduced to a string of propositions which invite the label 'truth' or 'error.' 'True or false?' would be an inappropriate question to address to a great deal of Scripture. [Commands are neither true nor false.]

"Second, the word *inerrancy* is a double negative, and I always prefer a single positive to a double negative. It is better to affirm that the Bible is true and therefore trustworthy....

"Third, the word inerrancy sends out the wrong signals and develops the wrong attitudes. Instead of encouraging us to search the Scriptures so that we may grow in grace and in the knowledge of God, it seems to turn us into detectives hunting for incriminating clues and to make us excessively defensive in relation to apparent discrepancies.

"Fourth, it is unwise and unfair to use *inerrancy* as a shibboleth by which to identify who is an evangelical and who is not. The hallmark of authentic evangelicalism ... is not whether we subscribe to an impeccable formula about the Bible but whether we live in practical submission to what the Bible teaches....

"Fifth, it is impossible to prove that the Bible contains no errors. When faced with an apparent discrepancy, the most Christian response is neither to make a premature negative judgment nor to resort to a contrived harmonization, but rather to suspend judgment, waiting patiently for further light to be given us" (*Evangelical Truth,* pp. 61-62).

There is an additional problem with the word *inerrant:* It must be carefully qualified. Even one of the most conservative statements about Scripture admits that the Bible contains grammatical irregularities, exaggerations, imprecise descriptions, inexact quotations, and observations based on a limited viewpoint ("The Chicago Statement on Biblical Inerrancy," Article XIII, printed in Norman L. Geisler, editor, *Inerrancy,* Zondervan, 1979, page 496).

In other words, *inerrant* does not mean "without error of any kind." Further, inerrancy applies only to the autographs, not to the copies that we have today. These qualifications seem to drain *inerrancy* of much of its meaning. The main point, as Millard Erickson says, is that "the Bible's assertions are fully true when judged in accordance with the purpose for which they were written" (*Introducing Christian Doctrine,* p. 64). That is a wise qualification.

For further reading

Achtemeier, Paul. *Inspiration and Authority.* Baker, 1998.

Arthur, Kay. *How to Study Your Bible.* Harvest House, 2010.

Marshall, I. Howard. *Biblical Inspiration.* Eerdmans, 1982.

McKnight, Scot. *The Blue Parakeet: Rethinking How You Read the Bible.* Zondervan, 2016.

McQuilken, Robertson. *Understanding and Applying the Bible.* Moody, 1992.

Mickelsen, A.B. and A.M. *Understanding Scripture.* Hendrickson, 1992.

Stott, John. *Understanding the Bible.* Zondervan, 1999.

Thompson, David. *Bible Study That Works.* Warner Press, 1994.

Veerman, Dave. *How to Apply the Bible.* Tyndale, 1993.

Wright, N.T. *Scripture and the Authority of God: How to Read the Bible Today.* HarperOne, 2013.

Michael Morrison

Bible Study Secrets

"I'm not getting as much as I would like to out of my personal Bible study. Do you have any tips on how to study the Bible?"

What advice do biblical scholars give to people who want to improve their Bible study? "People ask me this kind of question often," said Willard Swartley, professor of New Testament at the Associated Mennonite Biblical Seminary in Elkhart. Indiana. '"Usually I ask them if they have any method for studying the Bible."

Douglas Stuart, professor of Old Testament at

> "In any kind of Bible study, the key is always to ask questions of what you're reading. You will process the material only to the extent that you ask questions." — Robert H. Gundry, Professor of New Testament and Greek, Westmont College, Santa Barbara, California

Gordon-Conwell Theological Seminary in South Hamilton, Massachusetts, said, "I try to get people alerted to truly systematic Bible study and the methods that go with it."

"Method." The word kept cropping up in the interviews. A method — an organized procedure or system — of studying the Bible is what the scholars discussed.

Getting started

"First, I would recommend a couple of English versions of the Bible," said Robert H. Gundry, professor of New Testament and Greek at Westmont College in Santa Barbara, California. "I would use both a more staid, literally translated version and a more loosely translated one and make comparisons as I did my study." Since most of us don't know Hebrew or Greek, we read the Bible in translation. Comparing different translations gives insights into the meaning of the Scriptures.

> "Through meditation, the Scriptures challenge your value structure, and that's where spiritual growth takes place." — John Hartley, Professor of Old Testament, Azusa Pacific University, Azusa, California

Gundry recommends the New Revised Standard Version, the Revised Standard Version and the New American Standard Bible as good literal translations. For translations that allow some paraphrasing, he recommends the New International Version and the Good News Bible. Checking different translations allows you to see alternatives in text and meaning. These established versions will give you access to the most likely variations of text and nuances of meaning.

After you decide on the Bibles you will use, John Hartley, professor of Old Testament at Azusa Pacific University in Azusa, California, recommends you choose one version and read it all the way through. "It's important to gain perspective," he said. "This way, when you read the Gospel of Mark, you know what comes before it, what comes after it. Or if you pick up a prophet like Haggai, you have some understanding of where it is in the whole story of the Bible."

Hartley does not think the Bible has to be read in order, book by book. He has known people who have tried to read the Bible in sequence, cover to cover, who invariably got bogged down, usually in the ordinances and genealogies of Leviticus, and then gave up. Thus, Hartley advises that people regularly alternate the sections they read.

Clark Pinnock, professor of theology at McMaster Divinity College in Hamilton, Ontario, agrees with Hartley's approach. "One of the things I've done in the past," said Pinnock, "is to put bookmarks in different places of the Bible. For example, I'd start them at Genesis, Ezra, Matthew and Acts. Then I'd work ahead from all of those places, reading a few chapters from one book one day and a few from another book another day. This way I got a cross sampling of the Scriptures, and I covered the Bible in a year or so."

Having four entry places allows you flexibility in your study. If one place is less interesting, you

> "Ask questions of how the text engages you, at the level of your own way of thinking, your own beliefs, your own attitudes." — Willard Swartley, Professor of New Testament, Associated Mennonite Biblical Seminary, Elkhart, Indiana

can read from that section one day, and the next day read in a more inspirational place.

Even when you focus your study on individual books, the practice of studying two or more sections is effective. In one book you can study more intensely. In another, perhaps the Psalms or the Gospel of John, you can read for inspiration. These two approaches to the Bible — one for study and the other for inspiration —complement each other. Sometimes you're ready for a full-course meal; other times you want something lighter and easier to digest.

A closer focus

An old saying around Bible colleges goes, "When you realize that a story has a beginning, a middle and an end, you're then called a Bible scholar." Overly simple? Maybe not. Lifting verses out of context is often the first step in misunderstanding them. Effective Bible study focuses on the context, or landscape, of the Scriptures.

Thus, the next step in Bible study is to focus on individual books, not on individual verses or topics. Imagine a camera with a zoom lens. You start at the wide angle — the entire Bible — and then gradually zoom in on your subject, taking photos as you close in. Each photo will show less landscape but more detail, helping you understand your subject in the context of its surroundings.

"Context is king," continued Stuart. "The context of a word or a phrase or sentence or a paragraph is by far the most important indicator of its meaning." For example, the word *run* has more than a dozen possible meanings. A faucet can run if it needs a new washer, or a candidate can run for president. Words take on different meanings in different contexts, so do sentences and even paragraphs.

Pinnock said, "Generally, you'll want to read an individual book consecutively. You get the discourse of the entire book and see the individual verses in context."

Read inductively

Four of the five professors mentioned the inductive approach to Bible study. This approach has three steps: 1) observe, 2) determine the original meaning and 3) apply the meaning to your own personal situation. Though the professors had variations in their technique, in general terms, here's how inductive Bible study works.

Step one: observe. Select a book of the Bible; take a short one, like 1 John, to get started. (see sample below). Read through the book to get the

> "The purpose of Bible study is not to know the Scripture for its own sake, but to allow God to speak to you." — Clark Pinnock, Professor of Theology, McMaster Divinity College, Hamilton, Ontario

flow of ideas. Try to ignore the chapter divisions. Sometimes they unnaturally divide the book, breaking the flow of thought. You might want to take notes of what happens in the book. Don't yet focus on individual verses; focus on the flow of ideas.

Next, reread the book. When you do this, you will often see patterns of organization and thought that you may have missed the first time. Again, you might want to take notes. Try to limit yourself to observing what is happening in the book. Resist the urge to interpret just yet.

Step two: determine the original meaning. After

you're familiar with the contents and flow of the book, read background material about it in a survey of the Bible, a commentary or a study Bible. These introductions will help you place the book in historical and cultural context.

Introductions also give outlines of the books of the Bible. An outline helps you see the flow of ideas and subjects in the book and helps you divide it into logical sections. Outlines vary in detail and sometimes in the way they divide the book. Generally, the more detailed the outline, the more useful.

Next, reread the first section of the book as divided by the outline. Here you begin your in-depth study. Start asking questions. "In any kind of Bible study," advises Gundry, "the key is always to ask questions of what you're reading. You will process the material only to the extent that you ask questions."

As a starter list of questions, Swartley recommends asking what the repeated words or the key words of the text are. Since a section may be several chapters long, you may end up with 10 to 15 major theme words frequently repeated. Look these words up in a Bible dictionary to learn what they meant in biblical times. Add to your list names of places or people mentioned in the text, and look those up.

Continue asking questions. Are there other natural divisions in the section you are studying? How do individual verses fit in the context?

Answers to your questions are often within the Bible itself. If not, check a commentary. "If you go to a commentary just to read what it says, that's somewhat helpful," said Stuart. "But it's far more helpful to go to a commentary with a list of questions." This way you enter into a *dialogue* with the commentary and have more control over what you learn from it. If you go to the commentary first, you may listen to the commentary instead of the Bible.

Step two of the inductive method of Bible study helps you re-create the historical and cultural context of the scriptures. Your goal is to view the scriptures as their original audience viewed them.

(Move to step three for the section of the book you are studying, then repeat steps two and three for the other sections as divided by your outline.)

Step three: apply the meaning to your situation. "The purpose of Bible study is not to know the Scripture for its own sake," said Pinnock, "'but to allow God to speak to you." When the Word of God speaks to you, it challenges your values, your opinions, your actions — you. The Bible challenges you to change. James, the half-brother of Jesus, wrote: "Do not merely listen to the word, and so deceive yourselves. Do what it says" (James 1:22).

In the first two steps of the inductive method, you ask what God was saying to the original audience. Now you ask what he says to you. Take time for spiritual reflection. Meditate on the meaning of the text. At this point, you may want to reread the section in a different Bible version. How does its lesson apply? Is this lesson an inspirational teaching about God? Is it a lesson in the Christian walk with Jesus Christ? Or maybe a lesson in doctrine?

Ask why the writer believed this message to be important. Ask why it is important to you. How will remembering the lesson help you in your day-to-day life? "Through meditation, the Scriptures challenge your value structure, and that's where spiritual growth takes place," said Hartley. To guide the application of Scripture, some people like to take the words they have studied to God in prayer. They ask God to help them apply the biblical lessons for personal growth.

In addition to your private Bible study, spiritual reflection and prayer, you will also benefit when you discuss what you learn with other Christians. Ask how *they* view the original meaning of the text and how it applies today. How have they found the text helpful or challenging?

Meaningful dialogue with other Christians helps you see different perspectives on the Bible and on how to apply its teachings. Gundry said: "We are a community of faith, so we need to ask others what they think the Bible has to say. We need to learn from one another."

The Word of Life ¹That which was from the beginning, which we have heard, which we have seen with our eyes, which we have looked at and our hands have touched — this we <u>proclaim</u> concerning the Word of <u>life</u>. ²The <u>life</u> appeared; we have seen it and testify to it, and we <u>proclaim</u> to you the eternal <u>life</u>, which was with the Father and has appeared to us. ³We <u>proclaim</u> to you what we have seen and heard, so that you also may have <u>fellowship</u> with us. And our <u>fellowship</u> is with the Father and with his Son, Jesus Christ. ⁴We write this to make our joy complete.

Inductive Bible Study
Focus on 1 John 1-4

1 Observe

Read through the book you are studying. Take notes of what the book says. Reread the book. Pay special attention to the book's organization and structure.

2 Determine the original meaning

A. Read an introduction to the book.

The author of 1 John writes from

personal experience. He relates those experiences so that his readers may have assurance of eternal life (5:13).

B. Study the outline of the book in the introduction, as shown at right.
C. Read the first section of the book as divided by the outline.
D. As shown below, determine repeated and key words of the text and look them up in a Bible dictionary.

	1 John
I. Introduction	1:1-4
II. Walking in the light	1:5-2:27
a. in pureness	1:5-2:2
b. in fellowship	2:3-2:27
III. Walking as children of God	2:28-4:21
a. in love	2:28-3:24
b. in spirit	4:1-21
IV. Walking with the Son of God	5:1-12
V. Conclusion	5:13-21

The Word of Life

¹That which was from the beginning, which we have heard, which we have seen with our eyes, which we have looked at and our hands have touched — this we proclaim concerning the Word of life. ²The life appeared; we have seen it and testify to it, and we proclaim to you the eternal life, which was with the Father and has appeared to us. ³We proclaim to you what we have seen and heard, so that you also may have fellowship with us. And our fellowship is with the

E. Ask questions. Look for answers first in the text, then go to commentaries. Sample questions could be:
1. Why did John stress that he heard, saw and touched Jesus?
2. Why does John say that Jesus was "from the beginning"?

Father and with his Son, Jesus Christ. ⁴We write this to make our joy complete.

3. What is the significance of proclaiming Jesus Christ?
4. Why does John emphasize life and fellowship?

John was combating the false notion that Jesus Christ did not come in the flesh. John was emphasizing the centrality of the Incarnation to the Christian faith.

F. From background material and answers to questions, explain why John wrote what he did (see box at left).

3 Apply the text

It is vital to understand that Jesus Christ was fully God and fully human. God shared in our humanity. Through his atoning work on the cross, we have fellowship with God and with each other. God also gives us eternal life. Knowing this truth encourages us and makes our "joy complete."

The Bible for All Its Worth

Douglas Stuart is professor of Old Testament at Gordon-Conwell Theological Seminary, South Hamilton, Massachusetts. He has written numerous commentaries and books, including the acclaimed introduction to Bible study, *How to Read the Bible for All Its Worth,* which he co-authored with Gordon Fee.

Question: After people determine the original meaning of a biblical text, how should they apply the text they have studied to modern spiritual life?

Douglas Stuart: The first strategy is not to assume the original application has changed. Knowing the cultural background helps a person understand why a thing is said the way it is. But the Scripture was always written with the intention that there would be a modern time as well. God knew there would be a 20th century when he inspired the Bible, and the Scripture speaks to the 20th century.

The Bible is largely pancultural, panhistorical in its ability to convey information and in the kinds of ethical and behavioral standards it asks. Where it is culturally specific is more in the particular manifestations of that. For example, nothing in the book of Romans requires you to be a Greek in the ancient Roman Empire to understand it. Any modern person can figure out what he or she needs to know about ancient Greece to follow the descriptions and illustrations.

Q. Even though we need to know about the cultures of the Bible to understand the Scriptures, you're saying the Bible is not culturally bound?

A. Right. In fact, I would say the Bible was never really at home in any culture. The Old Testament teachings were not at home in ancient Canaan, nor were the teachings of the New Testament at home in the Roman Empire. A true orthodox Israelite's

"I encourage people to study a passage for all they can personally get out of it," says Douglas Stuart, a professor of the Old Testament.

beliefs were completely contrary to the culture. In those days, everybody worshiped by idolatry. Everybody.

We know of no culture at the time that was not idolatrous, and yet the Israelites were told not to be idolatrous. Today, we have plenty of non-idolatrous cultures. In this sense, the Old Testament is closer to some modern societies than to its own.

Likewise, the laws and standards we have in the Old Testament — a classless legal system — were contrary to everything anybody knew about in ancient times. All other ancient law systems were class conscious. There were different penalties if you were a noble, a free person or a slave. In the modern world, we have classless law, at least in theory. But that was unique in ancient times.

In several areas the Bible was hostile to its native environment, even more in Bible times than now. Of course, in some areas it was less hostile, so I think it evens out. Still, the Bible has never been completely at home in any culture. It is an otherworldly book.

Q. For the Bible to speak to us today, some people believe they need to resort to liberal approaches to Scripture. In your books, you disagree.

A. The vogue in liberalism is what is called the New Hermeneutic. That's not a new term, of course, but it is the vogue. The New Hermeneutic says that since we all read any literature partly through our own filter and bring our own sense of meaning to it, we should go right ahead and do that all the time with Scripture. I disagree with this approach.

In the New Hermeneutic, a person asks: "What do I want Scripture to say? How would I like it to speak to me?" A more objective view of Scripture, which I think should be that of conservatives, is to ask: "What did God put here? And, whether I like it or not, what am I supposed to do about it?"

For more on this topic, watch our interviews with Gordon Fee at https://www.gci.org/?s=gordon+fee.

George Hague

Inspiration, Authority, and Reliability of Scripture

The inspiration of Scripture

Affirmation: We accept the Bible as the inspired Word of God. The writers were inspired, moved by the Holy Spirit (2 Peter 1:21), and the resultant writings are inspired, as if breathed or spoken by God (2 Timothy 3:16). The Bible is therefore useful as a guide to salvation through faith in Christ, and sufficient for doctrine, correction, moral and ethical instruction (2 Timothy 3:15-17).

The New Testament affirms the inspiration of the Old Testament, including its function of pointing to Jesus Christ (Luke 24:44; John 5:46; Acts 10:43). Jesus used the Old Testament as thoroughly reliable words of God (Matthew 5:18; Mark 12:35; John 10:35). The sayings of Jesus are accepted as of divine authority (Matthew 24:35; Mark 8:38; John 6:63), and the letters of Paul are also considered Scripture (2 Peter 3:15-16). The early church quoted the New Testament in the same manner as the Old, treating all these writings as God-given words.[1]

Biblical authors were inspired, and the writings are inspired, but the Bible does not give many details about **how** God worked with humans to produce these documents. Numerous passages claim to be quotes directly from God (e.g., Exodus 20:1-17); others claim to be the result of ordinary research (Luke 1:1-4); some appear to be private letters (Philemon). Regardless of the method of inspiration, all these writings are considered canonical Scripture - an authoritative message from God to humans. The Bible reveals truths about God and about what God does so that we may know God and have a relationship with God.

But grammatical irregularities and stylistic differences indicate that God did not dictate every word. Rather, God allowed the divine message to be given in the phraseology of the human authors. Just as Jesus was God in human form, the Bible is God's word in human words.

Since the Bible is written with human words and grammar, people are able to understand much of the message. But they do not necessarily understand that the message is *true,* because spiritual truths are understood only with divine help (1 Corinthians 2:6-16). The objective Word of God becomes an effective Word of God only when the Holy Spirit enables a person to understand spiritual truths contained in it.[2] The effectiveness is not in the grammatical details - it is in the message being conveyed and the God-given willingness to submit to it.

Further details concerning the reliability of Scripture will be discussed below.

The authority of Scripture

Affirmation: God has all authority, and we accept the Bible as the primary authority by which God communicates to us what God wants us to believe and to do. The New Testament clarifies and sometimes supersedes the Old Testament guidance on faith and life.[3] The primary purpose of the Bible is its message about salvation, and that is its primary sphere of authority. It is a sufficient guide that tells us how we might be given eternal life with God. Those who believe the biblical revelation about God's grace and Jesus Christ will be saved; those who do not believe will not be saved (John 3:18; 14:6; Acts 4:12; 1 John 5:11-12). This message of salvation is essential.

The Bible also reveals divine commands and principles regarding the way we ought to live. A genuine faith in Christ as Lord and Savior transforms our lives and minds, with the result that our lives are brought progressively into greater submission to the will of God. Biblical instructions give us authoritative guidance on the will of God concerning how we should live and think and interact with one another.

The Bible is an authoritative revelation of truths about God, and we want to worship our Creator with as much understanding as possible. Moreover, we want to obey God's commands, not only to honor God but also because we believe that our all-wise and perfectly loving Creator has given us the best possible commands and guidance for life. Therefore, we want to understand the written message of God as best we can. But this is not always easy.

Humans are limited beings, and our minds are corrupted by sin, so even at our best we know only in part (1 Corinthians 13:12). Thus we find that the authority of God in the Bible is not only mediated by human language but also by our ability to understand its truths. Although our understanding is imperfect, the Bible is the standard by which our misunderstandings are corrected. God is able to give us sufficient understanding of biblical truths for us to have a saving relationship with God.[4]

Biblical interpretation is complicated by the fact that the Bible is written in many literary styles. Some passages are didactic, prescriptive, and concrete; others are narrative, imaginative and/or poetic. To communicate one spiritual truth, figures of speech may be used that may obscure other equally important truths revealed in other passages. Some commands are historically conditioned and others are timeless. To help us understand and submit to the authority of biblical principles, we humbly seek the guidance of the Author and study the Scriptures. We use reason to understand each biblical passage and point, and to discern what teachings are normative for us today.

Our ability to understand and to reason is shaped in part by our personal experiences and the traditions that have shaped our presuppositions. Reason, tradition, and experience should be subservient to Scripture; they should not contradict biblical authority. Nevertheless, because of different traditions and experiences, equally sincere people come to different conclusions about what the Bible teaches. Therefore we confidently teach our understanding of the Bible and simultaneously respect those who submit to biblical authority in different ways.

The reliability of Scripture

Affirmation: The Scriptures are a trustworthy guide for our relationships with God and with other humans. They give truth about faith, worship, salvation, morals and ethics (2 Timothy 3:15-16). But biblical commands cannot be applied simplistically, because some are superseded and some apply only in limited situations. We seek the illumination of the Holy Spirit and ask God to guide our reasoning and our use of tradition and experience so we might understand how to apply biblical principles.

The further we go from the stated purposes of the Bible, the less the Bible says about the subject and the less likely we are to have a complete statement about the subject. Statements about history and science are of special interest.

Historians find the Bible to be an accurate record of many ancient events, more reliable than other ancient writings. But its standard of accuracy is looser than the expectations of modern science and history, as can be discerned from parallel accounts in Scripture. The same event can be attributed to Satan or to God (2 Samuel 24:1; 1 Chronicles 21:1), to Jesus in vision or to Ananias (Acts 22:14-15; 26:16-18). Paul's companions stood and heard, but they also fell down and did not hear (Acts 9:7; 22:7, 9).

Most alleged discrepancies in the Bible are easily resolved, but these parallel accounts show that we must be cautious about taking biblical statements at face value. Even if we do not have a parallel account, it is hazardous to assume that unnamed intermediaries, for example, were not involved. This means that some biblical statements are true, but imprecise and incomplete, and therefore not a basis for a modern history. They may be used only with caution. Although biblical comments about salvation require the historical truth of certain events, such as the resurrection of Jesus, our faith does not require that we accept every biblical comment as historically or scientifically precise.[5]

Even one of the most conservative statements about Scripture admits that the Bible contains grammatical irregularities, exaggerations, imprecise descriptions, inexact quotations, variant selections, observations based on limited viewpoint, and free citations of the Old Testament.[6] When Scripture talks about the sun rising (Matthew 5:45), for example, its purpose is not to make a statement about astrophysics. When it calls a mustard seed the smallest seed (Matthew 13:31-32), it is not making a botanical claim. Genealogical lists may be incomplete (Matthew 1:8; 2 Chronicles 22-24), the length of kings' reigns may be misinterpreted due to co-regencies,[7] narrated events may be out of sequence (Matthew 4:18-22; 8:14; Luke 4:38-5:11), predicted events may not be fulfilled in every detail (Acts 21:11, 32-33; 27:10, 22), etc. Such irregularities encourage us to focus on the broad picture and the overall meaning, not tangential details.[8]

The truthfulness of the Bible should be evaluated according to its own "usage and purpose."[9] Yet its purpose rarely includes details of history and science,[10] and its demonstrable flexibility in word usage makes it unwise for us to insist on one meaning of a word when other meanings are possible. God inspired the ambiguities as well as the clear statements. Some things we need to know, and others we do not. God is not primarily concerned with whether we understand astrophysics, botany, and chronology. We err if we try to use his inspired book for purposes it was not designed for.

Christians come to different conclusions about the reliability of the Bible. Many insist that the Bible is more reliable in history and science than this position paper describes. We respect that view, for it is close to our own, but we do not think it theologically or biblically required. Other Christians insist that the Bible is less reliable than described herein. We respect their faith in Christ, but we repeat our belief, in summary, that the Bible is the inspired Word of God, authoritative and reliable in matters of faith, worship, morals, and ethics. We encourage all Christians to focus on these central and stated purposes of the Scriptures we have in common.

Endnotes

1 The testimony of the Bible to itself is summarized in I. Howard Marshall, *Biblical Inspiration,* Grand Rapids: Eerdmans, 1982, pages 19-30.

2 Revelation is both propositional and personal. See Marshall, pages 12-15.

3 Some parts of the Bible are more authoritative than others (e.g., circumcision and holy kisses) and do not function as a word of God in the same way other verses do. "The Bible...presents a progressive revelation, parts of which are now superseded in the light of what followed" (Marshall, page 58). The OT must be used on the basis of general principles, which suggests a similar approach for the NT.

4 William Hordern presents a neo-orthodox position in "The Nature of Revelation," in Millard Erickson, editor, *Readings in Christian Theology, Volume 1: The Living God,* 1973, pages 180-182. I do not have space to argue against the details of Hordern's view, but will say that any attempt to know God or Christ without relying on what Scripture says is suspect. "In subjectivism each man is his own authority, and if each man is his own authority there is neither truth nor authority" (Bernard Ramm, "The Pattern of Religious Authority," in Erickson, *Readings,* page 260).

5 I am avoiding the question whether all historical and scientific statements are true. I admit several passages for which I do not yet see a resolution.

One may wish to suspend judgment, which is a perfectly legitimate thing to do.... The Bible does contain what may be regarded as error and contradictions by modern standards but which are not in fact contrary to its own standards and purpose. (Marshall, 89, 71)

"Inerrancy" can never be demonstrated with a cogency which entitles it to rank as the foundation of a belief in inspiration. It must remain to those who hold it a doctrine of faith; a deduction from what they deem to be implied..." (James Orr, "Revelation and Inspiration," in Millard Erickson, editor, *Readings in Christian Theology, Volume 1: The Living God,* 1973, page 245)

6 International Conference on Biblical Inerrancy (ICBI). "The Chicago Statement on Biblical Inerrancy," Article XIII. Printed in Norman L. Geisler, editor. *Inerrancy.* Grand Rapids: Zondervan, 1979, page 496.

The analogy of Jesus, the Word made flesh, may offer a parallel. We accept his statements about God and salvation as completely true, and his life as perfectly sinless, but this does not necessitate that he never made a measurement mistake in his carpentry work. Likewise, the Bible may contain grammatical and other irregularities.

7 Dewey Beegle, "Inerrancy and the Phenomena of Scripture," in Millard Erickson, editor, *Readings in Christian Theology, Volume 1: The Living God,* Grand Rapids: Baker, 1973, pages 297-299, citing Edwin Thiele.

8 "One practical purpose for allowing the differences in parallel passages may be to give us a subtle clue that those are the kinds of things not worth quarrelling over!" (Alden Thompson, *Inspiration,* Hagerstown, Maryland: Review and Herald, 1991, page 70). Free citations of the OT suggest that meaning is more important than individual words, but a problem arises when the NT gives a different meaning to an OT passage.

9 ICBI, Article XIII. The qualifications in Article XIII make it difficult to accept some of the other articles, such as XI and XII, which say that Scripture never misleads us in matters of history and science. Galileo would disagree! "Having recognized that God's honour is not compromised by use of irregular grammar, etc., why is it so difficult to accept that his honour can be equally unaffected if he chooses to use equivalent irregularities in historical and scientific detail?" (James D.G. Dunn, "The Authority of Scripture According to Scripture," *Churchman* 96 (1982) 120.

10 "The Bible...nowhere claims to give instruction in (for instance) any of the natural sciences...and it would be an improper use of Scripture to treat it as making pronouncements on these matters" (J.I. Packer, *"Fundamentalism" and the Word of God,* Grand Rapids: Eerdmans, 1958, page 96). Perhaps all scientific statements in the Bible are phenomenological and therefore the concept of inerrancy is irrelevant for them.

Michael Morrison

The Importance of Doctrine

"I don't want to study doctrine," one person said. "I'm tired of doctrine. I want sermons to be short and inspiring — I don't want them to be doctrinal."

I can understand the feeling. Doctrinal arguments can be wearisome, and doctrine can turn people off. Yet I must point out that we still need doctrine — not in the sense of arguments, but in terms of understanding our faith. A "doctrine" is a "teaching," and the important teachings of the church are those relating to truth about God.

Sermons should be inspiring, but the kind of inspiration we need comes not from the speaker's skill, but from truth about God. For example, we can be inspired and have confidence about the future because of what God has done in Jesus Christ. We can be optimistic even in a troubled world because we have been taught about Jesus Christ. Our teachings and beliefs about Jesus are doctrines, truth about God, and the foundation of all that we do.

Enduring Christian faith is not built merely on good feelings, on brief moments of sensing God's presence in the beauty of the creation, or on a short inspirational story once a week. Good feelings and moments of inspiration are wonderful blessings — but those feelings alone cannot lead us into the changed life of unity and reconciliation with God that comes through knowing and believing in Jesus Christ. We need enduring faith, and that is built on knowing and understanding truth about God.

That is why doctrinal instruction is important, and why Christians need more than a 10-minute sermon once a week. We are dealing with eternal truths and ultimate realities, as well as the less important (but seemingly more urgent) matters of day-to-day life. Sometimes a profound point can be made in 10 minutes, but continually growing in understanding of who God is and what he has done needs a certain regular and on-going commitment of time.

What Jesus has done for us, as well as how that affects us and the way we live, must be explained again and again, continually, week after week, from many different angles, examining again and again the many different biblical lessons, prophecies, instructions and stories that God has given us to teach us about it. If most sermons are only 10 minutes long, we can easily see that it might take 20 years to cover all the subjects that are worth covering. But Christians need more than that.

It is easy to be simplistic in 10 minutes, to present only one side of the story. But Christian life is complex. People do not automatically grasp how the cross of Christ should affect the way we treat our neighbors, and they do not automatically believe everything they hear. Most aspects of Christianity take more than 10 minutes to explain. The sermon has to be for new people as well as for long-time members.

Need for classes

Ideally, churches would offer both discipleship classes and sermons. The classes would be more doctrinal and explanatory, with opportunity for questions and discussion. They would be geared toward specific groups, such as new Christians, teenagers, pre-teens and others. Then, the sermons could be shorter, with more of a motivational orientation, based on a short passage of Scripture. Motivation cannot come out of thin air or from a certain speaking style — it should come from truth about what God has done for us in Jesus Christ. The sermon must include some solid instruction, not just clever sayings and nice ideas.

Inspiration and exhortation cannot be separated from truth and discipleship. Bible study and doctrinal study is a form of worship, and may be done in a worship service. The sermon should be used for both instruction and encouragement. Doctrinal subjects can be covered through a series of biblical expository sermons.

A biblically grounded doctrinal sermon or Bible study takes greater mental energy, both in preparation and in listening, than a 10-minute "thought for the week." But Christians want to understand their faith, and Christian leaders and teachers should help them do so. Christians realize that faith in Christ goes much deeper than just good feelings and inspirational sayings, and they enjoy and appreciate being fed in all the good things the Word of God has to offer.

I am not advocating long sermons. There is no virtue in talking longer than people can pay attention. Some speakers can hold attention better than others, but even the best can't get 100 percent. However, speakers should do their best to explain the Word of God, explain something of its significance, to show how it relates to faith in Christ, how it relates to practical matters of life and death, and how it is based on what God has said and done. That will take some time, and it will take some work from the audience as well as from the speaker.

How long should a sermon be? It depends partly on the culture, on what the audience is used to. Many university classes are 50 minutes long, but they are not 50 minutes of lecture. The class is interactive, with opportunity for questions and discussion. A good length for a sermon may be about 30 minutes, with flexibility for special situations. Some speakers are less gifted and may be more effective if they give shorter sermons, giving some of the sermon time to other members for testimonials, stories or scriptural insights on a topic related to the sermon theme.

The ideal length also depends on how much spiritual nourishment people are getting during the week. Are they opening themselves to God's instruction in prayer, Bible study and small group fellowship? Sometimes it seems as if the people who do the most Bible study are also the most interested and excited about listening to sermons. They have a hunger for God. Christ is, after all, the most important thing in our lives and in our future.

I am convinced that doctrine is important — even though not all doctrines are equally important. For some people, it seems, earthquakes are just as important as the resurrection of Christ. Perhaps disasters seem more relevant to life today, but in actuality, Jesus' resurrection is always more important to us, even if we are in the middle of an earthquake. The doctrine of the resurrection is always relevant — especially when death is a real possibility! It is vital that all sermon and Bible study instruction be rooted in Jesus Christ.

How to avoid heresy

Christians need a strong doctrinal foundation that will help them discern crucial teachings from less-important ideas. Some Christians are attracted by New Age teachings or the teachings of quasi-Christian cults because of a lack of doctrinal grounding. We need to teach doctrine, because only doctrine will give people a defense against heresies that are preached with enthusiasm and confidence.

The early church had a great need for doctrine. The New Testament is filled with doctrine — with information about Jesus Christ and the difference he makes in our lives. But not all biblical teachings are of equal importance. For example, the teaching that the apostles numbered 12 is not as important as the teaching that Jesus was raised from the dead.

Core beliefs

The early church developed a short list of doctrines they felt were essential for new believers to know and accept. Different regional churches had slightly different lists, and in time these lists became more standardized. They are now called creeds, from the Latin word for "I believe." These creeds were simple statements of belief.

Our church also has a Statement of Beliefs, developed through much discussion in our doctrinal team. This provides a list of basic doctrines. It doesn't include everything, but even our Statement of Beliefs is longer than a list of what is essential to Christian faith. The doctrinal team has therefore developed a shorter list of ten essential beliefs, which we are calling a Doctrinal Summary. These are the core doctrines. These could form the basis for a series of sermons, and would provide a stable doctrinal foundation. Here is the Doctrinal Summary:

We believe:

- There is one God—Father, Son, and Holy Spirit.
- God the Father made all things through the Son, sent the Son for our salvation, and gives us the Holy Spirit.
- The Son of God, Jesus Christ, our Lord and Savior, was born of the virgin Mary, fully God and fully human, and is the perfect revelation of the Father and the perfect representative of humanity. He suffered and died on the cross for all human sin, was raised bodily on the third day, and ascended to heaven. Standing in for all humanity before the Father, Jesus Christ provides the perfect human response to God. Since he died for all, all died in him, and all will be made alive in him.

- The Holy Spirit brings sinners to repentance and faith, assures believers of their forgiveness and acceptance as God's dearly loved children, and works in them to conform them to the image of Jesus Christ.
- The Bible is the inspired and infallible Word of God that testifies to Jesus Christ. The Bible is fully authoritative for all matters of faith and salvation.
- Salvation comes only by God's grace and not by works, and it is experienced through faith in Jesus Christ. Christians respond to the joy of salvation when they gather in regular fellowship and live godly lives in Jesus Christ.
- We look forward to the resurrection of the dead and the life of the age to come.

Friends, I hope that these doctrines never become boring and never seem irrelevant. Granted, we human speakers can sometimes make them sound boring and irrelevant, but the doctrines themselves are vital for us all. These are short and inspiring doctrines. I am thankful that God has given his truth that is worth teaching again and again, as we follow the Teacher, Jesus Christ.

Joseph Tkach

The Gospel: It's Not Fair!

Jesus didn't carry any swords or spears. He didn't have an army behind him. His only weapon was his mouth, and it was his message that got him into trouble. He made people so angry that they wanted to kill him.

A dangerous message

His message was seen not merely as wrong—it was dangerous. It was subversive. It threatened to upset the social world of Judaism. But what kind of message could make the religious leaders so angry that they would kill the messenger?

One idea that could anger the religious leaders is found in Matthew 9:13: "I have not come to call the righteous, but the sinners." Jesus had a message of good news for sinners, but people who considered themselves good often thought that Jesus preached bad news.

Jesus invited prostitutes and tax collectors into the kingdom of God, and the good people didn't like that. "That's not fair," they may have said. "We have been working hard to be good, and why can they get into the kingdom without working hard? If you don't keep sinners out, it isn't fair!"

They thought that Jesus was saying that God is not fair. Even today, people don't like to hear that idea. Good Christian people want God to be fair—but he isn't.

Most people think that fairness requires equal treatment for everyone, but when it comes to salvation, God simply isn't fair.

More than fair

God is more than fair. His grace is far beyond anything we could deserve. God is generous, full of grace, full of mercy, loving us even though we don't deserve it.

That kind of message bothers religious leaders and all who say that the harder you work, the more you will get; if you behave better, you will get a better reward. Religious leaders like to have that kind of message, because it makes it easy to motivate people to work hard, to do right, to live right.

But Jesus says, It isn't so.

If you have dug a really deep pit for yourself, if you have messed up time and time again, if you have been the worst sort of sinner, you don't have to work your way out of the pit to be given salvation. God simply forgives you for the sake of Jesus. You don't have to deserve it—God simply does it. You just need to believe it. You need to trust God, to take him at his word: Your million-dollar debt is removed from the record.

That is good news for ordinary people.

But it seems that some people are distressed at this kind of news. "Look, I've been working hard to get out of the pit," they might say, "and I am almost out. You mean to tell me that 'those' people are pulled out of the pit instantly, without having to do any work at all? That's not fair!"

No, grace is not "fair"—it is grace—it is a gift we did not deserve. God can be generous to whomever he wants to be generous to, and the good news is that he offers his generosity to everyone. It is fair in the sense that it extends to everyone, even though this means that he forgives some people a big debt, and some people a smaller debt—the same arrangement for all even though there are different circumstances.

A parable of unfairness

Matthew 20 includes the parable of the workers in the vineyard. Some people worked all day long in the heat of the day. Some worked only half a day, and some worked only one hour, but they all got paid the same amount, a day's wage. Some got exactly what they agreed to, but others got more. However, the people who worked all day long said, "That's not fair. We worked all day long, and it's not fair to pay us the same as those who worked less" (see verse 12).

But the people who worked all day got exactly what they had agreed to before they began work (verse 4). The only reason they got upset was because other people got more than they deserved.

What did the boss say? It was this: "Don't I have the right to do what I want with my own money? Or are you envious because I am generous?" (verse 15).

The boss said they would be given a fair day's wage for a fair day's work, and they were—and yet they complained. Why? Because they compared themselves with others and they got the shorter end of the stick. They got their hopes up, and then they were disappointed.

But the landowner said: "I am doing you no wrong. If you think it's not fair, the problem is in what you expected, not in what you actually got. If it hadn't been for the amount I paid the newcomers, you would be quite happy with what I gave you. The problem is in your expectations, not in what I did. You accuse me of being bad, simply because I was good *to someone else*(see verse 15).

How would you react to this? What would you think if your boss gave a bonus to the newest employees, but not to the old faithful workers? It would not be very good for morale, would it? But Jesus was not giving us payroll advice here—he was telling a parable about the kingdom of God (verse 1).

The parable reflected something that was happening in Jesus' ministry. God was giving salvation to people who hadn't worked very hard, and the religious leaders said: "That's not fair. You can't be generous to them. We've been working hard, and they have hardly been working." Jesus replied, "I am bringing good news to sinners, not to the righteous." His teaching threatened to undermine the normal motive for doing good.

Where do we fit in?

We might like to think that we have worked all day long, bearing the burdens and the heat of the day, deserving a good reward. But we have not.

It doesn't matter how long you've been in the church or how many sacrifices you have made—those are nothing in comparison to what God is giving us. Paul worked harder than any of us; he made more sacrifices for the gospel than we realize, but he counted it all as a loss for Christ. It was nothing.

The time we've spent in the church is nothing to God. The work we've done is nothing compared to what he can do. Even at our best, as another parable says, we are unprofitable servants (Luke 17:10). Jesus has bought our entire lives; he has a fair claim on every thought and every action. We cannot possibly give him anything on top of that—even if we do everything he commands.

We are like the workers who worked only one hour and got a whole day's wage. We just barely got started, and we were paid like we actually did something useful. Is that fair? Maybe we shouldn't even ask the question. If the judgment is in our favor, we shouldn't ask for another opinion!

Do we think of ourselves as people who have worked long and hard? Do we think we deserve more than we are getting? Or do we see ourselves as people who are getting an undeserved gift, regardless of how long we've worked?

Joseph Tkach

The Message of Jesus: A Bible Study

This is a Bible study. Although you may get the gist of the answer by looking at the comments we append, the study will be more meaningful if you look up the Scriptures and take time to think about it, rather than reading through in a hurry.

1. When Jesus began his ministry, what did he preach? Mark 1:14-15. When he sent his disciples out, what did he tell them to preach? Matthew 10:7; Luke 10:9.

Comment: Some ancient Greek manuscripts of Mark 1:14-15 say that Jesus preached the kingdom of God; others say that he preached the gospel of God. It is not necessary here to discuss which manuscripts are better, but we will discuss the version that is familiar to most of us—Jesus preached, "The time is fulfilled, and the kingdom of God is at hand" (NIV 1984).

Jesus was announcing the kingdom—not just the king—as being near. He was talking about nearness in terms of *time,* not geography. "The time is fulfilled…." The time had come for God's kingdom to be established.

Likewise, when the disciples preached that the kingdom was near, they were not talking about the king, and they were not talking about a nearby territory. They were announcing that God's kingdom would soon be there. This was good news!

2. Was Jesus a king? John 18:37. But was he like the kings of this world? Were his disciples supposed to act the way rulers of this world act? Matthew 20:25-28. May we assume that God's kingdom is like the kingdoms of this world?

Comment: When we are studying something as important as the central message of Jesus Christ, it is not safe to make assumptions. God's thoughts are not like our thoughts, and his ways are not like ours. We need to look to Scripture to see what Jesus revealed about the kingdom.

The Jews had various assumptions about what the Messiah would do, but Jesus did not act the way they wanted him to. Their assumptions about the king were wrong, and their assumptions about the kingdom were wrong, too.

Just as their ancestors had wanted a king like the nations around them (1 Samuel 8:5), the first-century Jews also wanted a kingdom much like the kingdoms of this world—with a military leader who enforced laws in a particular territory. The Jews wanted the Messiah to bring a kingdom like that, but Jesus brought something different. Let's study a few more verses to learn about the kingdom Jesus preached.

3. Did Jesus say that the kingdom had already come upon the first-century Jews? Matthew 12:28. Were people already entering the kingdom of God? Luke 16:16; Matthew 21:31. How were they entering? Matthew 21:31-32. Is it possible to enter something that does not exist?

Comment: When Jesus preached the kingdom of God, he told people to believe the message and repent (Mark 1:15). He criticized those who did not believe and repent, but praised the people who did believe and repent, and said that they were entering the kingdom.

Jesus was talking about a spiritual move, not a geographic move. People enter God's kingdom by accepting his rule, not by moving to a new territory. They enter God's kingdom by repentance and faith—they accept his rule in their lives. They accept Jesus as their King, and he reigns over them. They become his subjects, doing his will. Paul said that Christians have already entered the kingdom (Colossians 1:13).

Jesus, the King, has already been crowned with

power and authority over all things (Matthew 28:18). He is already King. However, he does not force others to do his will, the way the kings of this world do. Rather, he reigns over those who willingly accept him as their King.

4. Did Jesus also speak of the kingdom of God as a future reality? Matthew 8:11; 13:43; Luke 13:28. Can something that exists right now expand and also exist in the future?

Comment: Jesus spoke of the kingdom as both a present-tense reality and a future glory. It exists now as a spiritual realm—in the world, but not part of the world—and it will later expand with power and glory when Jesus returns. The kingdom will then come in great power. God's power is already here, but it is veiled—present but usually not visible.

The kingdom is both present and future, already in existence but not yet visible in its fullness. The "already/not yet" nature of God's kingdom is similar to other spiritual realities:

- We are already saved, but the fullness of our salvation is yet future (Ephesians 2:5; 1 Peter 1:5).
- We have already been given eternal life, but its fullness will be given after we die (John 3:35; Mark 10:30).
- We will be like Christ, yet Christ is already being formed in us (Philippians 3:21; 2 Corinthians 3:18).
- We will live with God forever, but he already lives within us (1 Thessalonians 4:17; 1 John 4:13).

The Bible speaks of these spiritual truths not only as future gifts, but also as blessings we already enjoy in part.

In a similar way, Jesus spoke of the kingdom both as something that exists right now and something that will exist in a greater way when he returns. When he and his disciples announced that the kingdom was near, they meant the spiritual, invisible phase of the kingdom. For those who thought the kingdom would soon appear with power and glory, he told a parable to explain that there would be a delay (Luke 19:11-27)—but the parable also explains that some of the work of the kingdom must be done even before the kingdom appears in its fullness. Now is the time we are to believe, repent, be saved and enter the kingdom.

5. What did Jesus say would be preached throughout the world? Matthew 24:14. What did he commission his disciples to preach? Matthew 28:19-20; Mark 16:15-16; Luke 24:47. Should we conclude that preaching the kingdom is practically synonymous with preaching faith, repentance, forgiveness and making disciples?

Preaching in the book of Acts

What did the disciples preach about? Here are the verses in Acts that use the words for "preach":

4:2 — proclaiming that in Jesus there is the resurrection of the dead

5:42 — proclaiming Jesus as the Messiah

8:4 — proclaiming the word

8:5 — proclaimed the Messiah

8:12 — proclaiming the good news about the kingdom of God and the name of Jesus Christ

8:25, 40 — proclaiming the good news

8:35 — proclaimed the good news about Jesus

10:36 — preaching peace by Jesus Christ

11:20 — proclaiming the Lord Jesus

13:5 — proclaimed the word of God

13:32-33 — bringing the good news that God fulfilled the promise by raising Jesus

13:38 — proclaiming forgiveness of sins through Jesus

14:7, 21; 16:10 — proclaiming the good news

14:15 — bringing good news, that you should turn to God

15:7 — the message of the good news

15:35 — proclaimed the word of the Lord

17:3 — proclaiming the Messiah, Jesus

17:18 — telling the good news about Jesus and the resurrection

17:23 — proclaim what you worship as unknown

20:24 — testify to the good news of God's grace

20:27 — declaring the whole purpose of God

26:23 — proclaiming light to Jews and gentiles

Comment: According to Jesus, our goal when preaching is to make disciples, and we do that by preaching repentance and faith, baptizing those who believe and teaching them to obey what Jesus taught. For those who *reject* Jesus as King, the kingdom is a message of judgment. But for those who accept him, it is wonderfully good news — the good news is that we can enter the kingdom now!

Since the good news of the kingdom, which includes forgiveness, is experienced only through faith and repentance, these aspects of salvation are a prominent part of the gospel message. If people have faith in Jesus Christ and accept him as Lord, they enter his kingdom—even if they have never heard the word "kingdom." It is their *relationship* to Jesus Christ that is crucial; the precise terminology is not nearly as important.

When we preach the gospel of the kingdom, what should we say about it? In future studies we will see the way Jesus described the kingdom, what the original apostles preached, and what Paul emphasized as the most important part of the gospel message.

Preaching about what?

What are Jesus' disciples supposed to preach about? The answer can be seen by looking at scriptures that use the Greek words for "preach":

2 Tim. 4:2
Matt. 3:1; 4:17, 23; 9:35; 10:7; 24:14;26:1
Mark 1:4, 7, 14; 5:20; 6:12; 13:10; 14:9; 16:15
Luke 3:3; 4:18-19, 43; 8:1, 39; 9:2; 16:16; 24:47

Acts 5:42; 8:5, 12, 35; 9:20; 10:36, 42; 11:20; 17:18; 19:13; 20:25; 28:31
Rom. 10:8, 14
1 Cor. 1:23; 2:2; 15:11-12
2 Cor. 1:19; 4:5; 11:4
Gal. 1:16, 23; 2:2
Eph. 2:17; 3:8
Phil. 1:15
Col. 1:22-23
1 Thess. 2:9
1 Tim. 3:16

The gospel can be described in many ways — a message about the kingdom, about Jesus Christ, forgiveness, reconciliation, salvation or peace. The most common biblical description is the gospel of Jesus Christ.

"The gospel of ... "

Scripture describes the gospel in numerous ways. Here's how the word is most often used:

- good news of Jesus Christ — 15 times
- good news of God - 9 times
- good news of the kingdom - 7 times
- my gospel, our gospel - 6 times
- the gospel of peace - 2 times
- good news of God's grace - 1 time
- good news of the glory of Christ - 1 time
- gospel of your salvation - 1 time

Michael Morrison

Preaching in the Book of Acts
The Speeches of Peter

The church today is a continuation of first-century Christianity. We do not imitate every cultural detail of the church, but we do want to continue the faith and the message of the early church. To help us do this, let's turn to a record of what they did: the book of Acts. Evangelism is a major theme of the book. Let's examine it to see what the apostles preached.

The kingdom of God

Our first clue comes in verse 3: The resurrected Jesus taught the apostles "about the kingdom of God." However, despite the many evangelistic sermons described in the book of Acts, the word *kingdom* is not used in any of them. It is used only eight times in Acts:

- Jesus taught about the kingdom of God (1:3).
- The disciples asked about the kingdom (1:8).
- Philip taught the Samaritans about the kingdom of God and the name of Jesus Christ (8:12).
- Paul and Barnabas told the Christians in Antioch that we enter the kingdom of God through many hardships (14:22).
- Paul argued in the synagogue for three months about the kingdom of God (19:8).
- Paul told the Ephesian elders that he had preached the kingdom (20:25). But in verse 21 he characterized his message with the terms *repentance* and *faith;* in verse 24 he said he preached "the gospel of God's grace"; these seem to be equated with the gospel of the kingdom. (Luke never uses the phrase "gospel of the kingdom." The

only place he uses "gospel of" is here: "the gospel of God's grace.")
- To Roman Jews, Paul preached "the kingdom of God and tried to convince them about Jesus" (28:23).
- In Rome, Paul "preached the kingdom of God and taught about the Lord Jesus Christ" (28:31). Here, a message about the kingdom is linked to a message about Jesus Christ.

Although Jews believed in the coming kingdom of God and had the Old Testament prophecies of it, Paul argued about the kingdom for three months in the Ephesian synagogue. His concept of the kingdom must have been considerably different than what the Ephesian Jews believed. And no wonder! Paul's message about the kingdom was coupled with a message about Jesus and grace and faith.

That was Jesus' message, too. For 40 days after his resurrection, he taught the disciples about the kingdom. What did this entail? We can go to the Gospel of Luke to see what he talked about during that time. On the road to Emmaus, "he explained to them what was said in all the Scriptures *concerning himself*" (Luke 24:27). Later, he summarized his message: "Everything must be fulfilled that is written *about me* in the Law of Moses, the Prophets and the Psalms" (verse 44).

What was written? Here it is in a nutshell: "*The Christ* will suffer and rise from the dead on the third day, and *repentance* and *forgiveness* of sins will be preached *in his name* to all nations, beginning at Jerusalem" (verses 46-47). This is the kingdom message. As George Ladd wrote,

In the days after Jesus' resurrection, he continued to teach them about the Kingdom of God (1:3). We are undoubtedly to understand this to mean that he was instructing them in the relationship between his proclamation of the Kingdom of God and his death and resurrection. (George Eldon Ladd, *Theology of the New Testament* [Grand Rapids, Michigan: Eerdmans, 1963], page 332)

Jesus then reminded his disciples "You are *witnesses* of these things" (verse 48). That brings us back to the book of Acts. Let's see what the apostles preached.

Witnesses

What did the apostles preach about? Our next bit of evidence is in Acts 1:8. Jesus told his disciples that they would receive the Holy Spirit, and then he told them what that divine power would enable them to do: "You will be my *witnesses* in Jerusalem, and in all Judea and Samaria, and to the ends of the earth."

Witness is an important word in the book of Acts. It comes in several forms, both verbs and nouns, all built on the root *martyr-*. It refers to a witness in a courtroom, or the testimony that a witness gives in court. We get the English word *martyr* from this Greek root. People who were faithful **witnesses** to Jesus Christ sometimes became **martyrs** for their faith.

Let's survey the occurrences of the *martyr-* words in Acts to see what the disciples were witnessing to. They were giving evidence in support of a particular fact.

1:8 — witnesses of Jesus Christ
1:22 — witness of Jesus' resurrection
2:32 — witness of his resurrection
3:15 — witness of his resurrection
4:33 — they testified to the resurrection
5:32 — witnesses of his resurrection, exaltation and forgiveness
10:39 — witnesses of everything Jesus did
10:41 — the resurrected Jesus was seen by witnesses
10:43 — all the prophets testify about him and forgiveness

13:31 — those who saw the resurrected Jesus are his witnesses
14:3 — the Lord confirmed the message of his grace
22:15 — Paul will be Jesus' witness of what he saw and heard
22:18 — they will not accept Paul's testimony about the Lord
23:11 — Paul testified about Jesus in Jerusalem and Rome
26:16 — Paul was appointed a witness of what he saw of the Lord
26:22 — Paul testified, saying that the Scriptures predicted that the Christ would suffer, rise from the dead, and proclaim light to Jews and gentiles.[1]

The focus of the apostles' testimony is Jesus, his resurrection, and the fact that grace or forgiveness is available. Let's go back to the beginning of Acts and see how often that message is repeated.

Peter's Pentecost sermon

The first sermon that Luke includes in his apostolic history is Peter's comments to the crowd at Pentecost. This is not only a landmark event in the church, it is a foundational speech in the book of Acts. First, Peter tells the people that the Spirit-caused tongues are a fulfillment of Scripture and a sign that the "last days" had begun and people can be saved (2:16-21).

Ladd summarized it in this way:

The age of fulfilment was dawned. "This is what was spoken by the prophet Joel" (Acts 2:16). "But what God foretold by the mouth of all the prophets…he thus fulfilled" (Acts 3:18). "And all the prophets who have spoken, from Samuel and those who came afterwards, also proclaimed these days" (Acts 3:24). The apostles declared that the messianic age had dawned. (Ladd, page 329)

Peter then makes his point:

Men of Israel, listen to this: Jesus of Nazareth was a man accredited by God to you by miracles, wonders and signs…. This man was handed over to you by God's set purpose and foreknowledge; and you...put him to death by nailing him to the cross. But God raised him from the dead. (2:22-24)

Peter explains that David had predicted the Messiah's resurrection. The apostles are witnesses of Jesus' resurrection, and the exalted Jesus is now pouring out the Holy Spirit on his people. The conclusion: "Therefore let all Israel be assured of this: God has made this Jesus, whom you crucified, both Lord and Christ" (2:36). Jesus is the Messiah and the One we should obey.

The people believed. They had crucified the Messiah they had been hoping for! So what were they supposed to do? Peter told them the appropriate response of faith: repentance and baptism, with the result of forgiveness and the Holy Spirit (2:38). And Peter pleaded with them to do it (2:40).

Three thousand did, and their zeal is shown in Luke's summary statement: "They devoted themselves to the apostles' teaching and to the fellowship, to the breaking of bread and to prayer" (2:42). Their willingness to share was legendary (2:44-45). They met at the temple, broke bread at home and ate together, praising God (2:46-47). They quickly became a community, a fellowship.

Healing in Jesus' name

Peter's second sermon in Acts is reported in chapter 3. It is also given to a crowd of Jews at the temple, and it has some basic similarities to Peter's first sermon. A miracle was done; the people were amazed. They were ready to listen to Peter. What did he tell them? He told them about Jesus.

What ironies! The Jews wanted him killed, even though Pilate did not. Instead of accepting the true Messiah, they asked for a false one. They killed the author of life! (3:13-15). But God raised him and glorified him, Peter testified to the crowd.

The healing had been done by faith in the name of Jesus (3:15-16). The temple was the place of God's name (1 Kings 8:29), but the healing was done in the name of Jesus. We are soon told that there is no name, other than Jesus, by which we can be saved (4:12). The name of Jesus far surpasses the value of the temple.

Lame people were not allowed in the temple, but by faith in Jesus, this man, for the first time in his life, was permitted to praise God in the temple. Jesus, the Holy and Righteous One, makes it possible for more people to come to God. Readers would have already seen hints of that: "*Everyone* who calls on the name of the Lord will be saved" (2:21). "The promise is...for *all* who are far off — for *all* whom the Lord our God will call" (2:39). These are literary anticipations of the eventual opening of salvation to other previously restricted peoples, such as eunuchs, Samaritans and Gentiles.

Peter continues his sermon by noting the Messiah's sufferings had been predicted (3:18). The desired response: repentance, resulting in forgiveness, and waiting for the predicted return of the Messiah Jesus. After all, Moses had predicted that God would "raise up" (same Greek word as "resurrect") a prophet, and whoever rejects him will be expelled from the community of God's people (3:22-23). If they don't want to follow the leader God provides, then they won't be part of his people.

In Abraham's day, God promised to bless "*all* peoples on earth," and he is now blessing the Jews "first" (a subtle hint of others to come later) through the servant he raised up or resurrected, and the blessing comes through repentance (3:25-26). Luke summarizes the Peter's message in 4:2 — "The apostles were...proclaiming in Jesus the resurrection of the dead." The underlying implication is that Jesus' resurrection proves that we can also be resurrected if we are aligned with him.

Peter's witness to the Sanhedrin

The Sadducees, who did not believe in a resurrection, did not like the apostles' message. Peter and John were arrested and brought into court. The Jewish leaders asked Peter, "By what power or what name did you do this?" (4:7). They couldn't have asked a better question. Peter soon got to his point: "It is by the name of Jesus Christ of Nazareth, whom you crucified but whom God raised from the dead, that this man stands before you healed" (4:10). You rejected him, but God has made him the capstone and the only avenue of salvation.

The Sadducees still didn't like the message, so they told Peter "not to speak or teach at all in the name of Jesus" (4:17-18). But Peter replied that he had to speak about what he had seen and heard. He was a true witness, not one who could be forced to be silent or false.

Peter and John went back to the community of faith, and they all rejoiced in prayer. Their prayer acknowledged that the Scriptures predicted the conspiracy against the Messiah (4:25-27). It repeats the fact that everything had happened according to God's foreknowledge (4:28). They asked for boldness in speaking the word of God, and for miracles through the name of Jesus (4:29-30).

Luke gives another summary: The believers shared their possessions, and the apostles testified to the resurrection of the Lord Jesus (4:32-33). Grace and generosity are a result of Christian faith.

In answer to prayer, the apostles were bold, and many miracles were done (5:12-16). The Sadducees still didn't like it, and the apostles were jailed again (5:17-18). An angel released them, and told them to preach "the full message of this new life" (5:20). Here we see another phrase — new life — that characterizes the preaching of the apostolic church.

The apostles were again brought before the Sanhedrin and given opportunity to speak. Peter explained why he was disobeying the Jewish leaders' orders: "We must obey God rather than men!" (5:29). He was obeying God's orders to be a witness to the new life available through Jesus Christ. Peter then launched into his message:

> The God of our fathers raised Jesus from the dead — whom you had killed by hanging him on a tree. God exalted him to his own right hand as Prince and Savior that he might give repentance and forgiveness of sins to Israel. We are witnesses of these things, and so is the Holy Spirit, whom God has given to those who obey him. (5:30-32)

What kind of obedience was Peter referring to? Not the Jewish customs observed by the Sanhedrin. Rather, the obedience Peter had in mind here was belief in Jesus as the Christ, and obeying his command to preach salvation.

The Sadducees were even more angry at the message, and wanted to kill the apostles. But Gamaliel, a Pharisee (Luke is more favorable to Pharisees than to Sadducees), advised them to let the apostles go (5:33-39). Gamaliel's short speech may have been quoted partly for the benefit of Jewish Christians who did not like Paul's gospel to the Gentiles. The advice applies quite well: "Leave these men alone! Let them go! For if their purpose or activity is of human origin, it will fail. But if it is from God, you will not be able to stop these men; you will only find yourselves fighting against God" (5:38-39).

Despite the threat of death, the apostles rejoiced and "never stopped teaching and proclaiming the good news that Jesus is the Christ" (5:42). There's the gospel: Jesus is the Christ. His resurrection proves that he is the Messiah, the God-ordained agent of salvation.

The kerygma

Peter had a consistent message. He had seen something so life-changing that he simply had to tell others about it. He was filled with the Spirit, filled with zeal, filled with boldness, to tell others the good news. This gospel focuses on the resurrection of Jesus, but several other related facts are usually included.

This package of core facts is usually called the *kerygma* (a Greek noun meaning preaching). Here are the major components:

- Jesus' resurrection: God raised Jesus from the dead.
- Jesus' life and death: Jesus did many miracles, he suffered, he died by crucifixion.
- Jesus' exaltation: God glorified Jesus, raised him to his right hand as Messiah, Prince, Savior and Lord.
- Prediction: All this happened as predicted in Scripture. Jesus fulfills the promise of the Old Testament.

- Salvation: Because of Jesus' resurrection, people are exhorted to repent and are promised forgiveness, grace, salvation, and new life in his name.
- Restoration: Jesus Christ will return.[2]

This is the heart and core of the gospel — it is the message the apostles preached, despite threats of death. It's a life-transforming message, a message about new life, a message worth living for, and a message worth dying for. We see that in the next story Luke gives us.

Stephen, Philip and Saul

Stephen, a Greek-speaking Jew, was arrested, and he preached a long sermon before the Sanhedrin. He reminded them of a central lesson of Israelite history: They disobeyed, resisted the Holy Spirit and persecuted the prophets (7:51-52). Moses predicted that God would raise up a prophet (7:37), but they killed the prophets who predicted Christ, and now they had murdered him.

Stephen's last message was that the exalted Jesus, the Son of Man, was standing at the right hand of God (7:56). Stephen's stinging indictment of the Jewish leaders led to his martyrdom, and his last witness was to the forgiveness that can be obtained from the Lord Jesus (7:60).

Persecution intensified, and the Christians were scattered, but they did not stop preaching despite the threats of death. Philip went "to a city in Samaria and proclaimed the Christ there" (8:4-5). Miracles were done, and the crowds listened as Philip told them about the kingdom of God and the name of Jesus (8:6, 12). Many believed and were baptized. Philip eventually met the Ethiopian eunuch and accepted an invitation to speak. "Philip began with that very passage of Scripture [Isaiah 53:7-8] and told him the good news about Jesus" (8:35). The eunuch believed and was baptized.

Then we are introduced to the dramatic conversion and call of Saul of Tarsus. He was promised the Holy Spirit and was baptized (9:17-18). "At once he began to preach in the synagogues that Jesus is the Son of God…proving that Jesus is the Christ" (9:20, 22). That was the fundamental message. The Lord told Ananias that Saul had been chosen "to carry my name" (9:15). Paul was not preaching a new gospel, but a continuation of the same basic message taught by Christ and the apostles.

Peter's gospel message to Gentiles

Peter enters the story again, and his speech to Cornelius is pivotal. The leading Jewish apostle gives the kerygma to Gentiles. They, like Jews, can be saved through belief in the Messiah. God accepts people "from every nation who fear him and do what is right" (10:35).

Peter acknowledges that Cornelius already knows "the message God sent to the people of Israel, telling the good news of peace through Jesus Christ, who is Lord of all" (10:36). He knew the story, starting with the ministry of Jesus: "God anointed Jesus of Nazareth with the Holy Spirit and power, and…he went around doing good and healing…. We are witnesses of everything he did in the country of the Jews and in Jerusalem" (10:38-39).

The next item on the evangelistic summary: "They killed him by hanging him on a tree, but God raised him from the dead on the third day and caused him to be seen…by witnesses whom God had already chosen" (10:39-41).

Jesus commanded these witnesses to preach that Jesus is the Messiah — "the one whom God appointed as judge of the living and the dead" (10:42). As predicted in the Old Testament, "everyone who believes in him receives forgiveness of sins through his name" (10:43). This was a message Cornelius already knew. He believed, and the Holy Spirit gave evidence not only that God accepted Gentiles, but also that he accepted this message of salvation going to them as well as to Jews.

Peter continues to stress the now-familiar themes of the gospel. It is a message that brings salvation (11:14); it is a message about repentance and life (11:18).

Endnotes

[1] To be complete, here are all the other verses in Acts that use *martyr-* words. These do not indicate

what the apostles were commissioned to testify about, but show how the word can be used in other situations:

6:3 — men known to be full of the Spirit

6:13 — false witnesses gave testimony

7:44 — ancient Israelites had "the tabernacle of Testimony"

7:58 — witnesses at Stephen's trial

10:22 — Cornelius was respected by the people

13:22 — God testified concerning David

15:8 — God showed that he accepted Gentiles

16:2 — the brothers spoke well of Timothy

20:26 — Paul declared that he was innocent

22:5 — he can testify that Paul persecuted the church

22:12 — Ananias was highly respected by the Jews

22:20 — the blood of your martyr Stephen was shed

26:5 — they can testify that Paul was a strict Pharisee

2 Philippe Menoud gives us this summary of the kerygma:

> The preaching of the apostles...may be briefly summarized as follows:
> God has realized the promises of the OT and brought salvation to his people (Acts 2:16-21, 23; 3:18, 24; 10:43).
> This has taken place through the ministry, death, and resurrection of Jesus (2:22-24; 3:13-15; 10:37-39).
> Jesus has been exalted as "Lord and Christ" (2:36).
> The Holy Spirit in the church is the sign of Christ's present power and glory (2:33; 5:32).
> Salvation will reach its consummation in the return of Christ to judge the living and the dead (3:21; 10:42).
> The apostles have been chosen by God as witnesses of the ministry of Jesus and above all of his resurrection (2:32; 3:15; 10:40-41).
> They address to their hearers an appeal for repentance and offer to the believers forgiveness of sins and the gift of the Holy Spirit (2:38-39; 3:25-26; 5:31; 10:43).

In short, the primitive preaching of the apostles is a proclamation of the work of salvation made by God in Christ and a call to believe and be saved. (P.H. Menoud, "Preaching," *Interpreter's Dictionary of the Bible* [Nashville: Abingdon, 1962], volume 3, pages 868-869)

Michael Morrison

Sharing the Good News

After Jesus had been resurrected and had appeared to his disciples for several weeks, he took them to the Mount of Olives. The disciples asked him, "Lord, are you at this time going to restore the kingdom to Israel?" (Acts 1:6). In other words, where are we now in the prophetic timetable? Are we near the end?

And Jesus answered, "It is not for you to know the times or dates the Father has set by his own authority. But you will receive power when the Holy Spirit comes on you; and you will be my witnesses in Jerusalem, and in all Judea and Samaria, and to the ends of the earth" (verses 7-8). In other words, you don't need to know the prophetic timetable. What you need to do is to preach the gospel.

What Jesus said to the disciples is still true: Our place in prophecy is not to calculate dates, but to preach the gospel. We do not need to worry about the *next* phase of God's plan—we need to be diligent about the phase of history we are *currently* in. This is the church age, the gospel-preaching age, and we need to be doing the work he has assigned us.

Evangelism is central to our mission, as described in Jesus' "Great Commission": "Go and make disciples of all nations, baptizing them in the name of the Father and of the Son and of the Holy Spirit, and teaching them to obey everything I have commanded you" (Matthew 28:19-20).

For apostles only?

However, a few people have wondered: "The apostles were commanded to preach the gospel, but how do we know that it applies to us today? Isn't our role just to set a good example, and then give the gospel to people when they ask about it? The Bible does not actually command us to preach to the public, does it?"

Let's go back to Matthew 28:19-20. Jesus told his apostles to teach other people to obey everything he had commanded the disciples. And one of his commands to them was to preach, and as a result, the apostles taught believers to obey Jesus' command to preach the gospel. In effect, Jesus gave a self-perpetuating command. Future disciples were to carry on the commission. Matthew ended his book with a command that his readers needed to obey.

Verse 20 tells us that Jesus promised, "I am with you always, to the very end of the age." Jesus did not promise merely to be with the apostles, but with the church throughout the centuries. The commission is likewise applicable to all the church, from the earliest apostles even to the end of the age. The New Testament records the results of Christ being with and motivating apostles and many other believers to preach the gospel.

A word about 'preach'

Before we look at examples in the New Testament about the church carrying out the command to preach, let us take a moment to better understand the Greek words usually translated "preach" or "preaching." Some Christians are put off by the idea that all believers are told to "preach." They understand "preaching" as standing up in public and speaking convincingly and forcefully. Very few people are equipped to do that kind of "preaching."

But "preach" is only one of the possible ways the Greek words can be translated. One of the words commonly translated "preach" is *euaggelizo*, and it means "to bring or announce good news." Certainly, the common understanding of "preach" is an important way in which the good news is announced. But that common understanding is not the only way to bring the gospel.

In passages such as Luke 1:19 and 2:10, *euaggelizo* is translated "show" or "bring" the good news. Our concept of "preach" needs to expand to include the many other ways the gospel can be given to others. The concept intended with *euaggelizo* is that of a person or persons getting across the message of the good news of the gospel to other people. There are many ways in which that can be done in addition to preaching.

Another word usually translated "preach" is *kerysso,* and this means to proclaim, to make known. This can be done by public preaching, but it can be done in other ways too. The word used in Mark 16:15 and translated "preach" is *kerysso.*

Different translations often use different words to translate *kerysso* or *euaggelizo.* For example, in Luke 9:2, the King James Version translates *kyrusso* as "preach," while the New American Standard translates it "proclaim." In Luke 1:19, the KJV translates *euaggelizo* as "shew thee these glad tidings," while the NAS translates it as "bring you this good news" and the New International Version has it "tell you this good news."

Getting the gospel to others is not limited just to popular notions of preaching. On the contrary, informing others about the grace of God in Jesus Christ can take many forms, and all of us are gifted by the Spirit to bring the gospel to others in one way or another.

Evangelism in the early church

Throughout the book of Acts, we see the apostles carrying out Jesus' commission. They declared that Jesus is the Christ, that he was crucified and raised from the dead, and that salvation is available through him. It was a Christ-centered message, an "evangelistic" or "gospel-oriented" message.

But was the gospel proclaimed by the apostles alone? Not at all! Stephen did great works in the name of Christ, and argued that Jesus is the Christ (Acts 6:8-10). Before the Sanhedrin, he forcefully argued that Jesus is the Righteous One, the Messiah, predicted in the Scriptures (Acts 7:51-52). His dying words were a testimony to God's forgiveness of sins in Christ (verse 60).

God inspired Stephen, and he inspired many others. "On that day a great persecution broke out against the church at Jerusalem, and all except the apostles were scattered…. Those who had been scattered preached the word (*euaggelizo*) wherever they went" (Acts 8:1, 4). Even at risk of their lives, these lay Christians saw to it that the gospel was given to others. They were simply doing what Christians do naturally. They felt compelled—led by the Holy Spirit—to tell others the good news that God had blessed them with. Luke presents the story as a good example for us to follow.

Next, Philip went "to a city in Samaria and proclaimed the Christ there" (verse 5). God blessed this evangelism by converting some of the Samaritans. The gospel continued to expand.

> Those who had been scattered by the persecution in connection with Stephen traveled as far as Phoenicia, Cyprus and Antioch, telling the message only to Jews. Some of them, however, men from Cyprus and Cyrene, went to Antioch and began to speak to Greeks also, telling them the good news about the Lord Jesus. The Lord's hand was with them, and a great number of people believed and turned to the Lord. (Acts 11:19-21)

God inspired his people to tell the good news about Jesus, and he blessed the results.

Paul was given a special commission as an apostle to the Gentiles. But Luke tells us that Paul was not the only one who shared the good news with them. "Paul and Barnabas remained in Antioch, where they *and many others* taught and preached the word of the Lord" (Acts 15:34). Luke does not think that the commission applied only to the apostles. His book serves as an example of what future generations of the church should do.

Also in the book of Acts, we might note the example of Apollos, who "vigorously refuted the Jews in public debate, proving from the Scriptures that Jesus was the Christ" (Acts 18:28). Later, Paul rejoiced that even more people were preaching Christ (Philippians 1:15-18; *kyrusso* is used in verse

15; *kataggello,* meaning "proclaim," is used in verses 16 and 18).

Paul told Timothy (2 Timothy 4:5) to do the work of an evangelist (*euaggelistes*—a bringer of good news). God gives some of his people a gift for evangelism (Ephesians 4:11). Training can make their gift even more effective. The church could not fulfill its mission if all it ever did was wait for people to come to it. It needs to be intentional about going out in the name of Christ and reaching people with the good news.

Personal evangelism

At one level or another, evangelism involves every member of the church, every disciple of Jesus Christ. As we mature in the faith, each member should become more competent with the Christian message. "By this time you ought to be teachers," Hebrews 5:12 says, implying that anyone who has been a Christian for a while should be able to teach others the good news.

God has given the "message of reconciliation" to all who are reconciled by Jesus Christ (2 Corinthians 5:18-19). We are to encourage other people to be reconciled to God through the gospel of Jesus Christ.

As the church obeys the commands of Christ and we conduct ourselves "in a manner worthy of the gospel of Christ" (Philippians 1:27), people will indeed come to us and ask for help. This is evangelism by example, and it adds to rather than replaces our responsibility to be intentional about reaching others. We are to do both. Part of our example should be our willingness to give credit to the One who works within us.

We are a holy people, called to "declare the praises of him who called you out of darkness into his wonderful light" (1 Peter 2:9). How do we do this? In part, by living "such good lives among the pagans that, though they accuse you of doing wrong, they may see your good deeds and glorify God on the day he visits us" (verse 12).

It is in the context of setting a good example that Peter writes, "Always be prepared to give an answer to everyone who asks you to give the reason for the hope that you have" (1 Peter 3:15). Example and evangelism go hand in hand. Sometimes one comes first, sometimes the other does.

In the world today, the Christian way of life stands out. When society is pessimistic and apathetic, the Christian hope and purpose are more noticeable. People need and want the peace of Christ, whether they understand it yet or not. When they ask for help, we can explain in our own words why we have hope in Jesus Christ. A good example and a wise witness to our faith help preach the good news.

Paul encouraged Christians to live "without fault in a crooked and depraved generation, in which you shine like stars in the universe" (Philippians 2:15). But the Christian's role in the community does not stop with avoiding sin. Paul's very next words are "as you hold out the word of life" (verse 16). Their works were combined with their words. Good deeds go with the gospel, and the combination is an effective form of evangelism.

Prepared to give an answer

Each Christian should be able to explain the basics of the faith. Perhaps not in an eloquent way, and certainly not in an argumentative way, but in simple confidence. We know the peace of God in our lives. We know that we will be resurrected. We know that life is worthwhile. We know that our sins are forgiven. We know that God sent his Son to die for us, and that he now lives for us. We know he wants us to stop living for ourselves and start living for him (2 Corinthians 5:15).

Christians can't explain every verse of the Bible, but they can give their own testimony as to why they believe. They can't prove every point with an iron-clad argument, and they don't need to. What makes their testimony believable is their "good behavior in Christ" (1 Peter 3:16). When we give an answer for the hope that lies within us, the evidence is in our works as well as in our words. The two reinforce each other to make each more effective than they would have been on their own.

Not every member is equally gifted at explaining the grace of God, and not every member will do it in the same way. "Evangelism," in the sense of continually approaching others with the gospel, is a spiritual gift, and we cannot expect every Christian to have this particular gift. But all Christians are commanded to be ready to give an answer. All of us should want our neighbors to have the blessing of knowing Christ, rather than living in ignorance. All Christians should be ready to be used by God when appropriate situations arise.

Personal evangelism should not be ignored. The Holy Spirit leads each Christian in behavior and in word. That means that each of us should be a good example in the community and be a faithful witness of the faith that lies within us. If you are a more reserved person, if religion is not the first subject you want to bring up, that's OK. Be zealous for Christ in the way God has gifted you—but always be ready to give an answer. Being ready includes being willing, not just having the right words.

Christ's commission to bring the gospel to others is a continuing part of our work. That is why we are committed to the work of evangelism—this is one of the ways in which we obey Jesus Christ. This is part of our commission, part of our responsibility.

Joseph Tkach

Good News for Ordinary People

What Was the Message of Jesus Christ?

Almost 2,000 years ago, a Jewish carpenter began to preach. He was popular with some people, but he made others angry. Officials said he was a threat to national security, and they arranged for his death. His only weapon was his message. Bad people liked it, but "good" people didn't. He said it was about love—so why did anyone hate it? What was the message that got Jesus killed?

Here's another puzzle: If this message got Jesus killed, why did other people take up the message and preach it, too? Were they trying to get themselves killed? Why were they so bold with the message?

Let's examine what the Bible says about the message of Jesus. Let's see the words he used to describe it, and the words his followers used.

The gospel of the kingdom

Matthew describes the beginning of Jesus' preaching career in this way: "From that time Jesus began to proclaim, 'Repent, for the kingdom of heaven has come near'" (Matthew 4:17, New Revised Standard Version).

Verse 23 adds a little more: "Jesus went throughout Galilee, teaching in their synagogues and proclaiming the good news of the kingdom and curing every disease and every sickness among the people."

From these verses, we see that Jesus taught:

- good news (older translations say "gospel," which means the same thing)
- about "the kingdom"—the kingdom of heaven, or the reign of God
- the kingdom had come "near" and
- people should therefore repent, or turn toward God.

What is this "kingdom" of God? How was it near—in time or in location? How are people supposed to turn toward God? And if all this is good news, why did it create such a controversy among first-century Jews? Why would anyone kill the messenger of good news?

We need to keep reading.

"Good news"

In the Roman empire, the word for "good news" was used for official announcements. Jesus was announcing something about God's empire. Perhaps you can guess why some government officials might think that his message was dangerous: he was preaching about a kingdom. But they didn't understand what Jesus really meant.

How did Jesus use the word for "good news"? In the Gospels, the word is usually on its own—Jesus preached "the good news." The readers knew what it was—it was a shorthand way of saying "the message of Jesus."

But sometimes we are given a brief description of the good news. Once it is called "the good news of God" (Mark 1:14). But it is more often called "the gospel of the kingdom." The first three Gospels tell us that Jesus often preached about "the kingdom of God."

But this is not the only way to describe the message. The Gospel of John, for example, doesn't even use the word for "good news." John describes the message in other ways. And as we go forward in the Bible, the word "kingdom" becomes less common. The message is much more commonly called "the good news of Jesus Christ" (see box). It can also be called the good news of salvation, the good news of God's grace, and the good news of peace.

This creates another puzzle: The words "grace" and "kingdom," for example, are not normally interchangeable. Is the message about a kingdom, or is it about grace, or is it about Jesus Christ?

What did Jesus preach?

The Gospels use the word "preach" or "proclaim" more than 40 times. If we survey these, we will see that Jesus not only preached the good news about the kingdom, he also preached about repentance, forgiveness, justice, and rescue for the poor (Luke 4:18; 24:47).

Was Jesus leading some sort of poor-people's revolt? No, Jesus was not a political leader — he was a religious leader, a rabbi. His message was about God, repentance and forgiveness. But his message was especially good news for the poor — not to lift their economic burdens, but to lift their religious burdens. They were carrying a heavy load, and it wasn't fair.

Jesus preached justice for the poor, freedom for

> **The reason Jesus had to teach so much about the kingdom is because people had so many wrong ideas about it.**

the oppressed. But the people who were doing the oppression didn't like the message. The religious leaders didn't like the message of Jesus. It disturbed the peace, and threatened the status quo (Matthew 10:34).

Religion (even certain forms of Christianity) can be used to oppress people, to keep them in line, to burden them with guilt that they don't need to carry. But the message of Jesus can lift those burdens. It can help people see clearly, can help them be freed from religious bondage. Even today, people who oppress others do not like the message. Religious leaders who use religion as a tool of power do not like the message of Jesus.

The time is at hand

"The time is fulfilled," Jesus said, "and the kingdom of God has come near; repent, and believe in the good news" (Mark 1:15). What did Jesus mean by saying that the time was fulfilled? He meant that the time had arrived for the kingdom of God.

The kingdom of God is near, and in this passage Jesus is talking about nearness in terms of time. Jesus told his disciples to preach the same thing (Matthew 10:7).

The kingdom of God had been predicted hundreds of years earlier; it had been hoped for and prayed for. The Jewish people wanted the kingdom to come, and Jesus came and said, "I have good news! It's time for the kingdom of God!"

Today, we might have all sorts of ideas as to what a kingdom is, and what the kingdom of God might be. But if we have the wrong idea, then we will conclude that Jesus was a false prophet, because he did not bring the kind of kingdom that we expected. But if we do that, we are judging Jesus even before we give him a chance to explain what he means.

First-century Jews had their ideas about the kingdom, too, but Jesus did not bring what they expected. Many were disappointed — even his own disciples were disappointed. That's because they were hoping for a political kingdom, but Jesus did not bring a political kingdom. He brought a spiritual kingdom.

Jesus not only announced that the kingdom was near — he also had to explain what the kingdom was. The people had their ideas about it, but Jesus had to correct them. "The kingdom of God is like this…," Jesus often said, and he would give an illustration. The reason he had to teach so much about the kingdom is because the people had so many wrong ideas about it.

First-century Jews thought the kingdom would be a time of agricultural abundance, economic prosperity, military superiority and glory for the Jewish people. But Jesus never described the kingdom of God in these ways. He had something much better in mind.

Responding to the message

Jesus expected people to *respond* to his message. He urged them to believe it and to repent. Of course! Any speaker wants people to believe the message. But Jesus wants more than a simple acceptance that what he said was true — he wants them to believe that it is good! He wants them to receive it with joy.

The kingdom of God is bad news for people who oppress others. But if you are a victim of religious oppression, then the kingdom of God is good news. If you have been turned off to religion, then the message of Jesus is good news.

Jesus wanted people to repent. What does it mean to repent? In simple terms, it means a change of mind, a change of attitude. It means a change from not trusting God to trusting God. It means a change from not believing God to believing God. Since the kingdom is at hand, Jesus was saying, people need to have their hearts right with God.

Repentance is the flip side of believing the gospel. To have an attitude of *faith* is to believe that the news is good. We *want* the King to reign and rule. We trust that he will rule us well. We want to please him, rather than simply trying to avoid his anger. We rejoice that God's kingdom is near. And with joy, we give our allegiance and loyalty to him. That is what it means to repent and believe the good news of the kingdom of God.

When Jesus announced the gospel, there was an urgency about the message. Jesus didn't tell anyone to repent later. He told them to repent right away. The kingdom of God was at hand!

The message is just as urgent today. Jesus wants *us* to believe the gospel.

A Jewish kingdom?

What did first-century Jews think when they heard the phrase "kingdom of God"? They probably thought in terms of a normal human kingdom—a king, giving laws and ruling over people in a certain territory.

The Jews were ruled by Romans, but they wanted to be independent. They wanted God to restore the kingdom to Israel. They searched the Old Testament prophecies that promised Israel national greatness. They speculated about how and when God would rescue his people. They looked for a golden age in which Israel would be the richest and most powerful nation on earth.

The Dead Sea scrolls and other writings of the time show that the Jews wanted a Messiah, a person sent by God who would lead the nation to greatness again. The overall hope was that God would intervene and restore the Jewish nation to greatness.

Not what Jesus meant

When Jesus used the phrase "kingdom of God," many people would have thought of a nation like the kingdoms of this world. But this is not what Jesus meant. He did not lead or predict a revolt against Rome. The people wanted Jesus to be a military leader, but Jesus went out of his way to avoid their wishes (John 6:15). He told people to obey the Roman rulers and pay their taxes.

Jesus did not resist the government even when soldiers came to arrest him and crucify him. Jesus conquered spiritual enemies, not military ones. That is because spiritual enemies are far more oppressive than military ones. Spiritual freedom is far more important than political freedom.

> **God is Spirit, and the kingdom of God is a spiritual kingdom.**

Jesus' kingdom was not like the popular expectation. He used the phrase "kingdom of God" with a different meaning. His kingdom was not of this world (John 18:36). It was not like the kingdoms of this world. It was the kingdom of God, a supernatural kingdom. It was invisible to most people (John 3:3)—it could not be understood or experienced without the Holy Spirit (verse 6). God is Spirit, and the kingdom of God is a spiritual kingdom.

The disciples often misunderstood

But Jesus' disciples were ordinary Jews of first-century Jewish culture. The disciples had wrong ideas about the kingdom, too, and they often misunderstood what Jesus was teaching. Near the middle of his ministry, Jesus asked them, "Do you still not perceive or understand? Are your hearts hardened? Do you have eyes, and fail to see? Do you have ears, and fail to hear? And do you not remember?... Do you not yet understand?" (Mark 8:17-21).

Some people even stopped following Jesus because they couldn't understand what he was talking about (John 6:66). Others stayed even though they didn't understand (Mark 6:52). He asked Peter, "Are you also still without understanding?" (Matthew 15:16).

Christians today might find it encouraging that the disciples weren't particularly bright, and yet Jesus was patient with their mistakes. We make mistakes, too, and we don't always understand Jesus correctly, but we are in good company. We don't have to be super-smart to follow Jesus. He will lead us and teach us at the speed we need.

The wrong kind of Messiah

Matthew 16 tells us the interesting story of how Peter had a moment of wisdom, and then almost immediately stumbled into a horrible heresy. It begins with Jesus asking his disciples what the people thought of him (verse 13). Then he asked, "But who do you say that I am?" Peter answered, "You are the Messiah, the Son of the living God" (verses 15-16).

> "Wait," Jesus said. "Don't tell anybody who I am." Why not? We will see why if we keep reading.

Great answer!, said Jesus. You aren't smart enough to figure that out for yourself—no one is—God must have helped you (verse 17). So Jesus admitted to being the Messiah, the leader the Jewish people were eagerly waiting for. But wait, Jesus said. Don't tell anybody who I am (verse 20).

Surely this puzzled the disciples! Jesus was telling everyone that the kingdom of God was near. He just admitted to being the Messiah, the person everyone believed would bring the kingdom in. Why announce one truth but not the other?

We will see why if we keep reading: "From that time on, Jesus began to show his disciples that he must go to Jerusalem and undergo great suffering…and be killed, and on the third day be raised" (verse 21).

This did not match the disciples' ideas about a Messiah. Messiahs aren't supposed to suffer and be killed. So Peter took Jesus aside "and began to rebuke him, saying, 'God forbid it, Lord! This must never happen to you'" (verse 22).

Peter had just called Jesus the Messiah, the God-appointed national leader. Now he began to rebuke his own leader, as if he could teach him a thing or two. Perhaps he said, "Jesus, the Messiah isn't supposed to suffer and die—he is supposed to be a popular leader." Peter's idea of a Messiah was not the same as Jesus' idea.

Jesus had the right idea, and Peter and everybody else in Judea had the wrong idea. That's why Jesus didn't want the disciples to tell anybody he was the Messiah. They had the right word (it means someone anointed by God to do a certain task), but the wrong idea. Their understanding of "kingdom" probably wasn't much better than their understanding of Messiah.

That's why Jesus had to teach so much about the kingdom. It wasn't enough just to announce it—he had to explain what it was. The kingdom, like the Messiah, wasn't the way that people expected it would be. It was not the sort of kingdom that Greeks and Romans and Jews were familiar with.

Disciples would understand later

Jesus told the disciples to keep some things secret until after he had been raised back to life. But they did not understand (Mark 9:9-10). He predicted his own death and resurrection, but they still didn't understand (verses 31-32). These ideas didn't fit into their concept of what Jesus was all about.

The disciples were perplexed at the teaching of Jesus (Mark 10:24), and after more explanation, they were still perplexed (verse 26). They did not know what he meant (John 16:18). But Jesus said that the time would come when they would understand (verse 13).

Although Jesus had told them several times that he would be raised to life after being killed, they were devastated by his death and perplexed by the empty tomb. They did not understand, because it was all so different from what they had assumed.

Didn't Jesus preach that the kingdom of God was near? Didn't he say he was the Messiah? But when your Messiah is dead in the tomb, the kingdom of God seems a long way off. It just didn't make any sense. The disciples were afraid. They fled and locked the doors.

Shortly after Jesus was resurrected, he chided the disciples for how slow they were to believe (Luke 24:25). But they would soon understand it all. Near the end of his ministry, Jesus predicted that his gospel would to continue to be preached (Matthew 24:14). It would not be a different gospel, but the same good news, now going to all nations.

Now we need to turn to the book of Acts to see what the disciples preached. There we will learn more about what the gospel is.

Gospel statistics

What is the most common way to describe the good news? Here's how the word is most often used:

- good news of Jesus Christ — 15 times
- good news of God - 9 times
- good news of the kingdom - 7 times
- my gospel, our gospel - 6 times
- the gospel of peace - 2 times
- good news of God's grace - 1 time
- good news of the glory of Christ - 1 time
- gospel of your salvation - 1 time

The Bible does not require any particular label for the message of Jesus and the message of the church. We can convey the meaning without insisting on any particular word.

Michael Morrison

Grace

"If righteousness could be gained through the law," Paul wrote, "Christ died for nothing!" (Galatians 2:21). The only alternative, he says in this same verse, is "the grace of God." We are saved by grace, not by keeping the law.

These are alternatives that cannot be combined. We are not saved by grace plus works, but by grace alone. Paul makes it clear that we must choose either one or another. "Both" is not an option (Romans 11:6). "If the inheritance depends on the law, then it no longer depends on a promise; but God in his grace gave it to Abraham through a promise" (Galatians 3:18). Salvation does not depend on the law, but on God's grace.

"If a law had been given that could impart life, then righteousness would certainly have come by the law" (verse 21). If there could be any way that rule-keeping could lead to eternal life, then God would have saved us with the law. But it wasn't possible. The law cannot save anyone.

God wants us to have good behavior. He wants us to love others and by doing that, to fulfill the law. But he does not want us to ever think that our works are a reason for our salvation. His provision of grace implies that he has always known that we would never be "good enough" despite our best efforts. If our works contributed to our salvation, then we would have something to boast about. But God designed his plan of salvation in such a way that we cannot take any credit for saving ourselves (Ephesians 2:8-9). We can never claim to deserve anything; we can never claim that God owes us anything.

This goes to the heart of the Christian faith, and it makes Christianity unique. Other religions say that people can be good enough if they try hard enough. Christianity says that we cannot be good enough; we need grace.

On our own, we will never be good enough, and because of that, other religions are not good enough. The only way we can be saved is through the grace of God. We can never deserve to live forever, so the only way we can be given eternal life is for God to give us something that we don't deserve. This is what Paul is driving at when he uses the word *grace.* Salvation is a gift of God, something that we could never earn with even a thousand years of the law.

Jesus and mercy

"The law was given through Moses," John writes. "Grace and truth came through Jesus Christ" (John 1:17). John saw a contrast between the law and grace, between what we do and what we are given.

Nevertheless, Jesus didn't use the word *grace.* But his entire life was an example of grace, and his parables illustrated grace. He sometimes used the word *mercy* to describe what God gives us. "Blessed are the merciful," he said, "for they will be shown mercy" (Matthew 5:7). In this, he implied that we all need mercy. He noted here that we should be like God in this respect. If we value God's grace to us, we will give grace to others.

Later, when Jesus was asked why he associated with notorious sinners, he told people, "Go and learn what this means: 'I desire mercy, not sacrifice'" (Matthew 9:13, quoting Hosea 6:6). In other words, God wants us to show mercy more than he wants us to be perfectionists in law-keeping.

We do not want people to sin. But since we inevitably make mistakes, we need mercy. That is true of our relationships with one another, and true of our relationships with God, too. God wants us to know our need for mercy, and for us to have mercy toward others. Jesus gave us an example of this by the way he lived, when he ate with tax collectors and talked with sinners—he was showing by his behavior that God wants fellowship with us all, and he has taken all our sins upon himself and forgiven us so we can have fellowship with him.

Jesus told a parable of two debtors, one who owed an enormous amount, and the other who owed a lot less. The master forgave the servant who owed much, but that servant failed to forgive the servant who owed less. The master was angry and said, "Shouldn't you have had mercy on your fellow servant just as I had on you?" (Matthew 18:33).

Each of us should see ourselves as the first servant, who was forgiven an enormous debt. We have all fallen far short of what God wants us to be, so God shows us mercy—and he wants us to show mercy as well. We fall short in showing mercy, too, so we must continue to rely on God's mercy.

The parable of the good Samaritan concludes with a command for mercy (Luke 10:37). The tax collector who pleaded for mercy was the one who was set right with God (Luke 18:13-14). The wasteful son who came home was accepted without having to do anything to "deserve" it (Luke 15:20). Neither the widow of Nain nor her son did anything to deserve a resurrection; Jesus did it simply out of compassion (Luke 7:11-15).

The grace of our Lord Jesus Christ

The miracles of Jesus served temporary needs. The people who ate loaves and fishes became hungry again. The son who was raised eventually died again. But the grace of Jesus Christ continues to be extended to all of us through the supreme act of grace: his sacrificial death on the cross. This is how Jesus gave himself up for us, with eternal consequences rather than temporary ones.

Peter said, "It is through the grace of our Lord Jesus that we are saved" (Acts 15:11). The gospel was a message about God's grace (Acts 14:3; 20:24, 32). We are justified by grace "through the redemption that came by Christ Jesus" (Romans 3:24). God's grace is linked with the sacrifice of Jesus on

the cross (verse 25). Jesus died for us, for our sins, and we are saved because of what he did on the cross. We have redemption through his blood (Ephesians 1:7).

But God's grace goes further than forgiveness. Luke tells us that God's grace was on the disciples as they preached the gospel (Acts 4:33). God showed them favor, giving them help they did not deserve. Don't human fathers do the same? We not only give our children life when they had done nothing to earn it, we also give them food and clothing that they could not earn. That's part of love, and that is the way that God is. Grace is generosity.

When church members in Antioch sent Paul and Barnabas out on missionary trips, they commended them to the grace of God (Acts 14:26; 15:40). In other words, they put the missionaries into God's care, trusting God to take care of the travelers, trusting him to give them what they might need. That is included in his grace.

Spiritual gifts are a work of grace, too. "We have different gifts," Paul says, "according to the grace given us" (Romans 12:6). "To each one of us grace has been given as Christ apportioned it" (Ephesians 4:7). "Each one should use whatever gift he has received to serve others, faithfully administering God's grace in its various forms" (1 Peter 4:10).

God graced the believers with spiritual gifts (1 Corinthians 1:4-5). Paul was confident that God's grace would abound toward them as he enabled them to do even more work (2 Corinthians 9:8).

Every good thing is a gift of God, a result of grace rather than something we have earned. That is why we are to be thankful even for the simplest of blessings, for the singing of birds and the smells of flowers and the laughter of little children. Life itself is a luxury, not a necessity.

Paul's own ministry was given to him through grace (Romans 1:5; 15:15; 1 Corinthians 3:10; Galatians 2:9; Ephesians 3:7). Everything he did, he wanted to be according to God's grace (2 Corinthians 1:12). His strength and skills were a gift of grace (2 Corinthians 12:9). If God can save and use the biggest sinner of all (that's how Paul described himself), he can certainly forgive and use any of us. Nothing can separate us from his love, from his desire to give to us.

Response of grace

How should we respond to the grace of God? With grace, of course. We should be merciful, even as God is full of mercy (Luke 6:36). We are to forgive others, just as we have been forgiven. We are to serve others, just as we have been served. We are to be gracious toward others, giving them favor and kindness.

Our words are to be full of grace (Colossians 4:6). We are to be gracious (forgiving and giving) in marriage, in business, in church, with friends and family and strangers. It's supposed to make a difference in our lives and in our priorities.

Paul spoke of financial generosity as a work of grace, too: "We want you to know about the grace that God has given the Macedonian churches. Out of the most severe trial, their overflowing joy and their extreme poverty welled up in rich generosity. For I testify that they gave as much as they were able, and even beyond their ability" (2 Corinthians 8:1-3). They had been given much, and they in turn were willing to give much.

Giving is an act of grace (verse 6), and generosity—whether in finances, in time, in respect, or in other ways—is an appropriate way for us to respond to the grace of Jesus Christ, who gave himself for us so that we might be richly blessed (verse 9).

Joseph Tkach

Going on a Guilt Trip?

Guilt trips. They're all the rage, you know. Everybody's taking them. No date restrictions. Availability unlimited. People of all ages are welcome. But there are a few hidden costs.

Among other things, guilt trips cost you your stomach lining, your sleep, your sense of humor, your ability to have fun, your productivity and any realistic sense of who you really are and what your purpose really is.

But we stand in line for tickets anyway, as though it's our chief call and duty to leave the world of confidence and hope and set sail for the land of dread and gloom.

We stuff every mental container we own with depressing emotions, fear and blame, and then, with the whole load strapped on securely, we lug it across the gangplank and down the narrow hall to our inside stateroom deep in the bowels of the S.S. Guilty Conscience.

And yet we're religious people, people who know that God forgives sin and that we don't have to be crushed down with burdens of guilt.

Maybe that's the problem. Maybe religion is not the solution to guilt after all. Maybe, if the truth were known, we'd find that religion and guilt are sweethearts. After all, wherever you find one, the other will usually be buzzing nearby like some fat, annoying housefly.

That's because religion is designed to give people a list of things to do to stay on good terms with whatever deity they profess to worship. The trouble is, no one has ever kept their particular list of rules well enough to be absolutely sure their deity isn't one day going to hurl a nasty curse their way. Religion isn't enough. All it manages to do is make people feel worse for their failure. It pumps out guilt like some magic grinder gone mad. What people really need is some hope, some good news, not more religious talk about how bad they are.

Good news

Christians should know better, of course. We

have the gospel—the good news. Sad to say, however, a lot of us are experts at turning even the gospel into religion, which means we end up spending more time on guilt trips (or sending others on guilt trips) than we do resting at home with our Lord of grace.

Freedom from a guilty conscience is so foreign to most of us that as soon as it happens we start feeling guilty for not feeling guilty. It's as though we think we stand in better with God if we refuse to feel forgiven and clean.

Hebrews 10:19-22 says, "Therefore...since we have confidence to enter the Most Holy Place by the blood of Jesus...let us draw near to God with a sincere heart in full assurance of faith, having our hearts sprinkled to cleanse us from a guilty conscience...."

This passage speaks of confidence—confidence to be at home in the presence of God, not hiding guilt-ridden behind a trashcan in the corner. That confidence is not confidence in ourselves or in how well we've behaved; it's confidence in God himself who loves us so much that he sent his Son to remove our guilt and give us all the privileges of beloved children.

The gospel, thank God, is not religion. It is the end of religion. It's good news, the good news that God loves you so much that he sent his Son to bear the curse of your sinfulness and be raised from the dead so you can be forever at peace with him.

You don't need religion to be at peace with God; you just need to trust your Savior. You don't have to pack your guilt trip suitcase with plenty of fear, doubt, worry and anxiety. You don't have to wonder whether God really loves you, or really forgives you, or really has saved you.

Instead of a guilt trip, why not believe the good news—the good news that cleanses you from a guilty conscience?

J. Michael Feazell

What Is Salvation?

Salvation is a rescue operation. To understand salvation, we need to know what the problem was, what God did about it, and how we respond to it.

What humans are

When God made humans, he made them "in his own image," and he pronounced his creation "very good" (Genesis 1:26-27, 31). Humans were a wonderful creation: made from dust, but energized by the breath of God (Genesis 2:7).

"The image of God" probably includes intelligence, creativity and power over creation. It also includes the ability to have relationships and to make moral choices. We are in some way like God himself. That's because God has something special in mind for us, his children.

Genesis tells us that the first humans did something God had warned them not to do (Genesis 3:1-13). Their disobedience showed that they did not trust God, and it was a violation of his trust in them. By being faithless, they had broken the relationship and fallen short of what God wanted for them. They were becoming less like God. The result, said God, was struggle, pain and death (vv. 16-19). If they were not going to follow the Maker's instructions, they were going to end up doing things the hard way.

Humans are noble and crude at the same time. We can have high ideals, and yet be barbaric. We are like God, and yet ungodly. We are not the way we are supposed to be. Even though we have messed ourselves up, God still considers us to be made in his image (Genesis 9:6). The potential is still there for us to be like God. This is why he wants to rescue us, to save us, to restore the relationship he had with us.

God wants to give us eternal life, free from pain, on good terms with God and with each other. He wants our intelligence, creativity and power to be used for good. He wants us to be like he is, to be even better than the first humans were. This is salvation.

The center of the plan

We need to be rescued. And God has done this—but he did it in a way that no human would have expected. The Son of God became a human, lived a perfect life, and we killed him. And that, says God, is the salvation we need. What irony! We are saved by a victim! Our Creator became flesh so he could die for us. But God raised him back to life, and through Jesus, he promises to resurrect us, too.

In the death and resurrection of Jesus, the death and salvation of humanity is represented and made possible. His death is what our failures deserve, and as our Creator, he paid for all our failures. Though he did not deserve death, he willingly died for our sins, on our behalf.

Jesus Christ died for us, and was raised for us (Romans 4:25). Our old self died with him, and a new person is brought back to life with him (Romans 6:3-4). In one sacrifice, Jesus atoned "for the sins of the whole world" (1 John 2:2). The payment has already been made; the question now is how we are to receive the benefits. We participate in the plan through repentance and faith.

Repentance

Jesus came to call people to repentance (Luke 5:32). Peter told people to repent and turn to God for forgiveness (Acts 2:38; 3:19). Paul said people "must turn to God in repentance" (Acts 20:21). Repentance means to turn away from sin and toward God. Paul told the Athenians that God overlooked idolatry done in ignorance, but "now commands all people everywhere to repent" (Acts 17:30). They should stop their idolatry.

Paul was concerned that some of the Corinthian Christians might not repent of their sexual sins (2 Corinthians 12:21). For these people, repentance would mean a willingness to stop their immorality. Paul preached that people should "prove their repentance by their deeds" (Acts 26:20). We change our attitude and our behavior.

Part of our doctrinal foundation is "repentance from acts that lead to death" (Hebrews 6:1). But this does not mean perfect behavior—Christians are not perfect (1 John 1:8). Repentance means not that we arrive at our goal, but that we begin traveling in the right direction.

No longer do we please ourselves, but we live to please Christ (2 Corinthians 5:15; 1 Corinthians 6:20). Paul tells us, "Just as you used to offer the parts of your body in slavery to impurity and to ever-increasing wickedness, so now offer them in slavery to righteousness" (Romans 6:19).

Faith

However, simply telling people to repent is not going to rescue them from their failures. Humans have been told to obey for thousands of years, but they still need to be rescued. Something more is needed, and that is Christ. But we do not experience the blessing of forgiveness if we don't believe that Christ has done this for us. We need faith, or belief. The New Testament says much more about faith than it does repentance—the words for faith occur more than eight times as often.

Everyone who believes in Jesus is forgiven (Acts 10:43). "Believe in the Lord Jesus, and you will be saved" (Acts 16:31). The gospel "is the power of God for the salvation of everyone who believes" (Romans 1:16). Christians are known as believers, not as repenters. Belief is the defining characteristic.

Does this mean that we are to accept certain facts? The Greek word *can* mean that kind of belief, but more often it conveys the sense of trust. When Paul encourages us to believe in Jesus Christ, he is not emphasizing facts. (The devil knows the facts about Jesus, but he isn't saved.)

When we believe in Jesus Christ, we trust him. We know he is faithful and trustworthy. We can count on him to take care of us, to give us what he promises. We can trust him to rescue us from humanity's worst problems. When we turn to him for salvation, we admit that we need help, and that he can provide it.

Our faith does not save us—our faith must be in him, not something else. We commit ourselves to him, and he saves us. When we trust in Christ, we quit trying to save ourselves. Although we try to have good behavior, we do not think our efforts are saving us (diligent effort never made anyone perfect). Nor do we despair when our efforts fail. That's because we are trusting in Christ, not in ourselves, for our salvation. Our confidence is in him, not in our success or failure.

Faith is what motivates repentance. When we trust Jesus as our Savior, when we realize that God loves us so much that he sent his Son to die for us, when we know that he wants the best for us, then we become willing to live for him and please him. We make a choice—we give up the pointless and frustrating life we used to have, and accept his purpose and direction for what life is supposed to be.

Faith is the internal change that makes all the difference. Our faith doesn't earn anything or add anything to what Jesus has earned for us. Faith is simply the willingness to respond to what he has done. We are like slaves working in the clay pits, and Christ announces, "I have purchased your freedom." We are free to stay in the pits, or we can trust him and leave. The redemption has been done; our part is to accept it and act on it.

Grace

Salvation is God's gift to us, given by his grace, his generosity. We can't earn it, no matter what we do. "It is by grace you have been saved, through faith—and this is not from yourselves, it is the gift of God—not by works, so that no one can boast" (Ephesians 2:8-9). Even our faith is a gift of God. Even if we obey perfectly from now on, we do not deserve a reward (Luke 17:10).

We were created for good works (Ephesians 2:10), but good works cannot save us. They follow salvation, but they cannot earn it. As Paul says, if salvation could be achieved by law-keeping, then Christ died for nothing (Galatians 2:21). Grace does not give us permission to sin, but grace is given to us when we sin (Romans 6:15; 1 John 1:9). Whatever good works we do, we thank God for doing them in us (Galatians 2:20; Philippians 2:13).

God "has saved us and called us to a holy life — not because of anything we have done but because of his own purpose and grace" (2 Timothy 1:9). "He saved us, not because of righteous things we had done, but because of his mercy" (Titus 3:5).

Grace is the heart of the gospel: We are saved by God's gift, not by our works. The gospel is "the message of his grace" (Acts 14:3; 20:24). "It is through the grace of our Lord Jesus that we are saved" (Acts 15:11). "We are justified freely by his grace through the redemption that came by Christ Jesus" (Romans 3:24). We would be hopelessly in sin and condemnation, except for grace.

Our salvation depends on what Christ has done. He is the Savior, the one who rescues us. We cannot brag about our obedience, or our faith, because they are always defective. The only thing we can be proud of is what Christ has done (2 Corinthians 10:17-18) — and he did it for everyone, not just us.

Justification

The Bible explains salvation in many ways: ransom, redemption, forgiveness, reconciliation, adoption, justification, etc. That is because people understand their problem in different ways. For those who feel dirty, Christ offers cleansing. For those who feel enslaved, he offers redemption, or purchase. For those who feel guilt, he gives forgiveness.

For people who feel alienated and put at a distance, he offers reconciliation and friendship. For those who feel worthless, he gives an assurance of value. For people who don't feel like they belong, he describes salvation as adoption and inheritance. For those who are aimless, he gives purpose and direction. For those who are tired, he offers rest. For the fearful, he gives hope. For the anxious, he offers peace. Salvation is all this, and more.

Let's look at justification. The Greek word is often a courtroom term. People who are justified are declared "not guilty." They are exonerated, cleared, acquitted, declared OK. When God justifies us, he says that our sins will not be counted against us. They are removed from the record.

When we accept that Jesus died for us, when we acknowledge that we need a Savior, when we acknowledge that our sin deserves punishment and that Jesus bore the punishment of our sins for us, then we have faith, and God assures us that we are forgiven.

No one can be justified, or declared righteous, by observing the law (Romans 3:20), because the law does not save. It is only a standard that we fail to meet, and by that measurement, all of us fall short (v. 23). God "justifies those who have faith in Jesus" (v. 26). We are "justified by faith apart from observing the law" (v. 28).

To illustrate justification by faith, Paul uses the example of Abraham, who "believed God, and it was credited to him as righteousness" (Romans 4:3, quoting Genesis 15:6). Because Abraham trusted God, God counted him as righteous. This was long before the law was given, showing that justification is a gift of God, received by faith, not earned by law-keeping.

Justification is more than forgiveness, more than removing our debts. Justification means counting us as righteous, as having done something right. Our righteousness is not from our own works, but from Christ (1 Corinthians 1:30). It is through the obedience of Christ, Paul says, that believers are made righteous (Romans 5:19).

Paul even says that God "justifies the wicked" (Romans 4:5). God will consider a sinner righteous (and therefore accepted on the day of judgment) if the sinner trusts God. A person who trusts God will no longer want to be wicked, but this is a result and not a cause of salvation. People are "not justified by observing the law, but by faith in Jesus Christ" (Galatians 2:16).

A new start

Some people come to faith suddenly. Something clicks in their brain, a light goes on, and they accept Jesus as their Savior. Other people come to faith in a more gradual way, slowly realizing that they do trust in Christ and not in themselves for their salvation.

Either way, the Bible describes this as a new birth. When we have faith in Christ, we are born anew as children of God (John 1:12-13; Galatians 3:26; 1 John 5:1). The Holy Spirit begins to live within us (John 14:17), and God begins a new creation in us (2 Corinthians 5:17; Galatians 6:15). The old self dies, and a new person is being created (Ephesians 4:22-24)—God is changing us.

In Jesus Christ, and as we have faith in him, God is undoing the results of humanity's sin. As the Holy Spirit works within us, a new humanity is being formed. The Bible doesn't say exactly how this happens; it just says that it is being done. The process begins in this life and is finished in the next.

The goal is to make us more like Jesus Christ. He is the image of God in perfection (2 Corinthians 4:4; Colossians 1:15;Hebrews 1:3), and we must be transformed into his likeness (2 Corinthians 3:18; Galatians 4:19; Ephesians 4:13;Colossians 3:10). We are to be like him in spirit—in love, joy, peace, humility and other godly qualities. That's what the Holy Spirit does in us. He is restoring the image of God.

Salvation is also described as reconciliation—the repair of our relationship with God (Romans 5:10-11; 2 Corinthians 5:18-21; Ephesians 2:16; Colossians 1:20-22). No longer do we resist or ignore God—we love him. We are changed from enemies to friends. And even more than friends—God says that he adopts us as his own children (Romans 8:15; Ephesians 1:5). We are in his family, with rights, responsibilities and a glorious inheritance (Romans 8:16-17; Galatians 3:29;Ephesians 1:18; Colossians 1:12).

Eventually there will be no more pain and sorrow (Revelation 21:4), which means that no one will be making mistakes. Sin will be no more, and death will be no more (1 Corinthians 15:26). That goal may seem a long way off when we look at ourselves now, but the journey (just like any other journey) begins with a single step—the step of accepting Christ as Savior. Christ will complete the work he begins in us (Philippians 1:6).

And in the future, we will be even more like Christ (1 Corinthians 15:49; 1 John 3:2). We will be immortal, incorruptible, glorious and sinless. Our spiritual bodies will have supernatural powers. We will have a vitality, intelligence, creativity, power and love far beyond what we know now. The image of God, once tarnished by sin, will be restored even better than it was before.

Michael Morrison

Humans in the Image of God

God created the first humans in the image of God, in the likeness of God (Genesis 1:26-30). What does the "image of God" mean? In what way are we humans different than animals, and in what way are we like God? How has sin affected the image? Is this image relevant to Christian growth, sanctification and the ministry of the church?

I believe that the image of God refers primarily to humanity's moral capacities. Other theories about the image focus on a limited aspect of morality. Although sin has reduced our moral abilities, we continue to have moral abilities, and Christians are conformed closer to God's image as the Holy Spirit restores their moral abilities.

We will address three topics: 1) What is the image of God that sinful humanity now has? 2) What is the image that Christians are to become? and 3) How does the church assist in this transformation?

Part 1: The Image of God

Thesis: The image of God refers to intellectual and relational abilities not found in animals — the ability to think and reason, specifically to make moral decisions. Our ability has been corrupted by sin, but humans still have the potential for morality.

Humans were made in the "image" and "likeness" of God (Genesis 1:26). These two terms have similar meaning and will be used interchangeably in this paper.[1] But animals were not made in God's image.[2] Philip Hughes summarizes our uniqueness by saying that humanity, although having "affinities with the animal realm, is radically distinguished from all other earthly creatures by the fact that [humanity] alone has been created in the divine image and is intended by constitution to be a godly creature."[3]

Although humans were created to be God-like, we are now sinful and unlike God in our morality (Romans 3:10, 23). Nevertheless, we are still considered to be in God's image (Genesis 9:6; James 3:9). Four concepts have been proposed as this image:

- Thomas Aquinas located the image in the human ability to think and reason, to use language and art, far surpassing the abilities of any animals.[4]
- Leonard Verduin says that the image consists in our dominion over animals and plants, which continues despite our sinfulness.[5]
- A "widely accepted interpretation" is that the "image" is our ability to make moral decisions, which involve self-awareness and social awareness.[6]
- Emil Brunner says that it is our ability to have a relationship with God, reflected in the tendency of all societies to have forms of worship.[7]

These four are inter-related, but it seems that concept 3 is dominant. Our rational abilities are not ends in themselves — they enable us to make moral decisions, and our intellectual abilities are judged by morality. Morality also determines whether we are using dominion rightly and whether our relationships with God and humans are right.

Rationality and dominion help distinguish humans from animals, so they may be considered aspects of the image of God, but they do not constitute all that the image is. Rather, it is the purpose for which we use rationality and dominion that is of greater importance. People who have low intelligence and limited dominion are, if they love God

115

and neighbor, closer to the desired image of God than a wicked genius dictator is. Mental skills and rulership are God-like only if they are used in a moral way. Morality is the standard by which thoughts and actions are judged, so I conclude that, although cognition and dominion are aspects of the divine image, morality is a more significant aspect.[8]

Aquinas' emphasis on mental abilities is too broad, and the focus on dominion is too narrow. Humans are not unique in ruling, and we conform to the image of Christ primarily by submitting to rule, not by ruling. The manner of our rule is far more important than the fact of our rule — it is essential that we rule morally, in right relationship with God and other beings. Morality involves our relationships with other people, and also with the divine Being, but relationship in itself is not sufficient. The relative importance of morality and relationships will be further analyzed in the next section of this paper.

Part 2: Restoring the Image

Thesis: Jesus Christ is the perfect image of God. As we are re-created in his image, by his presence in us, we are being changed primarily in our morality — in our relationships with other humans and with God.

Ever since the Fall, humans have been corrupted morally. They are not like God in their morality, but yet they are still considered to be in God's image (Genesis 9:6; James 3:9). Our defect must be corrected, as shown in the next paragraph. Humans still have vestiges of moral potential. Even the natural human has a potential for morality — all societies have some concept of right and wrong (Romans 2:15).

Jesus Christ is the perfect image of God (2 Corinthians 4:4; Colossians 1:15; Hebrews 1:3), and Christians must be conformed to his likeness (2 Corinthians 3:18; Galatians 4:19;Ephesians 4:13; Colossians 3:10). Geoffrey Bromiley observes, "In Himself Christ already sums up all that humanity is to be.... He is a perfect representation of God."[9] He is our perfect example.[10] He is being formed in us and we are being conformed to his image. If we share in his humble estate in this life, we will share in his glory in the next age (Romans 8:29-30; 1 Corinthians 15:49; 1 John 3:2) — living more fully in his image.

In what way should we be conformed to the image of Jesus Christ? Jesus spoke about the morality of our thoughts, but he did not address rationality per se or the logic we use in forming conclusions. Although he took care of people's bodily needs, he did not indicate that health and wholeness were necessary for image completion. And he said more about subordination than about exercising dominion over animals and matter.

Knowledge is important (Romans 10:2; Ephesians 4:13), but not all facts are of equal importance. Jesus said that we ought to understand the Scriptures, to discern which portions are most important, and to make behavioral decisions on that basis (e.g., Matthew 23:23). We need to discern right from wrong behavior (Hebrews 5:14). Jesus' focus was on morality, which involves our relationships.

Karl Barth, noting that God is triune and that humans are male and female, argued that relationship is the divine image.[11] Bromiley and Hughes point out that his conclusion is not explicitly provable from Genesis 1.[12] Nevertheless, interpersonal relationships are important, for they are the sphere in which morality is manifested. They are a prominent part of Jesus' teaching and one of the ways in which we must become more Christ-like. Jesus advocated emotions such as love (an interpersonal attitude) and faith (an interaction with God).

Emil Brunner focused on our relationship with God.[13] This potential is a reflection of what God is, but it is misleading to isolate this as the only way in which humans are like God. Atheists are made in the image of God, so we can conclude that the image is not dependent on a good relationship. All creation has a relationship with God, but not all creatures are made in God's image. What kind of relationship is needed?

A right relationship with God leads to changes in our understanding of right and wrong behavior and to changes in our relationships with others. As we are being transformed more completely into the image of Christ, it is essential that we have a relationship with God. But the image of God has important practical implications, such as the necessity to avoid murder and hatred (Genesis 9:6; James 3:9; 1 John 4:20). We must not neglect the practical way in which the image of God expresses itself, and that is in terms of our morality — our relationships with others. These relationships give us experiences that help us understand our relationship with God. The quality of all our relationships is judged by morality, which again shows the priority of morality. Relationships are very important, since they are the sphere in which morality is exercised.

Part 3: Ministering to the Image of God

Thesis: The church should assist with the needs of every aspect of humanity: physical needs, knowledge and emotional needs involved in making moral decisions, and relational needs in society and with God.

Ephesians 4:12-13 summarizes some basic functions of the church: preparing God's people for works of service, and working toward unity in faith and the knowledge of Christ and maturity in him. Physical service, education, social needs and worship are all within the responsibility of the church.

Physical needs are important. Just as all humans have the duty to avoid bodily harm and cursing because of the image of God (Genesis 9:6; James 3:9), Christians have the duty to take positive actions for others.[14] The church not only teaches Christians to perform physical works of service that help the needy (James 2:15-17; Matthew 25:31-46; Galatians 6:10), it also sets an example of ministering to physical needs, as Jesus did. The church teaches social responsibility and morality to all who are being transformed closer to the image of Christ. It is often our failures in social areas that help us realize that our relationship with God is in need of repair.

The church preaches a message of reconciliation with God, which is a result of faith in Christ as Savior. Cognition and emotion work together to produce the faith-decision of the will — whether to believe (cognitive) and trust (emotive). The church teaches about God and Christ and exhorts people to accept the relationship with God that is offered through Christ and the Spirit. A love-based relationship with God, in turn, carries with it obligations regarding our relationship with other humans. Theology leads to ethics.

Christianity interrelates all aspects of humanity — worship, social obligations, rational decisions, and physical assistance. The church teaches relationship with God, faith in him, love for him, holy living (James 1:27; Hebrews 5:14; 1 John 3:1-3; 5:2), and love for other humans, a love that leads to practical service (James 1:27; Hebrews 10:25). The church teaches the proper use of dominion, rationality, creativity, and personality.

Conclusion

We are made in God's image, but the potential value of this image will not be realized unless we become conformed to the image of Christ in our morality. To be living in God's image, we must be in a right (i.e., moral) relationship with God and with other humans, using our minds and our authority to serve God and our fellow humans. This is what it means to be in the image of God and conformed to the perfect image, his Son.

Endnotes

[1] These terms are used interchangeably in Genesis 1:27; 5:1; 5:3; 9:6; they are used in Genesis 1:26 as synonyms in a typical Hebrew poetic parallel (Philip Edgcumbe Hughes, *The True Image: The Origin and Destiny of Man in Christ*. Grand Rapids: Eerdmans, 1989, p. 7).

[2] Animals could be killed, but humans were not to be killed because they were made in the image of God (Genesis 9:3, 6). Adam could not find any animal suitable as a companion (Genesis 2:20), and humans were given rulership over animals (Genesis 1:26-30).

[3] Hughes, p. 7. Humanity's similarities with animals include the fact that both are living *nepheshes* made of the earth, dependent on the breath of life

(Genesis 2:7, 19; 7:15). These material similarities with animals suggest that the image of God is not to be found in our matter, including shape or posture. Humans are in the image of God even if they are deformed.

[4] Thomas Aquinas, "Man to the Image of God," in Millard Erickson, editor, *Readings in Christian Theology, Volume 2: Man's Need and God's Gift,* Grand Rapids: Baker, 1976, pp. 37-43.

[5] Leonard Verduin, "A Dominion-Haver," in Erickson, pages 55-74.

[6] G.W. Bromiley, "Image of God," in G.W. Bromiley, editor, *International Standard Bible Encyclopedia,* vol. 2. Grand Rapids: Eerdmans, 1988, p. 804.

[7] Emil, Brunner, "Man and Creation," in Erickson, pages 45-54.

[8] Genesis 1:26 implies that the image of God is a qualitative rather than quantitative distinction. We are distinctly different than animals — not just more intelligent than apes and not just able to rule more of creation than elephants can. Some aspects of cognition and dominion are merely quantitative, which again suggests that they are not definitive of the image of God.

[9] Bromiley, p. 805. The metaphor of image is again paralleled by the metaphor of sonship, in that Christ is the Son in its fullest sense.

[10] Christ is more than an example, since he is the One who empowers the transformation we need and rectifies our failures along the way.

[11] Bromiley, p. 804.

[12] Bromiley (p. 804) and Hughes (pp. 18-20) point out that animals are created male and female, and that sexual activity is not necessary for image-bearing. Moreover, humans are not the only social animals, so this is a quantitative rather than a qualitative difference.

[13] Brunner, pp. 45-54.

[14] The practical implications of the image of God were seen by Tyndale and Latimer, who argued that it was more important to serve the needs of the living images of God than to give money to the church for lifeless images (Hughes, p. 21).

Michael Morrison

Responding to God's Grace in Our Relationships

How do we respond to God's grace? One way that we respond is by extending grace to others, in our families, neighborhoods, and workplaces. If we are going to live with God forever, we will also be living with each other forever. We were designed not for eternal isolation, but for living together and interacting with one another. Life's greatest joys come in our relationships with other people.

Life's greatest hurts come from other people, too. So if eternal life is going to be happy, we need to learn to get along with people without hurting them. The essential ingredient we need here is love. The most important commandment, Jesus said, is to love God, and the second-most-important command is, "Love your neighbor as yourself" (Mark 12:31).

If we are going to be like Jesus, we need to love people—even people who are hard to love. Jesus set the example for us, coming to die even for the people who hated him. As good parents know, love means a willingness to be inconvenienced, a willingness to set aside our own concerns to attend to the needs of someone else. Love is a lot more than good feelings—it must also include good actions.

Willing to serve

God is good not because he is powerful, but because he is good. He always uses his power to help other people, not to serve himself. We praise people who risk their lives to save others; we do not praise people who had the power but refused to use it. We admire self-sacrifice, not selfishness.

Jesus came to serve, not to lord it over people (Matthew 20:28). He told his disciples they should not be like power-hungry rulers, but should set an example by helping people. "Whoever wants to become great among you must be your servant" (verse 26). Jesus shows us what the Father is like (John 14:9)—not just what he was like 2,000 years ago, but what he is like all the time.

True greatness is not in power, but in service. God sets the example; as does Jesus. The meaning of life is not in having authority, but in helping other people. That is the only way that eternal life is going to be enjoyable for everyone.

Jesus set many examples of service. A special one happened the evening before his crucifixion. He got down and washed the 12 disciples' feet as a lesson in humility and service. "I have set you an example," he said, "that you should do as I have done for you" (John 13:15). Don't consider yourself too important to kneel down and help somebody. Leaders in the church should be servants.

Paul said we should "serve one another in love" (Galatians 5:13). "Carry each other's burdens," he wrote, "and in this way you will fulfill the law of Christ" (Galatians 6:2). "Do nothing out of selfish ambition or vain conceit, but in humility consider others better than yourselves" (Philippians 2:3).

If we are selfish, we will never be satisfied, but if we serve, we will find it self-rewarding. We are more satisfied when we help than when we take. Jesus told us this because it is so unlike the assumptions that most people make.

"This is love: not that we loved God, but that he loved us and sent his Son as an atoning sacrifice for our sins. Dear friends, since God so loved us, we also ought to love one another" (1 John 4:10-11). If we want to be like Jesus, if we want to have a meaningful life, then we need to serve others.

Serving in the church

One way that we serve others is by being active participants in a community of believers—a church. No church is perfect, just like no person is perfect, but the church is something that God designed to help us on our journey with Jesus. The church teaches us about Jesus, reminds us of his grace and promises, and gives us opportunities to worship together. The church helps us keep our purpose in focus.

The church also gives us opportunities to exercise patience and forgiveness. We may not like these "opportunities," but they still help us learn to be more like Jesus. Paul reminds us of the example we follow: "Bear with each other and forgive whatever grievances you may have against one another. Forgive as the Lord forgave you" (Colossians 3:13). "Be kind and compassionate to one another, forgiving each other, just as in Christ God forgave you" (Ephesians 4:32).

Educators know that we learn by listening, but we learn much more when we participate. Jesus taught his disciples not just in words, and not just in his example, but also by giving them work to do. "He sent them out to preach the kingdom of God and to heal the sick" (Luke 9:2). After his resurrection, he again assigned them work: "You will be my witnesses in Jerusalem, and in all Judea and Samaria, and to the ends of the earth" (Acts 1:8). They learned as they went.

If you want to be like Jesus, get involved in his work. He left it to us, not because we could do a better job than anyone else, but because it is for our good. We will learn more, and be changed more, by getting involved.

Different talents

Have you ever noticed that different people have different strengths? Believing in Jesus does not eliminate our differences. Being like Christ does not mean that we all look alike, dress alike and act alike. God purposely gives different strengths to different people (1 Corinthians 12:11). We are not to brag about our abilities, nor to wish we had someone else's (verses 14-26). Rather, we are to use our skills "for the common good" (verse 7).

Some people are very talented, but no one has all the talents that society needs. God makes sure that everybody is lacking something, so that we learn to work together. "Each one should use whatever gift he has received to serve others, faithfully administering God's grace in its various forms" (1 Peter 4:10). The church is a great place to learn to be like Jesus by serving other people.

We are to serve people's physical needs, and also their spiritual needs. One of the biggest spiritual needs that this world has is the message of salvation in Jesus Christ. The church is called to take this message to the world; each believer has a message that can encourage and help many others, and we will become more like Jesus if we become less self-conscious and more willing to share the message.

Why do we share the gospel? It is not a means of getting brownie points with God. It is not a way for us to brag about how good we are. Rather, it is a way to serve others, to help them with one of their most serious needs in life.

People need to know that God loves them, that their lives have meaning and purpose, that there is hope even when physical life seems pointless. God has good news for them, and we share it because people need it.

It is deeply satisfying to be used by God to help someone else. Sharing the gospel gives us a tremendous sense of significance, because we are taking part in a work of eternal worth, sharing in the work of God himself. That's part of what it means to be like God, to be like Jesus. God made us in such a way that we would find our deepest satisfactions in doing the work that he himself does. We were made for this!

Relationships of grace

We are saved by grace, not by our works. God sent Jesus to die for us, and he forgives us, not on the basis of our works, but because of his mercy. Now, if God is like that, and we were born to be like God, what does this say about our relationships with one another? It transforms them!

If we follow Jesus, grace should fill our families, our friendships and our workplaces. Being like Jesus means that we are not always demanding to get our own way. We are not bragging about ourselves or insulting others. Paul describes the results of God at work in our lives: "The fruit of [God's] Spirit is love, joy, peace, patience, kindness, goodness, faithfulness, gentleness and self-control" (Galatians 5:22-23).

"Honor one another above yourselves," Paul writes (Romans 12:10). "Live in harmony with one another" (verse 16). "Be completely humble and gentle; be patient, bearing with one another in love" (Ephesians 4:2).

"Encourage one another and build each other up.... Always try to be kind to each other and to everyone else" (1 Thessalonians 5:11, 15).

Husbands, how would it make a difference in the way you treat your wife? (See Ephesians 5:25.) Wives, how would it affect you? (See verse 22.)

Those who are employed, how would it affect your work? (See Ephesians 6:5-8.)

We all start out unlike Jesus. We start as sinners, as enemies of God, as selfish, self-seeking people. But that is precisely what we need to be saved from, to be rescued from. There's a lot of changing that needs to happen.

If we are to be like Jesus, our relationships may have to change a lot. It won't be easy, and it won't happen overnight. It takes time, so we need patience with the process, both in ourselves and in others. We need faith that God will finish the work he has started in us.

God has the most fulfilled, most satisfying life possible—and he wants us to enjoy eternal life, too. He wants us to be like he is. God is "compassionate and gracious ... slow to anger, abounding in love and faithfulness, maintaining love to thousands, and forgiving wickedness, rebellion and sin" (Exodus 34:6-7).

Joseph Tkach

Grace: A License to Sin?

It is a constant wonder how we guardians of the true faith can become so skilled at gumming up the greatest news in the universe. We hold in trust the Good News of all good news — God gives free grace to sinners for Christ's sake — and then we break our necks to hide it behind a great wall of rules, regulations and laws.

"You must not take grace too far or you will turn it into license to sin!" we admonish one another, as though lack of license has ever stopped anybody from sinning.

Hasn't anyone noticed? We are all sinners, for crying out loud, even all we religious, God-fearing, church-going Christians. Always have been, always will be, in this life. It is only by God's pure

and unfettered grace, as demonstrated once for all through Jesus Christ, that we are made something else — righteous — and not by avoiding sin, but by trusting him.

It seems that our vigilant efforts to prevent anyone from "turning grace into license to sin" has resulted, ironically, in our managing to turn sin into a barrier to accepting grace. The church promises grace, then delivers condemnation. The church headlines the gospel, then preaches hellfire. The church disguises its moralistic hook with gospel bait, reels in the unwary catch and plops him or her into the hot greasy frying pan of salvation by works.

Consider how the gospel is plowed under by

the relentless glacier of denominational "right-ness," doctrinal "exactness" and behavioral "standards." Christian church against Christian church, warring over phraseology, terminology, dress codes, political stands, seating arrangements, music styles, architecture…the list seems endless. We all seem to have at least a mild case of the "our-way-is-God's-way-die-you-heretic" virus.

Certainly, right doctrine is important. But surely we need look no farther than the Nicene Creed or the Apostles Creed for those doctrinal "is-sues" that really matter. Yet, many Christian churches still refuse Communion to fellow believ-ers who don't belong to the "right" denomina-tional brand name or haven't jumped through all the required theological hoops.

The underlying message of religious behavior-ism, "Behave right (according to our particular standards), or go straight to hell," buries the gospel under layer after layer of religious hair-splitting, nit-picking and measurement-taking. That isn't the gospel. It's religion. It holds out salvation like some phantom carrot-and-stick reached only through a lifetime of unquantifiable good deeds. It is a soul-sapping lie against the truth of God.

Jesus did not bring some "new and better" brand of religion. He brought the gospel, which is good news for sinners, which we all are. For the sake of Christ, God has thrown away all the report cards, homework records and detention notes in the world and given everybody a 4.0 GPA and a gold-plated invitation to eternal life.

Only some of us, it seems, "don't want no char-ity." We'd rather feel like we have been — or through discipline and devotion have become — the right and proper sort of person upon whom God could appropriately bestow eternal life. We have been good Christians, and we don't want to be lumped in with a bunch of immoral losers who do nothing more than put their trust in the Christ we have worked so hard for so long to imitate and obey. (We thank you, O God, that we are not like the rest of people — greedy, dishonest, adulterous or, for that matter, like this embezzler.)

Suppose we take up a challenge: give up the charade. Drop the legalism and the fear tactics. Quit pretending to be worthy and righteous, admit we are hopeless sinners without anything to our credit, and put our trust in Jesus Christ, for whose sake God justifies the ungodly (Romans 4:5).

Drop the nonsense about how that would mean people could "just go out and sin all we want, since we're already forgiven." Nobody who trusts God wants to sin. When you trust God to love you and forgive you, you want to be like Jesus; you don't want to sin. But when we do sin, in spite of the fact that we don't want to, we have an advocate with the Father, 1 John 2:1-2 tells us (and he tells us that so we won't sin, not so that we will, verse 1 says).

It's like Paul told Titus:

> The grace of God that brings salvation has appeared to all men. It teaches us to say "No" to ungodliness and worldly passions, and to live self-controlled, upright and godly lives in this present age, while we wait for the blessed hope — the glorious appearing of our great God and Savior, Jesus Christ, who gave himself for us to redeem us from all wickedness and to purify for himself a peo-ple that are his very own, eager to do what is good. (Titus 2:11-14)

It's *grace* that teaches us to say no to ungodli-ness. It's *grace* that makes us eager to do what is good. Knowing we're already forgiven and ac-cepted does not lead us into the devil's workshop, but into deeper fellowship with our Lord and Sav-ior. The gospel really is that simple. It really is good news.

J. Michael Feazell

What Is the Church?

The Bible says that people who have faith in Christ become part of the "church." What is the church? How is it organized? What is its purpose?

Jesus is building his church

Jesus said, "I will build my church" (Matthew 16:18). The church is important to him — he loved it so much that he gave his life for it (Ephesians 5:25). If we have the mind of Christ, we will love the church, too, and give ourselves to it.

The Greek word for "church" is *ekklesia,* which means an assembly. In Acts 19:39, 41, it is used for a large group of townspeople. But among Christians, the word *ekklesia* came to have a special meaning: all who believe in Jesus Christ.

For example, the first time that Luke uses the word, he writes, "great fear seized the whole church" (Acts 5:11). He does not have to explain what the word meant, for his readers were already familiar with it. "The church" means the disciples of Christ. It refers to people, not to a building.

Each local group of believers is a church. Paul wrote to "the church of God in Corinth" (1 Corinthians 1:2); he referred to "all the churches of Christ" (Romans 16:16) and the "church of the Laodiceans" (Colossians 4:16). But he could also use the word *church* to refer to all believers everywhere: "Christ loved the church and gave himself up for her" (Ephesians 5:25).

The church exists in several levels. At one level is the universal church, which includes everyone worldwide who accepts Jesus Christ as Lord and Savior. Local churches are a different level, including people who regularly meet together. Denominations are an intermediate level, containing groups of congregations that work more closely together because of shared history and beliefs.

Local congregations sometimes include unbelievers — family members who have not accepted Jesus as Savior, yet nevertheless meet regularly with believers. Local congregations sometimes include people who consider themselves to be Christians, but may not be. Experience shows that some of these will later acknowledge that they were not really Christians.

Why we need the church

Some people claim to believe in Jesus Christ but do not want to attend any of his churches. The New Testament shows that the normal pattern is for believers to meet together (Hebrews 10:25). Paul repeatedly exhorts Christians to do different things to "one another" (Romans 12:10; 15:7; 1 Corinthians 12:25; Galatians 5:13; Ephesians 4:32; Philippians 2:3; Colossians 3:13; 1 Thessalonians 5:13). It is difficult for people to obey these commands if they do not meet with other believers.

A local congregation can give us a sense of belonging, of being involved with other believers. It can give us some spiritual safety, so that we are not blown around by strange ideas. A congregation can give us friendship, fellowship and encouragement. It can teach us things we would never learn on our own. A congregation can help train our children, help us work together for more effective ministry and give us opportunities to serve that help us grow in ways we did not expect. In general, the value that we get out of a local congregation is in proportion to the amount of involvement we give to it.

But perhaps the most important reason for each believer to participate in a local congregation is that members need each other. God has given different abilities to different believers, and he wants us to work together "for the common good" (1 Corinthians 12:4-7). If only part of the work force shows up, it is no surprise that the congregation is not able to do as much as we would like, or to be as healthy as we would like. Unfortunately, some people find it easier to criticize than to help.

Our time, our abilities, and our resources are needed to fulfill the work and mission of the church. The commitment of mission-focused people is essential in order for the church to effectively reflect Jesus and his love to the world. Jesus said to pray for laborers (Matthew 9:38). He wants each of us to be working, not sitting on the sidelines.

Individuals who try to be Christian without the church fail to use their strengths to help the people the Bible says we should be helping. The church is a mutual-aid society, and we help each other, knowing that the day may come (and in fact is already here) that we will need to be helped.

Descriptions of the church

The church is described in several ways: the people of God, the family of God, the bride of Christ. We are a building, a temple and a body. Jesus described us as sheep, a field of grain and a vineyard. Each analogy describes a different aspect of the church.

Many of Jesus' parables of the kingdom describe the church, too. Like a mustard seed, the church started small and yet has grown large (Matthew 13:31-32). The church is like a field in which weeds are scattered among the wheat (verses 24-30). It is like a fishnet that catches bad fish as well as good (verses 47-50). The church is like a vineyard in which some people work a long time and others only a short time (Matthew 20:1-16). The church is like servants who were given money to invest for the master, and some produce more fruit than others (Matthew 25:14-30).

Jesus described himself as a shepherd, and his disciples as sheep (Matthew 26:31); his mission was to seek lost sheep (Matthew 18:11-14). He described his people as sheep that must be fed and cared for (John 21:15-17). Paul and Peter used the same analogy, saying that church leaders should be shepherds of the flock (Acts 20:28; 1 Peter 5:2).

"You are…God's building," Paul says (1 Corinthians 3:9). The foundation is Jesus Christ (verse 11), and people are the structure built on it. Peter said that we are all "living stones…being built into a spiritual house" (1 Peter 2:5). As we are built together, we "become a dwelling in which God lives by his Spirit" (Ephesians 2:22). We are the temple of God, the temple of the Holy Spirit (1 Corinthians 3:17; 6:19). Although God may be worshiped in any place, the church has worship as one of its purposes.

We are "the people of God," 1 Peter 2:10 tells us. We are what the people of Israel were supposed to be: "a chosen people, a royal priesthood, a holy nation, a people belonging to God" (verse 9; see Exodus 19:6). We belong to God, because Christ purchased us with his blood (Revelation 5:9). We are his children, and his family (Ephesians 3:15). As his people, we are given a great inheritance, and in response we are to try to please him and bring praise to his name.

Scripture also calls us the bride of Christ—a phrase that suggests his love for us, and a tremendous change within ourselves, that we might have such a close relationship with the Son of God. In some of his parables, people are invited to attend the wedding banquet, but in this analogy, we are invited to be the bride.

"Let us rejoice and be glad and give him glory! For the wedding of the Lamb has come, and his bride has made herself ready" (Revelation 19:7). How do we become ready for this? It is a gift: "Fine linen, bright and clean, was given her to wear" (verse 8). Christ cleanses us "by the washing with water through the word" (Ephesians 5:26). He presents the church to himself, having made her radiant, spotless, holy and righteous (verse 27). He is working in us.

Working together

The picture of the church that best illustrates the way that members relate to one another is that of the body. "You are the body of Christ," Paul says, "and each one of you is a part of it" (1 Corinthians 12:27). Jesus Christ "is the head of the body, the church" (Colossians 1:18), and we are all members of the body. If we are united to Christ, we are united to one another, too, and we have responsibilities to one another.

No one can say, "I don't need you" (1 Corinthians 12:21), and no one can say, "I don't belong in the church" (verse 18). God distributes our abilities so that we work together for the common good, helping one another and being *helped* by working together. "There should be no division in the body" (verse 25). Paul frequently warned against the sin of divisiveness, even saying that a person who causes division should be put out of the church (Romans 16:17; Titus 3:10). Christ causes the church to grow "as each part does its work" — as the various members cooperate (Ephesians 4:16).

Unfortunately, the Christian world is divided into denominations that sometimes squabble with one another. The church is not yet perfect, since none of its members is perfect. Nevertheless, Christ wants the church to be united (John 17:21). This does not require a merger of organizations, but it does suggest a common purpose.

True unity can be found only as we draw closer to Christ, preach his gospel, and live as he would. The goal is to promote him, not ourselves. The existence of different denominations has a side benefit, however: Through diverse approaches, more people are reached with the message of Christ in a way they understand.

Organization

The Christian world has three basic approaches to church organization and leadership: hierarchy, democracy and representative. These are called episcopal, congregational and presbyterian. Variations exist within each type, but in general, the episcopal model means that a denominational officer has the power to set policy and ordain pastors. In the congregational model, church members choose their policies and their pastors. In a presbyterian system, power is divided between the denomination and the congregations. Elders are elected and given power to govern.

The New Testament does not require any particular church structure. It talks about overseers (bishops), elders and shepherds (pastors) as if these were different words for the same type of church leader. Peter told the elders to be shepherds and overseers (1 Peter 5:1-2). Similarly, Paul told a group of elders that they were overseers and shepherds (Acts 20:17, 28).

The Jerusalem church was led by a group of elders; the church in Philippi was led by several overseers (Acts 15:2-6; Philippians 1:1). When Paul told Titus to ordain elders, he wrote one verse about elders and then several about overseers, as if these were synonymous terms for church leaders (Titus 1:5-9). In the book of Hebrews, the leaders are simply called "leaders" (Hebrews 13:7).

Some church leaders were also called "teachers" (1 Corinthians 12:29; James 3:1). The grammar of Ephesians 4:11implies that pastors and teachers were in the same category. One of the primary functions of a church leader is teaching — one of the qualifications for leadership is that the person must be "able to teach" (1 Timothy 3:2).

One thing is consistent in this: Certain people were designated as leaders. The local churches had some organization, though the exact title didn't seem to matter much. Believers were exhorted to respect and obey these leaders (1 Thessalonians 5:12; 1 Timothy 5:17; Hebrews 13:17). If the leader commands something wrong, people should not obey, but for the most part, members are to support their leaders.

What do leaders do? They "direct the affairs of the church" (1 Timothy 5:17). They shepherd the flock, leading by example and by teaching. They watch over the church (Acts 20:28). They should not lord it over others, but serve them (1 Peter 5:2-3). They are to "prepare God's people for works of service, so that the body of Christ may be built up" (Ephesians 4:12).

How are leaders chosen? We are told in only a few cases: Paul appointed elders (Acts 14:23), implied that Timothy would choose overseers (1 Timothy 3:1-7), and authorized Titus to appoint elders (Titus 1:5). At least in these cases, there was a hierarchy. We do not find any examples of church members choosing their own elders.

Deacons

However, in Acts 6:1-6 we see members choosing some leaders to help distribute food to the needy, and the apostles then appointed them for this work. In that way the apostles could concentrate on spiritual matters, and the physical needs could also be taken care of (verse 2). This distinction between spiritual leadership and physical leadership is also seen in 1 Peter 4:11-12.

Leaders who serve in manual work are often called deacons, from the Greek word *diakoneo,* which means to serve. Although all members and leaders are to serve, some are specifically appointed for service roles. At least one woman is called a deacon (Romans 16:1). Paul gave Timothy a list of traits needed in a deacon (1 Timothy 3:8-12), but he did not specify what they did. Consequently different denominations assign them different roles, ranging from custodial work to financial management.

The important thing in leadership is not what people are called, how they are structured or how they are appointed. The important thing is the purpose of leadership: to help God's people grow in maturity so that we become more like Christ (Ephesians 4:13).

Purposes of the church

Christ has built his church, given his people gifts and leadership, and he has given us work to do. What are the purposes of the church?

A major purpose of the church is worship. God has called us that we "may declare the praises of him" who called us "out of darkness into his wonderful light" (1 Peter 2:9). God seeks people who will worship him (John 4:23), who will love him above everything else (Matthew 4:10). Everything we do, whether as individuals or as a congregation, should be for his glory (1 Corinthians 10:31). We are called to "continually offer to God a sacrifice of praise" (Hebrews 13:15). We are commanded, "Speak to one another with psalms, hymns and spiritual songs" (Ephesians 5:19). When we gather, we sing praises to God, we pray to him and we listen to his word. These are forms of worship. So is the Lord's Supper, baptism and obedience.

Teaching is another purpose of the church. It is at the heart of the Great Commission: "teaching them to obey everything I have commanded you" (Matthew 28:20). Church leaders should teach, and members should teach one another (Colossians 3:16). We should encourage one another (1 Corinthians 14:31; 1 Thessalonians 5:11; Hebrews 10:25). Small groups provide an excellent setting for this mutual ministry.

If we want to be spiritual, Paul says, we should want to "build up the church" (1 Corinthians 14:12). The goal is to edify, strengthen, encourage and comfort (verse 3). The entire meeting should "be done for the strengthening of the church" (verse 26). We are to be disciples, people who learn and apply the word of God. The early church was praised because they "devoted themselves to the apostles' teaching and to the fellowship, to the breaking of bread and to prayer" (Acts 2:42).

Ministry is a third major purpose of the church. Paul writes, "As we have opportunity, let us do good to all people, especially to those who belong to the family of believers" (Galatians 6:10). Our first duty is to our family, and then to the church and then to the world around us. The second-greatest commandment is to love our neighbors (Matthew 22:39).

This world has many physical needs, and we should not ignore them. But the greatest need is the gospel, and we should not ignore that, either. As part of our ministry to the world, the church is to preach the good news of salvation through Jesus Christ. No other organization will do this work—it is the mission of the church. Every worker is needed—some on the front lines, and some in support. Some will plant, some will nurture and some will harvest, and as we work together, Christ will cause the church to grow (Ephesians 4:16).

Michael Morrison

Six Functions of the Church

Why do we meet together each week for worship and instruction? With a lot less bother, couldn't we worship at home, read the Bible and listen to a sermon on the radio or the internet?

In the first century, people gathered weekly to hear the Scriptures — but today we have our own copies of the Bible to read. Then why not stay at home to read the Bible on our own? It would be easier — cheaper, too. Through modern technology, everyone in the world could listen to the best preachers in the world, every week! We could have a menu of options, and listen only to the sermons that apply to us, or only to subjects we like. Wouldn't it be lovely?

Well, not really. I believe that stay-at-home Christians are missing out on many important aspects of Christianity. I hope to address these in this article, both to encourage faithful attendees to get more out of our meetings, and to encourage others to return to weekly attendance.

To understand why we gather each week, it is helpful to ask, Why did God create the church? What purposes does it have? By learning the functions of the church, we can then see how our weekly meetings serve various purposes in God's desire for his children.

God's commands are not arbitrary things just to see if we will jump when he says *jump*. No, his commands are given for our own good. When we are young Christians, we may not understand *why* he commands certain things, and we need to obey even before we know all the reasons why. We simply trust God, that he knows best, and we do what he says. A young Christian may attend church simply because that's what Christians are expected to do. A young Christian may attend simply because Hebrews 10:25 says, "Let us not give up meeting together."

So far, so good. But as we mature in the faith, we should come to a deeper understanding of *why* God tells his people to meet together.

Many commands

Let's begin exploring this subject by noting that Hebrews is not the only book that commands Christians to assemble with one another. "Love one another," Jesus tells his disciples (John 13:34). When Jesus says "one another," he is not referring to our duty to love all human beings. Rather, he is referring to the need for disciples to love other disciples — it must be a mutual love. This love is an identifying characteristic of Jesus' disciples (verse 35).

Mutual love does not express itself in accidental meetings at the grocery store and sporting events. Jesus' command assumes that his disciples are meeting with one another on a regular basis. Christians should have regular fellowship with other Christians. "Do good to all people, especially to those who belong to the family of believers," Paul wrote (Galatians 6:10). To obey this command, it is essential that we know who the family of believers is. We need to see them, and we need to see their needs.

"Serve one another," Paul wrote to the church in Galatia (Galatians 5:13). Although we should serve unbelievers in certain ways, Paul is not using this verse to tell us that. He is not commanding us to serve the world. Rather, he is commanding *mutual service among those who follow Jesus Christ.* "Carry each other's burdens, and in this way you will fulfill the law of Christ" (Galatians 6:2). But how can we carry each other's burdens unless we know what those burdens are — and how can we know unless we meet each other regularly?

"If we walk in the light…we have fellowship

with one another," John wrote (1 John 1:7). John is talking about spiritual fellowship, not casual acquaintances with unbelievers. If we walk in the light, we seek out other believers with whom to have fellowship. Similarly, Paul wrote, "Accept one another" (Romans 15:7). "Be kind and compassionate to one another, forgiving each other" (Ephesians 4:32). Christians have special responsibilities *toward one another.*

Throughout the New Testament, the early Christians met with one another to worship together, to learn together, to share their lives with one another (for example, Acts 2:41-47). Everywhere Paul went, he raised up churches, rather than leaving scattered believers. They were eager to share their faith and zeal with one another. This is the biblical pattern.

But some people today complain that they don't get anything out of the sermons. That may be true, but it's not an excuse to stop attending the meetings. Such people need to change their perspective from "get" to "give." We attend worship services not just to get, but also to *give* — to give worship to God with our whole heart and to give service to other members of the congregation.

How can we serve others at church services? By teaching children, helping clean the building, singing hymns and special music, arranging chairs, greeting people, etc. We provide an atmosphere in which others can get something out of the sermons. We talk with others, and find out needs to pray about and things to do to help others during the week. If you aren't getting anything out of the sermons, then at least attend in order to give to others.

Paul wrote, "Encourage one another and build each other up" (1 Thessalonians 4:18). "Spur one another on toward love and good deeds" (Hebrews 10:24). This is the reason given in the context of the Hebrews 10:25 command for regular assemblies. We are to encourage others, to be a source of positive words, whatsoever things are true and lovely and of good report.

Consider Jesus as an example. He regularly attended synagogue and regularly heard readings of Scripture that didn't add anything to his understanding, but he went anyway, to worship. Maybe it was boring to an educated man like Paul, but he didn't let that stop him, either.

Duty and desire

People who believe that Jesus has saved them from eternal death ought to be excited about it. They enjoy getting together with others to praise their Savior. Sometimes we have bad days and don't feel like attending. But even if it is not our desire at the moment, it is still our duty. We can't go through life doing only the things we *feel* like doing — not if we follow Jesus Christ as our Lord. He did not seek to do his own will, but the Father's. Sometimes that's what it boils down to for us. When all else fails, the old saying goes, read the instructions — and the instructions tell us to attend.

But why? What is the church for? The church has many functions. To help bring out different aspects of the church's work, some Christians have used a four- or five-fold scheme. For this article, I will use six categories.

1) Worship

Our relationship with God is both private and public, and we need both. Let's begin with our public interaction with God — worship. It is possible to worship God when we are all alone, but the term *worship* usually suggests something we do in public. The English word *worship* is related to the word *worth*. We declare God's worth when we worship him.

This declaration of worth is made both privately, in our prayers, and publicly, in words and songs of praise. 1 Peter 2:9 says that we are called to declare God's praises. The implication is that this a *public* declaration. Both Old and New Testaments show God's people worshiping *together,* as a community.

The biblical model, in both Old and New Testaments, is that songs are often a part of worship. Songs express some of the emotion we have with God. Songs can express fear, faith, love, joy, confidence, awe and a wide range of other emotions we have in our relationship with God. Not everyone in the congregation has the same emotion at the same time, but we nevertheless sing together. Some members would express the same emotion in different ways, with different songs and different styles. Nevertheless, we still sing together. "Speak to one another with psalms, hymns and spiritual songs" (Ephesians 5:19). We have to meet together to do this!

Music should be an expression of unity — yet often it is a cause for disagreement. Different cultures and different age groups express praise for God in different ways. Most churches have several cultures represented. Some members want to learn new songs; some want to use old songs. It seems that God likes both. He enjoys the psalms that are thousands of years old; he also enjoys new songs. It is helpful to note that some of the old songs — the psalms — command new songs:

> Sing joyfully to the Lord, you righteous; it is fitting for the upright to praise him. Praise the Lord with the harp; make music to him on the ten-stringed lyre. Sing to him *a new song;* play skillfully, and shout for joy. (Psalm 33:1-3)

In our music, we need to consider the needs of people who may be attending our services for the first time. We need music that they will find meaningful, music that expresses joy in a way that they comprehend as joyful. If we sing only the songs that we like, it sends the message that we care about our own comfort more than we care about other people. We cannot wait until new people start attending before we start learning some contemporary-style songs. We need to learn them so we can sing them meaningfully.

Music is only one aspect of our worship services. Worship includes more than expressing emotion. Our relationship with God also involves our minds, our thought processes. Some of our interaction with God comes in the form of prayer. As a gathered people of God, we speak to God. We praise him not only in poetry and song, but also in ordinary words and normal speech. And the Scriptural example is that we pray together, as well as individually.

God is not only love, but also truth. There is an emotional component and a factual component. So we need truth in our worship services, and we find truth in the Word of God. The Bible is our ultimate authority, the basis for all that we do. Sermons must be based in that authority, and our songs should be truthful.

But truth is not some vague idea that we can discuss without emotion. God's truth affects our lives and hearts. It demands a response from us. It requires all our heart, mind, soul and strength. That is why sermons need to be relevant to life. Sermons should convey concepts that affect how we live and how we think throughout the week, in the home and on the job.

Sermons need to be true, based on Scripture. Sermons need to be practical, directed to real life. Sermons need to be emotive, calling for a heart-felt response. Our worship includes listening to God's Word, and responding to it with repentance and with joy for the salvation he gives.

We can listen to sermons at home. There are many good sermons available. But this is not the full church experience. As a form of worship, it is only partial involvement. It is missing the community aspect of worship, in which we sing praises together, in which we respond together to the Word of God, in which we exhort one another to put the truth into practice in our lives.

Some believers cannot attend services because of ill health. They are missing out — as most of them know quite well. We pray for them, and we also know that it is our duty to visit them to make mutual ministry possible for them (James 1:27). Although shut-in Christians may need to be served in physical ways, they are often able to serve others in emotional or spiritual ways. Even so, stay-at-home Christianity is an exception based on necessity. It is not what Jesus wants his able-bodied disciples to do.

2) Spiritual disciplines

Worship services are only *part* of our worship. The Word of God must enter our hearts and minds to affect what we do throughout the week.

Worship can change its format, but it should never stop. Part of our worship response to God involves personal prayer and Bible study. People who are becoming more spiritually mature hunger to learn from God in his Word. They are eager to give him their requests, praise him, share their lives with him, and be aware of his constant presence in their lives.

Our dedication to God involves our heart, mind, soul and strength. Prayer and study should be our desire, but if they are not yet our desire, we need to do them anyway. This is the advice John Wesley was once given. At that time in his life, he said, he had an intellectual grasp of Christianity, but he did not *feel* faith in his heart. So he was advised: Preach faith until you have faith — and once you have it, you will certainly preach it! He knew he had a duty to preach faith, so he did his duty. And in time, God gave him what he lacked: heart-felt faith. What he had formerly done out of duty, he now did out of desire. God had given him the desire that he needed. God will do the same for us.

Prayer and study are sometimes called spiritual disciplines. "Discipline" may sound like a punishment, perhaps an unpleasant thing we have to force ourselves to do. But the real meaning of the term *discipline* is something that "disciples" us, that is, teaches us or helps us learn. Spiritual leaders throughout the ages have found that certain activities help us learn about God, love him and become more like him.

There are many practices that help us walk with God. We are familiar with prayer, study, meditation and fasting. There are other disciplines we can also learn from, such as simplicity, generosity, celebration or visiting widows. Church attendance is also a spiritual discipline, giving benefits for the individual relationship with God. We may also learn more about prayer, study and other spiritual habits by attending small groups in which we see how other Christians worship.

Real faith leads to obedience — even when that obedience is not comfortable, even when it is boring, even when it requires us to change our behavior. We worship him in spirit and in truth, at church meetings, at home, on the job and everywhere we go. The church is composed of God's people, and God's people have private worship as well as public worship. Both are necessary functions of the church.

Six Functions of the Church

Part 2

3) Discipleship

Throughout the New Testament, we see spiritual leaders teaching others. This is part of the Christian lifestyle; it is part of the great commission. "Go and make disciples of all nations…*teaching* them to obey everything I have commanded you" (Matthew 28:19-20). Everybody must be either a learner or a teacher, and we are usually both at the same time. "Teach and admonish one another with all wisdom" (Colossians 3:16). We must be learning from one another, from other Christians. The church is an educational institution as well as a place of worship and transformation.

Paul told Timothy, "The things you have heard me say in the presence of many witnesses entrust to reliable people who will also be qualified to teach others" (2 Timothy 2:2). Every Christian should be able to teach the basics of the faith, to give an answer concerning our hope in Jesus Christ.

What about people who have already learned? They should become teachers, to pass the truth along to new generations. Teaching is often done by pastors. But Paul commands *every* Christian to teach. Small groups provide one way in which this is done. Mature Christians can teach both in word and in example. They can tell others how Christ has helped them. When their faith is weak, they can seek the encouragement of others. When their faith is strong, they can help the weak.

It is not good for a Christian to be alone. "Two are better than one, because they have a good return for their work: If one falls down, his friend can help him up. But pity the man who falls and has no one to help him up!… Though one may be overpowered, two can defend themselves. A cord of three strands is not quickly broken" (Ecclesiastes 4:9-12).

By working together, we help one another grow. Discipleship is often a mutual process, one member helping another member. But some discipleship flows more purposefully, with more direction given to it. God has appointed some people in his church for that very reason:

It was he who gave some to be apostles, some to be prophets, some to be evangelists, and some to be pastors and teachers, to prepare God's people for works of service, so that the body of Christ may be built up until we all reach unity in the faith and in the knowledge of the Son of God and become mature, attaining to the whole measure of the fullness of Christ. (Ephesians 4:11-13)

God provides leaders who have the role of preparing others for their roles. The result is growth, maturity and unity, if we allow the process to work as God intended. Some Christian growth and learning comes from peers; some comes from people in the church who have the specific assignment of teaching and modeling the Christian life. People who isolate themselves are missing out on this aspect of the faith.

We have much to learn — and much to apply. Local congregations need to offer Bible studies, classes for new believers, training in evangelism, etc. We need to encourage lay ministry by giving permission, giving training, giving tools, giving control and getting out of the way!

4) Fellowship

The church is sometimes called a fellowship; it is a network of relationships. We all need to give and to receive fellowship. We all need to give and receive love. Fellowship means a lot more than talking to each other about sports, gossip and news. It means sharing lives, sharing emotions, bearing one another's burdens, encouraging one another and helping those who have need.

Most people put a mask on to hide their needs from others. If we are really going to help one another, we need to get close enough to one another to see behind the masks. It means that we have to let our own mask fall down a bit so others can see our needs. Small groups are a good place in which to do this. We get to know people a little better and feel a little safer with them. Often, they are strong in the area in which we are weak, and we are strong where they are weak. So by supporting one another, we both become stronger. Even the apostle Paul, although he was a giant in the faith, felt that he could be strengthened in faith by other Christians (Romans 1:12).

In ancient times, people didn't move very often. Communities would develop in which people knew each other. But in industrialized societies today, people often do not know their neighbors. People are often cut off from families and friends. People wear masks all the time, never feeling safe enough to let people know who they really are inside.

Ancient churches did not need to emphasize small groups — they formed them naturally. The reason we find it necessary to emphasize them today is that society has changed so much. To form the interpersonal connections that ought to be part of Christian churches, we need to go out of our way to establish Christian friendship/study/prayer circles.

This will take time. It takes time to fulfill our Christian responsibilities. It takes time to serve others. It even takes time to find out what kinds of service they need. But if we have accepted Jesus as our Lord, our time is not our own. Jesus Christ makes demands on our lives. He demands total commitment, not a pretend-Christianity.

5) Service

When I list "service" as a separate category here, I am emphasizing physical service, not the service of teaching or the service of encouraging others. A teacher is also a washer of feet, a person who illustrates the meaning of Christianity by *doing* what Jesus would do. Jesus took care of physical needs such as food and health. In a physical way, he gave his body and his life for us. The early church gave physical help, sharing their possessions with needy people, collecting offerings for the hungry.

Service should be done both inside and outside the church: "As we have opportunity, let us do good to all people, especially to those who belong to the family of believers" (Galatians 6:10). Folks who isolate themselves from other believers are falling short in this aspect of Christianity. The concept of spiritual gifts is important here. God has placed each of us in the body "for the common good" (1 Corinthians 12:7). Each of us has abilities that can help others.

Which spiritual gifts do you have? You can take a questionnaire to find out, but much of the questionnaire is based on your experience. What have you done in the past that turned out well? What do other people say you are good at? How have you helped others in the past? The best test of spiritual gifts is serving within the Christian community. Try a variety of roles in the church, and ask others what you do best. Volunteer. Every member should have at least one role in the church. Small groups provide many opportunities for involvement, and many opportunities for feedback on what you do well and what you enjoy doing.

The Christian community also serves the world around us, not only in word, but also in deeds that go with those words. God did not just speak — he also took action. Actions can demonstrate the love of God working in our hearts, as we help the poor, as we offer comfort to the discouraged, as we help victims make sense of their lives. It is those who need practical help who are often the most responsive to the gospel message.

Physical service may be seen as supporting the gospel. It is a method of supporting evangelism.

But service should be done with no strings attached, no attempt to get something in return. We serve simply because God has given us some resources and has opened our eyes to see a need. Jesus fed and healed many people without any immediate appeal for them to become his disciples. He did it simply because it needed to be done, and he saw a need that he could fill.

6) Evangelism

"Go into all the world and preach the gospel," Jesus commands us. Frankly, we need a lot of improvement in this area. We have been too conditioned to keep our faith to ourselves. People cannot be converted unless the Father is calling them, but that does not mean that we shouldn't preach the gospel! Jesus told us that we should.

To be effective stewards of the gospel message, we cannot just let other people do it. We cannot be content to hire other people to do it. Those forms of evangelism are not wrong, but they are not enough. Evangelism needs a personal face. When God wanted to send a message to people, he used people to do it. He sent his own Son, God in the flesh, to preach. Today he sends his children, humans in whom the Spirit is living, to preach the message and give it appropriate shape in each culture.

We need to be active, willing and *eager* to share the faith. We need enthusiasm about the gospel, an enthusiasm that communicates *at least something* about Christianity to our neighbors. (Do they know that we *are* Christians? Does it look like we are *happy* to be Christians?) We are growing and improving in this, but we need more growth.

I encourage all of us to give thought to how we might be Christian witnesses to those around us. I encourage every member to obey the command to be prepared to give an answer. I encourage every member to read about evangelism, and to apply what they read. We can all learn together and spur one another on to good works. Small groups can provide some training for evangelism, and small groups can often become places of evangelism.

In some cases, members may learn faster than their pastors. That's OK. The pastor can then learn from the member. God has given them different spiritual gifts. To some of our members, he has given a gift for evangelism that needs to be awakened and directed. If the pastor cannot equip this person for this form of ministry, the pastor at least ought to encourage the person to learn, and implement, and provide examples for others, so that the whole church might grow.

Conclusion

I have commented at length on the purposes of the church, and I have highlighted areas in which we need growth. I hope that people find it helpful to see the bigger picture of what we are doing.

Most people who read this article are faithful and supportive. However, I would like to add a few words for people who don't attend anymore. I cannot know your heart. I do not know all your hurts and questions. But I do know that you are missing out on a significant percentage of the Christian life. The biblical picture throughout is that Christians meet together regularly. If you are not, please consider attending again. There is so much God wants to do in your life. Christianity works best when we work together.

Joseph Tkach

Ministry Means Service

When the Bible talks about "ministry," what is it talking about? When it says that Christians are to be involved in "works of ministry," what does it mean? This article examines the concept of ministry by seeing how the biblical writers were inspired to use the words for ministry. This can help us understand a little better what we are to be doing in the church and in the world. It also gives us a context in which we can examine other topics about ministry.

Some of the words, although Greek, are not completely foreign to us. For example, our English word "deacon" is related to the Greek word *diakonia,* which is sometimes translated "ministry." The English word "liturgy" comes from *leitourgia,* which can also be translated "ministry."

The word *diakonia* is used to describe the "ministry of the word" (Acts 6:4), the "ministry of the Spirit" (2 Corinthians 3:8) and the "ministry of reconciliation" (2 Corinthians 5:18). *Leitourgia* is used to describe the ministry that Jesus has received as our High Priest (Hebrews 8:6). Similar Greek words can also be used for ministry, ministers and ministering. The Corinthian Christians were a result of Paul's ministry (*diakoneo*), and Paul considered himself a "minister [*leitourgos*] of Christ Jesus" (2 Corinthians 3:3; Romans 15:16).

We can learn much about ministry by seeing how the New Testament uses these words and other words with similar meaning. These give us the tone or flavor of New Testament ministry. We will see that every Christian has a ministry.

Diakonos Service

Diakonos means "a person who serves." We get the English word "deacon" from it.

In Philippians 1:1 and 1 Timothy 3:8-13 it denotes an office in the church. But almost everywhere else, the word is used in a more general sense. It refers to apostles, preachers and lay members more often than it does to deacons. The general sense of the word is "assistant." It indicates not just work in general, but work that benefits someone else. Paul used the word *diakonos* to describe himself as a servant of the Lord (1 Corinthians 3:5), a servant of God (2 Corinthians 6:4), a servant of the new covenant (2 Corinthians 3:6), a servant of the gospel (Ephesians 3:7; Colossians 1:23) and a servant of the church (verse 25).

Paul said that many of his co-workers were also servants: the woman Phoebe (Romans 16:1) and the men Tychicus (Ephesians 6:21; Colossians 4:7), Timothy (1 Timothy 4:6) and Epaphras (Colossians 1:7). Jesus said that his followers should be servants (Matthew 20:26;23:11; John 12:26). All Christians must do the work of a deacon. We are all deacons of Christ, deacons of his message and deacons of one another.

Diakoneo is the verb form of *diakonos;* it means "serve." The most specific meaning of *diakoneo* is to work with food to serve other people. Martha "served" at a dinner (John 12:2;Luke 10:40). Jesus told parables about servants who were expected to prepare food and serve their masters (Luke 17:8; 22:27). In the early church, seven men were chosen "to wait on tables" (Acts 6:2-3).

Diakoneo can refer to more general types of service, too. Jesus served his disciples (Matthew 20:28; Mark 10:45). Jesus' disciples should also serve (Luke 22:27; John 12:26). When we serve others, we are showing love to God (Hebrews 6:10) — a point also made in the parable of sheep and goats. This parable shows that serving can include not only supplying food and drink, but also clothing and other needs (Matthew 25:44).

Some people served Paul in prison (Philemon 13; 2 Timothy 1:18). Serving can include financial assistance: Several women served Jesus from their own possessions (Luke 8:3). Paul collected an offering to serve the saints in Jerusalem (Romans 15:25).

Diakoneo often means manual labor, but service to others can also be done through speaking. When Jesus said that he served his disciples, he included his teaching. The gospel is included when Paul says that the Corinthian church was a result of his serving (2 Corinthians 3:3).

1 Peter 4:10-11 uses the word in both a general sense and then in a more specific sense: "Each one should use whatever gift he has received to *serve* others, faithfully administering God's grace in its various forms. If anyone speaks, he should do it as one speaking the very words of God. If anyone *serves*, he should do it with the strength God provides."

Everyone should serve (in a general sense), but each serves in a different way — some serve by speaking and some serve by manual labor. It is this latter type of service that forms the core of the office of deacon (1 Timothy 3:10, 13). No matter what type of serving is done, it should be done with the strength God provides, so that he gets the praise and glory (1 Peter 4:11).

Diakonia is another word in the *diakonos* family. It denotes the result of serving — "service" or "ministry." It is translated in a variety of ways. Martha was busy with dinner "preparation" (Luke 10:40). In the early church, there was a daily "distribution" of food for widows (Acts 6:1). Famine relief was also called a ministry (Acts 11:29; 12:25; Romans 15:31; 2 Corinthians 8:4; 9:1, 12-13). When Macedonian believers supported Paul, it was a ministry to him (2 Corinthians 11:8).

Diakonia is often used to refer to a spiritual ministry. The apostles had a "ministry of the word" (Acts 6:4). Paul said that his ministry was "the task of testifying to the gospel of God's grace" (Acts 20:24). Paul's message of reconciliation was his ministry (2 Corinthians 5:18). The new covenant is a "ministry that brings righteousness" (2 Corinthians 3:8-9).

All members are encouraged to have a ministry. Church leaders exist "to prepare God's people for works of *service*" (Ephesians 4:12) — "to equip the saints for the work of ministry" (NRSV). There are different kinds of ministry (1 Corinthians 12:5), but they should all be used "for the common good" (verse 7). Those who have been given a gift of (manual) ministry should use that gift (Romans 12:7). Those who have other gifts should likewise use them to serve others (1 Peter 4:10).

Doulos Service

Paul frequently called himself a *doulos* — a slave or servant of Jesus Christ. In Jewish society, a *doulos* was usually a servant. In Greek society, he was usually a slave. However, this type of service is not restricted to slaves and apostles — it is commanded for all Christians. This is another description of our ministry.

Christ himself took on the nature of a servant (Philippians 2:7), and he quoted the proverb, "No servant is greater than his master" (Matthew 10:24-25; John 15:20-21). Since our Master served as a servant, shouldn't we also be servants? In Christianity, greatness is measured by service. "Whoever wants to be first must be slave of all" (Matthew 20:27; Mark 10:44).

Numerous people were called slave-servants of God: Moses, Simeon, Mary, Paul, Timothy, Silas, Luke, Epaphras, Tychicus, Peter, John, James and Jude. All of God's people are commanded to be servants (1 Peter 2:16). Service is part of what it means to be a Christian. Many of Jesus' parables included servants; these parables have extra meaning for Christians, the servants of Christ.

Doulos also has metaphorical uses — sinners are slaves of whatever has power over them (2 Peter 2:19). Christ frees us from the slavery of the fear of death (Hebrews 2:15). He frees us from the slavery of sin (John 8:34; Romans 6:16-20) by redeeming us, purchasing us with his own blood. He frees us from "the yoke of slavery" (Galatians 5:1) so that we may serve him in the new way of the Spirit (Romans 7:6). We become slaves to obedience, slaves to righteousness (Romans 6:16-22).

Christians are "slaves of Christ" (1 Corinthians 7:22; Ephesians 6:6). We are all admonished to serve the Lord (Romans 12:11; 14:18; 1 Thessalonians 1:9), and one of the primary responsibilities our Lord and Master gives us is to serve one another in love (Galatians 5:13). As slaves of Christ and slaves of one another, we serve one another by using the gifts God gives us (see appendix below).

Paul calls us slaves, but he also says that we are not slaves (Galatians 4:7). In some ways we are like slaves, but in other ways we are not. With respect to obedience, our obligation to Christ is like that of a slave — we are to obey. But with respect to reward, we are much better than slaves. "As long as the heir is a child, he is no different from a slave…. You are no longer a slave, but a son; and since you are a son, God has made you also an heir" (Galatians 4:1, 7).

"A slave has no permanent place in the family, but a son belongs to it forever" (John 8:35). "I no longer call you servants…. Instead, I have called you friends" (John 15:15).

Worship service

Some Greek words for service also mean worship. *Latreia* and *latreuo* denote religious service or worship. (We see the root word *latr-* in the English word *idolatry*.) The NIV uses "serve" and "worship" almost interchangeably for these words. Worship was done at the temple (Luke 2:37;Acts 7:7; Romans 9:4; Hebrews 8:5; 9:1, 6, 9; 10:2; 13:10). In Revelation, the saints "serve" God in his heavenly temple (Revelation 7:15) and will "serve" him always (Revelation 22:3).

Christ has cleansed us so that we may "serve" God (Hebrews 9:14). We are exhorted to "worship" God (Hebrews 12:28). Christians "worship" by the Spirit of God (Philippians 3:3). Paul exhorts us to be living sacrifices, which is our "reasonable service" (KJV), a "spiritual act of worship" (Romans 12:1, NIV). Our service to God is not centered on a temple, but is done wherever we are.

Leitourg- words come from the Greek words *laos* (people) and *ergon* (work). They originally referred to a public service, but they eventually came to refer specifically to religious service and worship. We get the English word *liturgy* from these Greek words.

This was the type of service Jewish priests performed (Luke 1:23; Hebrews 10:11; 9:21). This religious service is now done by Jesus, our High Priest (Hebrews 8:2, 6). In the context of priests and sacrifices, Paul said that he was a "minister" of Jesus Christ (Romans 15:16).

A practical service such as famine relief could be called a *leitourgia* (Romans 15:27; 2 Corinthians 9:12). By using a *leitourg-* word, Paul was reminding his readers that this seemingly ordinary service to the saints was actually an act of worship, a religious activity. All Christians can perform religious service (Acts 13:2; Philippians 2:17).

Ministry of all believers

There is a progression in the way worship words are used. In the old covenant, God required the Israelites to serve him through a priesthood, a sacrificial system and a temple. In the new covenant, *all* Christians worship God through spiritual sacrifices, and we all serve God in the Spirit. The ministry of worship has been given to all the people.

This is one reason the 16th-century Reformers taught "the priesthood of all believers." Jesus Christ is the High Priest, and all Christians are priests (1 Peter 2:5, 9; Revelation 1:6). Every Christian can enter the heavenly Holy of holies because of the once-for-all sacrifice of Jesus Christ (Hebrews 10:19). Christians offer spiritual sacrifices (1 Peter 2:5; Romans 12:1). We also have the priestly duty of interceding for one another in prayers and in practical action.

The Reformers also noted that Christians serve God through their secular work — their vocation or "calling" — as well as through their involvement in the church. A person who grows food is providing a service to society; a person who works in a factory or teaches school does, too. Christian homemakers and government employees are also serving others.

"Whatever you do, do it all for the glory of God"

(1 Corinthians 10:31). All work — in the home, in the store, in the car and in the office — is an act of worship to God. We are his slaves — full-time ministers in his service.

Summary

The New Testament says the same thing in many different ways: Christians are commanded to serve one another. None of the words for service or ministry is restricted to the ordained clergy. All members are enslaved to one another. We all have obligations to one another. Whether our service is in word or in deed, it is a religious duty for all Christians. Whether we are ordained or not, we are all called to serve the Lord by serving one another.

As slave-servants, we are ministering to one another, to the church, to the gospel and to the Lord. God has given each of us a ministry. We should minister to one another's needs. God has given us abilities so that we will use them to serve others. All Christians — whether men, women, deacons or elders — are called to be ministers.

Appendix A: *Allelon*

The Greek word *allelon* gives us a helpful introduction to the ways in which Christians should serve each other, because this Greek word means "one another" or "each other." It is often used to describe our mutual obligations — the responsibility that all members have toward one another.

Perhaps the most comprehensive command Jesus gave was the well-known "Love one another" (John 13:34). "As I have loved you, so you must love one another. By this everyone will know that you are my disciples, if you love one another" (verses 34-35). This command is such a fundamental statement of our Christian duty that it is given again in John 15:12, 17; Romans 13:8; 1 Thessalonians 4:9; 1 Peter 1:22; 1 John 3:11, 23; 4:7, 11-12; and 2 John 5. This is the attitude in which we should always interact with one another.

Paul developed the command a little further: "Be devoted to one another in brotherly love. Honor one another above yourselves" (Romans 12:10). "Serve one another in love" (Galatians 5:13). He prayed that the Lord would help the Thessalonians' love to increase not only for each other, but that their love would also increase for everyone else (1 Thessalonians 3:12). "Always try to be kind to each other *and* to everyone else" (1 Thessalonians 5:15). In his second letter to the Thessalonians, he thanked God that their mutual love was indeed increasing (2 Thessalonians 1:3).

In Christ, we belong to each other and form one body (Romans 12:5). We are members of one another (Ephesians 4:25). "We have fellowship with one another" (1 John 1:7). Paul prayed that the Roman Christians would have "a spirit of unity among yourselves as you follow Christ Jesus" (Romans 15:5). To avoid division in the body, Paul wanted members to "have equal concern for each other" (1 Corinthians 12:25). "Offer hospitality to one another" (1 Peter 4:9).

We see further development of the command in the words of Jesus: "Be at peace with each other" (Mark 9:50). Paul put it this way: "Live in peace with each other" (1 Thessalonians 5:13*). [An asterisk indicates that the pronoun is *heautou* instead of *allelon;* the meaning is often the same.] "Live in harmony with one another" (Romans 12:16). Paul shows how this is done: "Do not be conceited" (same verse). "Be completely humble and gentle; be patient, bearing with one another in love" (Ephesians 4:2). "Do nothing out of selfish ambition or vain conceit, but in humility consider [each other] better than yourselves" (Philippians 2:3). "Clothe yourselves with humility toward one another" (1 Peter 5:5).

"Stop passing judgment on one another," Paul writes (Romans 14:13). "Accept one another, then, just as Christ accepted you" (Romans 15:7). "Bear with each other and forgive whatever grievances you may have against one another. Forgive as the Lord forgave you" (Colossians 3:13). "Be kind and compassionate to one another, forgiving each other, just as in Christ God forgave you" (Ephesians 4:32). "Confess your sins to each other and pray for each other" (James 5:16).

"Serve one another," Paul wrote (Galatians 5:13). Peter gives the same point: "Each one should use whatever gift he has received to serve others" (1 Peter 4:10*). Jesus had given the same lesson when he told his disciples to "wash one another's feet" (John 13:14). "Submit to one another out of reverence for Christ" (Ephesians 5:21). "Carry each other's burdens, and in this way you will fulfill the law of Christ" (Galatians 6:2).

Paul wanted the Roman Christians and himself to be "mutually encouraged by each other's faith" (Romans 1:12). One purpose of our weekly meetings is to "spur one another on toward love and good deeds...encourage one another" (Hebrews 10:24-25). "Encourage one another daily" (Hebrews 3:13*). "Encourage one another and build each other up" (1 Thessalonians 4:18; 5:11). "Build yourselves up in your most holy faith" (Jude 20*).

Paul wanted "mutual edification" (Romans 14:19). "Teach and admonish one another with all wisdom, and as you sing psalms, hymns and spiritual songs" (Colossians 3:16*; Ephesians 5:19*). Paul was confident that the Romans could "instruct one another" (Romans 15:14).

These are some of the ways in which Christians, as servants of Jesus Christ, minister to one another. None of these types of service or ministry is restricted to ordained elders or pastors.

Appendix B: Gifts of the Holy Spirit

The "gifts" of the Spirit are God-given abilities distributed as God knows is best for different aspects of Christian service. There are different kinds of spiritual gifts, Paul tells us, even though they are all inspired by the same Spirit (1 Corinthians 12:4). God gives these special abilities "for the common good" — so Christians can help one another (verse 7).

But not everyone has the same spiritual gift or ability, just as not every part of the human body performs the function of seeing, hearing or walking. Feet, hands, eyes and other parts serve different functions. By contributing to the body as a whole, the various parts serve one another. So it is in the church, the body of Christ (verses 14-27).

God distributes the gifts: one power to one person, another gift to the next person, a third ability to another, just as God determines (verses 8-11). God appoints people with various spiritual functions: apostles, prophets, teachers, miracle-workers, healers, helpers, administrators and speaking in different kinds of tongues (verse 28). By dividing the gifts in this way, God encourages members to work with and help one another. Through a division of labor, God encourages us to work with one another to be more efficient. As we work together, Christ gives his church growth (Ephesians 4:15-16).

What are the gifts? Paul lists some in 1 Corinthians 12:28-30: church leadership positions such as apostle, prophet and teacher, or gifts of miracles, healings and tongues, or less spectacular but equally necessary abilities such as helping others and administration. Another list is in verses 7-10: messages of wisdom and knowledge, faith and healing and miracles, inspired messages of prophecy, tongues or interpretations, or a special gift for distinguishing between spirits. The precise difference between wisdom and knowledge, or faith and healing and miracles may not be important in this list; Paul is simply making the point that spiritual gifts come in many varieties, although they are all "for the common good."

Romans 12:6-8 gives another list of gifts (none of the lists is complete): prophesying, serving, teaching, encouraging, giving to others, leading others or showing mercy. Some of these service gifts should be found in all Christians, but some people are distinctly better at certain activities than other people are. As God gives us these abilities, we should apply them as best we can for the common good of the body of Christ.

The gifts in these lists come in three major categories: church leadership, speaking, and serving others. Peter summarizes "gifts" under the categories of speaking and serving (1 Peter 4:11). "Each one should use whatever gift he has received to serve others, faithfully administering God's grace in its various forms" (verse 10).

Paul said that God had given (the Greek verb is similar to the noun used for "gift") the Philippian Christians the ability to believe in Christ and also the opportunity to suffer for him (Philippians 1:29-30). Suffering patiently and faithfully can be a useful spiritual gift. Paul says he was given a "thorn in the flesh" (2 Corinthians 12:7), which emphasized Paul's weaknesses, therefore showing that the power of his message came not from himself but from God (verses 8-10).

Paul referred to marital status, whether married or not, as a gift (1 Corinthians 7:7). Any of life's circumstances can be considered a gift of God if we are able to use it to glorify Christ and serve others. It does not matter how spectacular or seemingly ordinary the gift is – what matters is how it is used (1 Corinthians 13:1-4). Love, a fruit of the Spirit that all Christians must have, is the test of whether an ability or gift is good.

All gifts should be used to glorify Christ and to benefit others.

Michael Morrison

Christian Life

When we accept Jesus Christ as our Savior, we have begun the Christian life. But accepting Christ is only a beginning—God isn't finished with us yet.

After we come to faith, what do we do? How does faith make a difference in the way we live? What does God want to do with us? How does he want to change us? And how do we make the transformation easier?

God's goal in our lives

God wants each of us to "be conformed to the likeness of his Son" (Rom. 8:29). We are in the process of "being transformed into his likeness with ever-increasing glory" (2 Cor. 3:18). Paul worked so that Christ would be "formed" in the believers (Gal. 4:19). He described our goal in this way: "Attaining to the whole measure of the fullness of Christ" (Eph. 4:13).

We believe that Christians should gather in regular fellowship and live lives of faith that make evident the good news that humans enter the kingdom of God by putting their trust in Jesus Christ.

As children of God, we are to become more like the Son of God. He is not only our Savior, he is also our example, showing us what humans should be like. When we believe in Christ, we have a new identity and a new purpose for living. Our new identity is "child of God." Our purpose is "to be like God in true righteousness and holiness" (Eph. 4:22-24)—we are to act like the new person that we are.

What an enormous goal! We are to be like God. God is changing us to be more like himself—more like Jesus, who showed us what God is like when living in the flesh.

Obviously, we cannot make ourselves Godlike. But God can—and he is! He does not do this against our will, but only as we agree to what he is doing. And by the Holy Spirit working in our hearts and minds, he is helping us agree. "It is God who works in you to will and to act according to his good purpose" (Phil. 2:13).

We do not need to be like Christ in carpentry skills, cultural customs or physical appearance. Rather, we are to be like him "in true righteousness and holiness." In our morality and in our devotion to God, we are to be like Jesus Christ. That is the purpose of the Christian life, that we grow to be more like him.

We need to be changed on the inside, in our thoughts. Paul says, "Be transformed by the renewing of your mind" (Rom. 12:2). We are "being renewed in knowledge in the image of [our] Creator" (Col. 3:10). When we think like Christ, we will be like him.

Submitting ourselves

God is the one who does the work, but we are involved. We can resist his work, or we can submit ourselves to cooperating with it. In the history of Christianity, three practices stand out: prayer, Bible study and worship. Millions of Christians have found that these practices (sometimes called spiritual disciplines) help us to present ourselves to God for him to do his work in our hearts and minds.

In prayer, we acknowledge our need for God. We are reminded that he is our standard, the reference point for our lives. We grow in love for God by praising his power and thanking him for his mercy. We set each day in its proper context, praising him for every good thing and acknowledging his purpose for our lives. We confess our needs and seek his help, not just for our physical needs but also for the spiritual transformation that we also need.

Prayer was a constant part of Jesus' life, and if he needed it, we need it even more. But sometimes it is difficult. We don't always know what to say, what to ask, or how to praise. It isn't easy to set aside time. But we need to—regularly.

In prayer, we not only talk to God, we also listen to what he says as the Holy Spirit may bring certain thoughts to our minds. How do we know whether those ideas are from God, or merely from our own brain? To discern the difference, we need training in the mind of God—training that we get in Bible study.

Scripture was important to Jesus. He knew it well and considered it authoritative. He used Scripture to reject the devil's temptations (Matt. 4:1-11). He said that we should not "live on bread alone"—we also need "every word that comes from the mouth of God" (v. 4).

We need the words of Scripture. God caused these books to be written for our instruction and encouragement (2 Tim. 3:16). Scripture helps change our thoughts to be more like Christ's.

The early Christians devoted themselves to learning doctrine from the apostles (Acts 2:42). We get the same teachings from the New Testament. Part of God's plan for our transformation is the study of Scripture. He doesn't force us to do it—it's our choice.

It isn't always easy—for two reasons. First, parts of the Bible are hard to understand, and sometimes the meaning is debatable. There is depth in Scripture that can last a lifetime. We understand some of it the first time, a little more the second time, and a little more the third time. So we can't expect to understand it all right away. It's helpful to focus on what we do understand, not on what we don't.

However, for most people, the hardest part about Bible study is taking the time to do it. We need to make it a habit, a regular discipline. Many Christians find it helpful to read a small portion of the Bible each day, thinking and praying about it. Devotional books are often helpful. The main thing is to form a habit, and keep at it.

Worship is a third discipline that helps us grow to become more like Christ. Jesus said that God is looking for people who will worship him sincerely (John 4:23). The early Christians devoted themselves to fellowship, breaking bread and prayer (Acts 2:42). They gathered for worship. The more we worship God, the closer to him we will be. Our faith will be stronger when we are in frequent contact with others who have faith.

There are many other spiritual disciplines, or tools for spiritual growth. These include meditation, fasting, solitude, simplicity, generosity, service and others. In all these, we must remember that spiritual growth is not our own achievement. We do not become like Christ through self-discipline. Rather, the disciplines are merely a way to let God do his work with less resistance from us.

Jesus Christ as Lord

In the New Testament, one of the most common titles of Christ is *kyrios,* usually translated as "Lord." This Greek word could refer to a landowner, a government official or another person of authority. It could also refer to God, as it frequently did in the Greek translation of the Old Testament.

When the Roman emperor wanted people to call him *kyrios,* he was claiming to be *the* lord, the supreme authority—and Christians refused. Instead of saying "Nero is Lord," they would say "Christ is Lord," even though it sometimes cost them their lives. Although they obeyed Roman laws whenever they could (Rom. 13:1-7), they could give unqualified allegiance only to Jesus Christ. Only he has supreme authority. He is the Lord.

Peter tells us, "In your hearts set apart Christ as Lord" (1 Pet. 3:15). As our Lord, Jesus is two things: Protector and Boss. We are to trust him and obey him. He who gave his life for us can be counted on to give us what we need.

This does not mean everything we want, and it doesn't always mean health and money. In fact, Jesus may let us go through many trials (Acts 14:22; Heb. 12:5-11), but we need to trust that he knows what he's doing, that it is for our good. He also promises to help us through them (1 Cor. 10:13).

The apostle Paul had many trials, but he "learned to be content whatever the circumstances" (Phil. 4:11). Sometimes he was poor, and sometimes he had plenty, and Christ was his source of strength even when he was hungry (vv. 12-13). His Lord provided as much as he needed at the time. Sometimes he provided a way to escape a trial; sometimes he provided strength to endure it.

Our Lord is also our Master, who gives commands and expects us to obey. Paul talked about the obedience that comes with faith (Rom. 1:5); James said that faith without obedience is dead (Jas. 2:17). In our actions, we show whether we trust Christ. He died for us, and in response, we live for him and serve him (2 Cor. 5:15). We offer ourselves to God, to be used in righteousness (Rom. 6:12-13).

Faith, hope and love

Why should we obey God? The simplest reason is: It's our duty. Through his death on the cross, Christ has purchased us (Acts 20:28), and it is only fair that we do what he says. We are children of God, and we are to do what he commands. Of course, we do not obey in order to be saved. Salvation comes first, and obedience should follow.

But obedience goes deeper than duty. Obedience should come from the heart, done because we want to, not grudgingly, because we have to. So why should we want to obey? There are three main reasons: faith, hope and love.

In faith, we believe that God's commands are for our own good. He loves us and wants to help us, not give us unnecessary burdens. As our Creator, he has the wisdom to know how we should live, what works best and what causes the most happiness in the long run. And we have to trust him in that; his perspective is much better than ours.

Obedience expresses faith in his wisdom and love. Obedience is what he made us for (Eph. 2:10), and life works better if we are in tune with the way we were made.

Obedience also involves hope in a future blessing. If there is no future life, then Christianity would be foolish (1 Cor. 15:14-18). Jesus promised that his disciples would find eternal life worth far more than anything they might have to give up in this age (Mark 10:29-30). Everyone who is saved will have the joy of knowing God in eternal life, but there are also rewards in addition to eternal joy.

Jesus encouraged his disciples to "store up for yourselves treasures in heaven" (Matt. 6:19-21). Several of his parables indicate that we will be rewarded for what we do in this life. God rewards those who seek him (Heb. 11:6).

Paul also wrote about rewards: "The Lord will reward everyone for whatever good he does" (Eph. 6:8). This is not talking about salvation, but about rewards in addition to salvation. He described the judgment as a fire that tests the quality of every person's work. "If what he has built survives, he will receive his reward" (1 Cor. 3:14). If it is burned up, he will lose it, but he will still be saved (v. 15).

But reward is not the only reason we work, for we are children of the King, not employees who do only what we get paid for. Our final motive for obedience is love. This includes love for people around us, because they will be better off if we obey God than if we do not. God's instructions are sensible, not arbitrary rules. They help people get along with other people.

But most of all, it is our love for God that causes us to want to obey him. He has done so much for us, that we cannot help but be thankful and want to please him. "If you love me," Jesus says, "you will obey what I command" (John 14:15). "If anyone loves me, he will obey my teaching" (v. 23). John later wrote, "This is love for God: to obey his commands" (1 John 5:3). "The man who says, 'I know him,' but does not do what he commands is a liar.... But if anyone obeys his word, God's love is truly made complete in him" (1 John 2:4-5).

Obedience can also tell other people that we love God. Obedience says that he is great and good and wise, and we adore him. Obedience says that God is important to us, that he is valuable, that he deserves our loyalty. Let your good deeds be seen, Jesus said, so that people can see them "and praise your Father in heaven" (Matt. 5:16).

"Live such good lives among the pagans," Peter wrote, "that, though they accuse you of doing wrong, they may see your good deeds and glorify God on the day he visits us" (1 Pet. 2:12). A good example can help people be favorably disposed to God. "Whatever happens, conduct yourselves in a manner worthy of the gospel of Christ" (Phil. 1:27).

Help the gospel be associated with good things, not bad. Our love for God means that we want to bring him favorable publicity, so that others will come to love him, too. A bad example will bring the gospel into disrepute (Titus 2:5). Those who flaunt their sins cannot be counted as members in good standing (1 Cor. 5:1-13).

Sanctification

Much of what we have been discussing comes under the theological term *sanctification,* which means "making holy." Through his death on the cross, Christ has already sanctified us (Heb. 10:10). That means he has set us apart for himself, for his use. We are holy, and Scripture frequently calls us "saints" — which means "holy ones." We are dedicated to God.

But in another sense, we are still in the process of being made holy (v. 14). The work is not yet done. Perhaps you've noticed that our behavior isn't always what it ought to be. In the process of sanctification, our thoughts and behaviors are being brought into conformity with what they ought to be. We are holy children of God, and we ought to live like it.

Although God enables and energizes this process, Christians have an active part in it. They are repeatedly told to think, speak and act in certain ways. "Continue to work out your salvation with fear and trembling, for it is God who works in you to will and to act according to his good purpose"

(Phil. 2:12).

God "has saved us and called us to a holy life," Paul wrote (2 Tim. 1:9). He exhorts us to offer our bodies as living sacrifices, doing the will of God (Rom. 12:1-2). He encourages us to "live a life worthy of the Lord" and to "please him in every way: bearing fruit in every good work, growing in the knowledge of God" (Col. 1:10).

"It is God's will that you should be sanctified ... that each of you should learn to control his own body in a way that is holy and honorable.... For God did not call us to be impure, but to live a holy life" (1 Thess. 4:3-7). "Make every effort to live in peace with all men and to be holy; without holiness no one will see the Lord" (Heb. 12:14).

To be like Jesus, to live like Jesus — this may seem like an unrealistic goal. But it is our goal nonetheless, for God is the one doing the work in us. Despite our inabilities, we can be confident that he will finish the work in us (Phil. 1:6). Although our progress may sometimes seem slow, we trust in Christ, not in ourselves.

Paul expressed an excellent attitude: "Not that I ... have already been made perfect, but I press on to take hold of that for which Christ Jesus took hold of me" (Phil. 3:12). Christ has taken hold of us for his purpose, which is that we are to be conformed into his image. So we press onward, confident in him, striving to do his will.

"One thing I do: Forgetting what is behind and straining toward what is ahead, I press on toward the goal to win the prize for which God has called me heavenward in Christ Jesus" (vv. 13-14).

Press onward!

Michael Morrison

Obeying God

"I still don't get one thing. If we are forgiven already, what's to stop us from continuing to sin? I mean, I realize we are saved by God's mercy and not by being good, and I realize we could never be good enough anyway, and I realize that even our goodness is tainted with sin, but still, doesn't God want us to stop sinning?"

You're worried that if we put too much emphasis on grace, people won't care how they behave?

"Yes, I guess I am."

I have never met a Christian who did not care about how he or she behaves. It just comes with the territory—Christians care about how they behave. But I have met lots of Christians who have serious trouble believing that God could keep on loving them and forgiving them in spite of how rotten they behave.

Most of us Christians have an easy time seeing our sins and trying to do better. What we have trouble with is handing off our deep sense of guilt and failure to Christ. Most of us are always and ever struggling to overcome something, but our moments of deep peace and guiltless rest in God's total and unconditional love for us are few and far between.

"Well, that supports my point. If we would quit sinning, then we wouldn't have to suffer from guilt."

You said you realized that even our goodness is tainted with sin, and you are right about that. It is. If we are honest with ourselves (and as Christians, we ought to feel free to be honest with ourselves), we know we are never guilt-free. But in Christ, we *are* guilt-free, not because of us, but because of him.

God accounts us righteous in Christ. All we can do is believe it, because we can't see actual evidence of it. We might see a little, or even a lot, of improvement in this or that aspect of our lives, but we never see anything close to perfection (unless we are delusional).

In other words, yes, we should fight sin in our lives, and because Christ lives in us, we do. But we should never measure God's love for us by our success levels in achieving sinlessness. God wants us to trust *him* to be our righteousness.

When we trust him to be our righteousness three things happen:

- We realize we are not righteous (that is, we are sinners in need of mercy; that's what we mean by repentance—admitting we are sinners in need of mercy).
- We realize his Word, his promise to forgive us and save us, is good.
- We rest in him.

God got hot with Israel over *unbelief* (Psalm 106:6-7, 21, 24; Hebrews 3:9, 12, 19). They would not trust him to do what he said he would do for them, which was to save them, to be their salvation, to take care of them. Instead of trusting him, they would make treaties with neighboring countries, or sacrifice to the gods of other nations, or trust in their own military strength.

(And hand in hand with their untrust, they would oppress the poor and weak among them. Not trusting God to take care of us always leads to walking all over the poor and weak. That is because when you try to make your own way in the world, you have to adopt the ways of the world, play by the world's rules—survival of the fittest.)

Trusting in God means that when we are hurt or taken advantage of, or when problems arise or tragedy strikes, all is not lost, because Christ was raised from the dead for us. It means that we know we have nothing to lose because everything we have was given to us by God in the first place.

It means we can cast all our cares on him because he cares for us. And that takes faith, because God's deliverance from the many things that fall on us in this life very seldom comes in ways that make sense to us.

Sometimes deliverance doesn't come in this life at all. In the same way, overcoming all our sins doesn't come in this life, which means we have to *trust* him when he says he doesn't count our sins against us (Romans 4:1-8) and that our new lives are hidden with Christ in God (Colossians 3:3).

Holy in Christ

Sin is our enemy as well as God's enemy. It destroys the creation, including us. But God has moved powerfully, decisively and once for all in Christ to redeem the creation, including us, from the corruption of sin. The outcome of the war with sin has already been determined through the death and resurrection of the incarnate Son of God. The devil, along with the sin and death he champions, has already been defeated, but he still exercises influence in the world until Christ returns.

By God's grace, we are *God's* children. Our hearts are turned to him, devoted to him and sanctified by him. We have tasted his goodness and experienced his love, and we have given our allegiance to him. We fight sin in our lives and strive to walk in righteousness because he lives in us.

Christ's victory is our victory. In other words, what Christ did, he did for us, and he stands for us with God. We are holy because, and only because, we are in Christ. That is something we can see only with the eyes of faith—we have to trust God that it is so.

Christian life a paradox

Here is another way of putting it: God has given us an active part in Christ's victory. We stand clean and forgiven in Christ's blood even while we seek to live in harmony with God's perfect love. A repentant heart and commitment to obedience

characterize our lives of faith in Christ, yet we routinely fall far short of Christ's ideal.

When we fail, which is continually, we can trust in the forgiveness of our God who loves us so much that he gave his Son to redeem us. In Christ we stand, and we stand only because we are in Christ, who is *for us,* as opposed to *against us.*

In Christ, even though we are sinners, we are righteous. Even when our commitment flags, Christ's commitment to us does not—God is faithful even when we falter (2 Timothy 2:13). There is no condemnation for those who are in Christ (Romans 8:1).

If all this sounds like a paradox, it is. At least, it is from our perspective. But from God's perspective, it is the way the universe is put together. God loves and redeems, and he has made all things new in Christ. We are dead in sin, yet we are alive in Christ (Ephesians 2:5;Colossians 2:13). We still sin, yet God no longer considers us sinners (Romans 4:8). Our real lives, which are a new creation, are hidden in God with Christ (Colossians 3:3). Just as the old creation is judged, the new creation is saved.

Does that make sin OK? The question misses the point. Sin is not OK. It is never OK. But it is defeated. Its teeth have been pulled. It is on its last legs. It still slaps you around and might even kill you, but God has you covered forever.

Jesus confirms the ideals of the life of the kingdom in Matthew 5. The old categories of the law of Moses are transcended by Jesus' description of the transformed heart that reflects the new life in him. It is a heart that puts others ahead of self, that not only avoids hurting others but also actively loves others. It is a pattern of life that cannot be measured by mere outward appearances, but flows instead from a new creation, a new interior, a new birth.

It is the heart of Christ. And as such, it is a heart we are *given,* not one that we work up with moral energy and personal commitment.

"Why does Jesus say that anyone who does not keep the whole law and teach it will be called least in the kingdom of heaven?"

Because it is true. But remember, it is in Jesus that we keep the whole law, not in ourselves. It is Jesus who has kept it for us. The law condemns us because we cannot help but fail to keep it (Galatians 3:10-14). In Christ, there is no condemnation.

We become law keepers only by putting our faith in Jesus, who himself alone is our righteousness. Don't let anyone tell you otherwise. We don't begin to have what it takes to stand righteous in the presence of God. Jesus does, and the gospel is God's good news that God has *in Christ* made us everything he wants us to be. He has already done it.

Because we can't see any physical evidence of that, we can know it only by faith in the One who gives us the gift (Galatians 3:22). That's why God pleads, "Trust me!"

One other point, while we're on the topic: When Jesus refers to the law in Matthew 5, he is obviously not talking about the whole old covenant law. Otherwise we would all be wearing blue tassels and phylacteries and sacrificing lambs. Whatever way Jesus is defining "law" here, we are law keepers only through faith in him, not through our ever-bungling efforts to avoid sin.

Devotion born of trust

Jesus is our Savior, Lord and Teacher. We can start with the confidence that we are indeed forgiven and saved, purely as God's free gift to us through his Son. Jesus is our Savior. With that sure trust in God's true word of grace, and because his love is growing in us from the moment we believed him, we can (in his strength) devote ourselves to doing whatever he says. Jesus is our Lord, which also means he is our Master, our King, our Ruler.

We come to know God better and understand his will more fully by listening to what he has given us about himself in the Bible. Some of the ways we listen to him are: reading the Bible, listening to our teachers in the church (Ephesians 4:11-14), reading devotional writing by Christian teachers, as well as "listening" to God's prompting of our wills during prayer. Jesus is our Teacher.

"So, you're saying that obedience really is important?"

Yes. We are commanded to obey God. If we believe in God's mercy and love through Christ, then the Holy Spirit works in us to lead us to desire to obey God, and to actually obey him.

"So, that's what we mean by 'bearing fruit'?"

Exactly. We bear fruit, but it is not really that we are doing it ourselves. It is the Holy Spirit working in us to bear it. But the beauty is that the Spirit makes us able to cooperate with his work in such a way that we are indeed pleasing God and bring glory to him through Christ.

"But, back to the original problem. We fall short a lot."

Yes, we do. But again, we can rest in the confidence that God has already forgiven us, already saved us and already made us his saints. In that confidence we don't have to languish in discouragement; we can get up and continue our struggle against sin, resting in the sure and unlimited love of God. Our failures, lapses and sins are not the measure of who we are in Christ; his faithful word and his victory for us are.

"So, we really are in a battle against sin."

Of course we are. But the victory does not depend on us; it depends on Christ, and he has already won. We are living out the implications of his victory in our personal struggles, and because the victory is already his, our God-given part in his victory is not at stake.

Our part has already been secured by the Son of God. By God's gracious will for us, we are indeed safe in Christ, and we can take joy and rest in God's presence if we believe his word about that. (If we won't believe God's word about that, then, of course, we won't be able to rest in his joy. God doesn't force people not to stew in hell, but hell is not his choice for them.)

Teaching right living

"But shouldn't the church teach people

right ways to live?"

Yes, it should. And as it does so, it needs to keep in mind that teaching right ways to live is not the same as teaching people how to be loved by God or how to be saved. The two must be kept separate. God already loves us and has already saved us, even though we are sinners. Right living can help us avoid loads of trouble, pain and heartache, but it can't make God love us or save us any more than he already has.

"But doesn't it please God when we live right?"

Yes, it does. It pleases God because he loves to see us living in tune with him and with the persons he has made us to be in Christ. Likewise, he hates to see us torturing ourselves and living in fear and despair, out of harmony with the new creation he has made of us in Christ. Do we stop loving our children when they ignore our rules and warnings and get themselves hurt? God loves us even more than we are able to love our children.

With the new covenant in Christ, God has eclipsed the old system of reward for righteousness and punishment for sin (Hebrews 10:9-10). That system bound everybody under sin and death (Galatians 3:21-22). Because of our utter helplessness, weakness and bondage, he has taken on himself for us the consequences of sin, and he, as the righteous Human for all humans, shares with us the rewards of his righteousness. Those rewards for righteousness are reconciliation and unity with God. We receive everything Christ has done for us only one way: *in faith,* and without faith, or trust in God that his word of the gospel is true, we will not accept his love, reconciliation and eternal life.

What this means is that we must get rid of the notion that our behavior determines how God feels about us. God alone determines how God feels about us, not our good works or our bad works. God decided before all time that he loves us, and his Son is the perfect Human for us in our place so that God's love for us may be complete and eternal precisely because its essence is his love for his Son. He will be faithful even when we are not faithful,

because in Christ we are reconciled with the Father, and it is in Christ that he loves us for the sake of Christ.

So, when we teach people to live rightly, we are teaching them, and ourselves, how to live free of the bondage and pain that accompanies sin. We are not teaching how to be better than others, more loved of God than others, more important to God than others, or even more righteous than others. That is because our righteousness is only in Christ, and we walk in that righteousness only by faith in him, not by avoiding illicit drugs, sex and violence.

To be sure, life is indescribably smoother if we do avoid illicit sex, drugs and violence. But we need to remember that the blood of Jesus is just as necessary for indifference, laziness, stubbornness, selfishness, gossip, judgmentalness, secret envy and the like as it is for blatant adultery, grand theft, heroin trafficking and murder. We are all sinners, regardless of how much success we achieve in right living, and we all stand in need of mercy at the foot of Jesus' cross.

Faith in the faithful One

Still, the church does have the role of teaching right living, and every one of us does have an obligation to God to commit ourselves to doing everything God wants us to do. God gives us all this instruction about right living because it is good for us, and because it reflects the way he is toward us. The more we trust in God to save us from our sins, the more we desire to turn away from sin. Yet it is God himself, reigning in his divine freedom to save sinners in Christ, who actually delivers us from sin.

When we pore over pornography or engage in casual sex, we are reinforcing empty illusions about human intimacy that corrupt our ability to find real and fulfilling intimacy. In other words, we are robbing ourselves of the very thing that led us to the porn site or the one-night stand in the first place, the need for an honest, trusting, intimate relationship.

Besides that, we are defrauding and taking advantage of other children of God for our own gratification, whether by indulging in photographic images of their shame and ignorance, or by participating with them in their own painful journey of humiliation and indignity. We are ignoring God's warning to avoid the attractive but dangerous trap door in our quest for the real thing he made us to need and desire.

When we resort to fraud or larceny, we are turning our backs on God's promise to be our provider and see us through. We are finding our own solutions to our needs or wants, overlooking the consequences our actions will bring to others, and robbing ourselves of the peace of heart that God wants us to experience with him through the deepening trust that comes of patience.

Church of forgiven sinners

Whatever instruction the church gives in paths of right living needs to be framed in humility and love. The same Bible from which we draw God's pearls of wisdom about human conduct provides us his testimony about his Son who died to save us from our failure to heed perfectly such instruction.

Every teacher of the Bible is himself or herself a sinner. As fellow sinners with the world, then, we must guard against the tendency of the church to allow its proclamation to descend into a mere rattle of condemnation against people who don't walk in the precepts of the Bible. To become a voice of condemnation does violence to the gospel and reduces the Christian proclamation into merely another religion vainly trying to hold together a powerless façade of human morality.

The church (I'm talking about the people, not the buildings) is the place in the world where the gospel visibly intersects human history. It is the place where sinners have found out they are clean and forgiven, and where these forgiven sinners continually offer to God their worship, praises and thanksgiving.

It is where this good news of the gospel is celebrated and affirmed for everyone who will listen. It is where the love of Christ can take root in the world. It is where men, women and children of faith have been made able, by their Savior and Lord in whom they trust, to be like him in the world—a friend of despised people and sinners.

Wherever the church comes into contact with the world, the world should be the better for it. The poor should be hearing good news. Prisoners should be hearing about the release that transcends physical freedom. People in bondage to personal and societal sin should be finding mercy, kindness and hope.

The cleansing, purifying light of Christ's truth and love and peace should be finding its way into dark fears, lost hopes and tortured souls. And this should be happening because the crucified Christ is risen and living in his people, not because the church found an ancient book of laws it can use to more effectively declare sinners condemned.

Jesus did not come to condemn the world, but to save it (John 3:17). That is why the gospel is *good news!* How sweet it is when the proclamation of the church is the same good news.

J. Michael Feazell

Responding to Jesus With Prayer

How do we respond to the risen Jesus? The book of Hebrews tells us: Since Jesus has risen into heaven as our great high priest, then we can have confidence to enter God's presence, and because of that, we should enter his presence (Hebrews 10:19-22).

"Since we have a great high priest who has gone through the heavens, Jesus the Son of God, let us hold firmly to the faith we profess.... Let us then approach the throne of grace with confidence, so that we may receive mercy and find grace to help us in our time of need" (Hebrews 4:14-16). In other words, since Jesus has risen from the dead, we should pray, and we should do it with confidence.

The risen Jesus makes a difference in our lives through prayer. Because he is now in heaven, we have the guarantee that our prayers will be heard. We pray "in Jesus' name" — he intercedes for us — he prays for us! God listens to us just as well as he listens to Jesus himself.

There are many misconceptions about prayer. Let's discuss what prayer is, and how we pray.

Prayer: a cry for help

Some people make prayer sound like a duty, as a work that faithful Christians must perform. Some make it sound like we ought to pray seven times a day, or three times a day, or all night long, or rise before dawn, or spend at least two hours every day, following the example of this or that famous person.

I think Christians should pray not as a duty, but out of need. After all, prayers are requests. There are no biblical commands for us to pray at certain times or in certain ways. We are not told to follow Jesus' example in praying all night, or Daniel's example of facing Jerusalem.

But Scripture everywhere assumes that God's people do pray. We are not told to pray for specific lengths of time, but all the time (1 Thessalonians 5:17; Ephesians 6:18). We are not told to kneel or stand or lie on the floor when we pray. Rather, we are told to pray while doing everything (Philippians 4:6).

Why so much prayer?

Prayer is, in its simplest sense, a request. The most common Hebrew and Greek words for prayer mean "ask." Whenever we ask God for anything, we are praying — and it is right that we ask. Paul told the Philippians to ask for whatever they wanted (Philippians 4:6).

That is why we should pray: We are to ask God for the things we need. The better we know ourselves, the more we will know that we are incredibly needy people. Of ourselves, we can do nothing. If we want to accomplish anything worthwhile, we must seek God's help. We must depend on him. Prayer is a cry for help. And since our needs never end, our prayers should never cease.

Rely on God

Self-reliance is sin. It is arrogant for us tiny creatures to think that we can do whatever we want, that we can control our own destinies, that we can decide for ourselves what is right and what is wrong. Humans do not have the wisdom or the power. The universe exists only because Christ is upholding it by the word of his power (Hebrews 1:3). We exist only because our Creator supplies our needs (Acts 14:17).

Yet (I speak from experience) even believers sometimes forget about our minute-by-minute need for God, and we may go through the day with scarcely a thought, scarcely a thanks for what God is doing for us. He is upholding us even as we ignore him.

Even when we face problems, we sometimes struggle on and on, trying to solve the problems with our own strength, with our own strategies, instead of realizing that needs and desires should be shared with God in prayer (Philippians 4:6). We act as if everything depends on us, when everything actually depends on God. He knows our needs, and he wants us to trust him.

Thankfully, the Holy Spirit intercedes for us, even when we are too unthinking to ask for ourselves (Romans 8:26-27). The Holy Spirit stands in the gap and helps us in ways that we do not know. So when we fail to pray constantly, the Holy Spirit steps in. Even so, we cannot turn all prayer over to the Holy Spirit and let him do all the talking while we go through life unawares.

We need to pray. We will be happier, less stressed, more fulfilled, if we keep in mind that we live in the presence of God, that in him we live and move and have our being (Acts 17:28). The more we are aware of God, the better our understanding of life will be, for God is the frame of reference that we need. When we see life in his context, we see it accurately.

God is not a genie who grants our every wish. That is because we often do not understand what we really need. We may pray for escape from a trial, but God is using that trial to teach us something far more important than temporary comfort. We may pray for a neighbor to come to Christ, but God knows this may not be the right time. God may want us to be more involved in the person's life.

Frankly, there are so many things wrong with this world that we should have many desires, for ourselves, for our churches and for this world. We have much to pray about.

Prayer is our cry for help. In prayer, we admit that we are not self-sufficient, that we cannot handle everything on our own. In prayer, we acknowledge a relationship between God and us, a relationship in which God has promised to provide our needs and to bless us in ways he knows are best. Prayer is an act of worship, for it acknowledges that God has power and that he is dependable.

Thanks

God supplies our needs, and it is appropriate for us to thank him for doing so. Every breath we take is a gift from him. All the beauty in nature is a gift from him. The wonderful variety of sights, sounds, smells and textures is a gift from him. Our conversations with God should include thanks as well as requests. This is a form of praise, to acknowledge that he is the giver of every good thing.

As we thank God, we remind ourselves of our place in the universe—a place of great honor as a target of God's affection, and a place of dependence on his graciousness. Giving thanks is a way to know who we are and why we exist; it reminds us that the universe functions only through his gift.

Some may say: "I already know that. Why do I have to keep saying it?" I think it is only through saying it that we are really mindful of it; it is too easy for us to go through the day without really being aware that life functions best if we remember it as a gift. This is supported by the biblical commands for us to be thankful, and to continually give thanks to God in our prayers (1 Thessalonians 5:17-18).

The Bible similarly tells us to pray with persistence, giving the same request again and again. We know by faith that God heard us the first time, and that he knows our earnestness even without our persistence, so I conclude that his command for our persistence is really for our own good. We need to tell ourselves again and again what the desires of our heart are, and that we trust God with them.

This does not mean that prayer is just a means of talking to ourselves, or of reminding ourselves of abstract truths. No, Scripture assures us that prayer is a genuine conversation with God. Our requests really go to heaven, and are really heard and answered by God. Our thanks really go to God; we must see him in the picture. Often, it is in prayer that God speaks to us, when we grow in our understanding of what he wants us to think or do.

We have never-ending thanks for what God does for us day to day, thanks for the promises he has made for our future, and thanks for what he has already done in Christ to ensure that future. Our thankfulness for Jesus Christ turns naturally to dedicating ourselves to doing what God wants us to do. We eagerly want to respond with faithful allegiance to one who loves us so much.

Our existence, our joy, our pleasures, our sanity, are all dependent on God's day-to-day favor toward us through Jesus Christ. We have much to be thankful for—indeed, everything we have and ever hope to have is a gift for which we need to be thankful.

Our thanks should include our appreciation for who God is, and here our prayers blend thanks and praise. We praise his power, his wisdom, his mercy, the beauty of his love. We praise him for who he is, not just for what he gives us, for in actuality, he gives us himself.

My cry for help

Finally, my friends, I ask you to pray for your local church. It takes God's strength for your congregation to make a difference for the kingdom in your community. You need divine help to work together and to tackle the impossible. In other words, you need to pray. Pray for your local leaders, too. Those who lead worship music need divine blessing. Those who speak should speak the words of God (1 Peter 4:11), and this cannot be done from human wisdom.

Pray for me, too. Even the most talented human could not do the work God sets before me. I need divine help, and I pray for it, and I receive it. And just as Paul asked his churches to pray for him (Colossians 4:2-3, etc.), I ask you to pray for me, too. The difficulties I face personally, and the difficulties I face in serving the church, mean that I need God's help. We all need help. We all need to pray.

Joseph Tkach

The Role of the Law in Christian Life

At the heart of Paul's theology, in the center of his good news message about Jesus Christ, is the doctrine of justification by faith. God accepts us when we believe in his Son — he accepts us as righteous on the basis of what Christ has done, not on the basis of what we have done.

This may be interpreted as bad news by people who think they've done pretty well. Such people tend not to like the idea that God would lower his standards and accept people who aren't as good as they are, who haven't tried as hard as they have.

However, this is incredibly good news for those of us who know that we have messed up pretty badly, and that we could never redeem ourselves, no matter how many good things we do. We realize there is no special merit in doing the things we should have done. We know we can never make up for the fact that we have let God down — all we can do is rely on his mercy.

A demonstration of justice

The good news is that God has guaranteed that mercy. He sent his Son to die for us. Because of Jesus' death for us, God remains righteous even though he declares the wicked to be justified (Romans 4:5; 5:6). God presented Jesus "as a sacrifice of atonement…to demonstrate his justice" in leaving sin unpunished (Romans 3:25).

As odd as it may sound, the death of Christ was a demonstration of God's justice — because it shows that God has the right to forgive sin. In forgiving us, God does not just pretend that sin does not matter. Rather, he shows how much it matters by sending his Son to die for us, that is, by taking our sins upon himself. God has done everything that was needed so that he can justify the ungodly — he does not violate his own righteousness when he declares us righteous and acceptable.

This is grace. Since Christ died for us, we can be forgiven. Paul makes it clear that we are justified by faith (Acts 13:38; Romans 3:22, 26; 4:24; 5:1; etc.). We are accepted by God as his children — this is the heart of the good news of God's kingdom. We don't deserve it — it comes by grace — but it is guaranteed by God. The means of salvation is a gift of God (Ephesians 2:8).

Which law to obey?

So far, so good, say some people. God brings you into his kingdom if you have faith. Now that you are here, they say, you should obey God. Specifically, you should obey the commandments he has given his people, commandments we find in the Holy Scriptures — clear commands regarding circumcision, festivals, Sabbaths, etc.

This was the Galatian heresy: false teachers said that Christians had to have both the old and the new covenants, both Moses and Christ, both law and faith, both merit and grace. It was an emphasis on continuity, on covenant faithfulness, on living by every word of God. It sounded logical, it sounded worshipful, but it was fundamentally flawed.

It is true that Christians should obey God, but the Law of Moses is the wrong law. The book of Galatians makes it clear that the Law of Moses is obsolete. Its authority has expired, and we are no longer "under the law." Paul even says that the Sinai covenant produced a religion of bondage (Galatians 4:24-25), but that Christians are free.

We are children of the promise, children of the free woman (3:29; 4:31). "It is for freedom that Christ has set us free. Stand firm, then, and do not let yourselves be burdened again by a yoke of slavery" (5:1). If you try to be justified by the law, then you will be alienated from Christ, and you will have fallen out of grace (verse 4). Paul emphasizes that we "were called to be free" (verse 13).

Not only is the old covenant the wrong law, Paul's point is that we cannot be saved by any law. "If righteousness could be gained through the law, Christ died for nothing!" (Galatians 2:21). If a different law could have given us life, then God would have given us the life-giving law. But the very nature of law prevents it from giving us life. All a law can do is set forth requirements and prescribe penalties for failure. Since we all fail at some point, the law prescribes penalties. It cannot give us life.

Since we never achieve perfect obedience in this life, we can never look to law as a standard for salvation. We can never say, Grace covered my past sins, but now my salvation depends on my obedience. If that were true, we would all be doomed. Our acceptance with God is *always* on the basis of grace and faith, and never on the basis of our obedience. We can never say that we deserve eternity with our Creator.

Loyalty to God

What then is the role of law in a Christian's life? We know that Christians do not "sin deliberately so that grace may abound." We know that Christians want to please the God who saved them. We know that sin caused our Savior to suffer and die, so we do not want to have anything to do with sin. We want to obey God as best we can, even though we know we can't do it perfectly. We are obeying not because we earn anything through obedience, but because we love God and want to obey him. We are his children, not hired servants.

Our relationship with God is based on faith, not a list of rules. It is a personal loyalty to God, a loyalty that leads us to obey, but a loyalty that always looks directly to God, not to a list of rules as a gauge of our relationship. We never boast of obedience, nor despair of falling short. God has already made fully sufficient provision for justifying us even when we were wicked and ungodly.

When we are used to thinking of religion as a list of rules, Paul's teachings seem self-contradictory. If our salvation doesn't depend on the law, the reasoning seems to go, then why would anybody want to obey? Surely there has to be some kind of threat involved, or else the people of God would quickly jump into immorality. I exaggerate to make a point. The point is that we need to think about law in a different way, and we need to think of Christianity in a different way.

When people see laws and commands only in terms of reward and punishment, then they are naturally bewildered about the role of law when it is neither a basis of reward nor of punishment. Christ has removed it from such roles.

Why then should anybody obey? We need to reorient our thinking about law — away from thoughts of reward and punishment, away from a standard that we are measured by. We need to think of God's laws as a matter of personal loyalty, as integral and natural to a personal relationship.

A new form of righteousness

God's law, which for us is the law of Christ (1 Corinthians 9:21), provides forgiveness for every transgression (except that of rejecting the forgiveness provided by Christ). This forgiveness is received by faith, not by penance, not by good works, not by our paying a price (Romans 3:28). This is not the kind of "law" that we are used to.

Christianity is a faith, not a list of rules. It is a belief in God's grace, in his love, in his promise and power to forgive and cleanse. God grants his children not only forgiveness of sin, but also a new life — a life in Christ. Where once we lived for ourselves, now we live for Christ. And we do so because the Holy Spirit resides in us, not because we have suddenly become righteous ourselves.

The New Testament does give us rules and behavioral expectations, but these should be seen as the *result* of a faith relationship, not as the *basis* for it. They are not the measurement of our righteous standing before God — and that's good, because we all fall short. We have no righteousness of our own, but when we put our confidence in Christ, God counts us as righteous (Romans 4:23-25). We have peace with God, not directly ourselves, but through Christ (Romans 5:1-2).

There is now a new righteousness that God has made known (Romans 3:21). It is a righteousness that does not come from the law. It is a righteousness that comes only from God himself (verse 22). The law and the prophets testified to this new righteousness, but it does not come from them; it comes only from God (verse 21).

This new righteousness comes from God through faith, to all who believe. Everyone is a sinner, and the only way we can have righteousness, the only way we can have peace with God, is by God giving it to us (verses 22-23). All who believe are made righteous, or justified, freely, by God's grace through the redemption that comes through Jesus Christ (verses 23-24).

The fruit of the Spirit

Our righteousness, then, is not really ours — it is Christ's. God attributes the righteousness of the only righteous human, Jesus, to us, if we are united to him by faith. More than that, he actually works in us to live righteously. That is why the good that Christians do is called "fruit of the Spirit" (Galatians 5:16-26). It is fruit of the Spirit because it is done only because God lives in us. The fruit is his, not ours.

God produces the fruit of the Spirit in us through faith, not because we "set our wills" or "try really hard" to be good. The root of righteous living is faith, not personal virtue. Sin is no longer our master, because we are not under law, but under grace (Romans 6:14).

We strive to be found in Christ (Philippians 3:7-9), not to be found personally good. Christians are not pursuing a righteousness of our own that comes from the law, but the righteousness that comes from God through faith in Christ (verse 9). When we pursue knowing and loving God, our lives will naturally (because God is at work in us) begin to produce righteous fruit. We can't become righteous by trying to become righteous; we can become righteous only by trusting God, who makes believers righteous.

When our minds are set on knowing and loving Christ, the Spirit brings forth righteous fruit in us (Romans 8:5). When our minds are set on the desires of sin, we bring forth fruit of sin. The way to righteousness is through faith, and faith is strengthened when we are spending our time with Christ. It is through Christ, and not through ourselves, that we fully meet the righteous requirements of the law (verses 3-4).

As Christ loved us, so we are to love one another (John 13:34-35). In this kind of love, the whole law is summed up (Galatians 5:14). That is why John sums up God's law for us (which Paul calls the law of Christ) in the commands that we are to believe in Christ and that we are to love one another (1 John 3:23-24). Only when our trust rests in Christ can we love one another as he loved us.

Communion with Christ

It is only because we are in Christ that we are able to live righteously. And that is not because we can do so, but because he already defeated sin for us. It is God who makes us stand firm in Christ (2 Corinthians 1:20). It is not our doing. All the glory is his because he has done every bit of it.

When we are in close communion, or fellowship, with Christ, we remember who we are and to whom we belong. We remember how destructive sin is, and that we have been set free from its power (Romans 8:1-4). We are inclined to heed the prompting of the Spirit and follow his lead (verses 12-16).

Our minds are led by the Spirit when we are spending time with Christ. But when we put our minds on the things of the sinful nature, we forget that we belong to Christ, that he has defeated the power of sin for us, that we are saved and that God loves us. All those things remain true, but our ability to see and believe them becomes clouded. In that condition, we are easy prey for the sinful nature.

We are no match for sin. It "so easily entangles" us, Hebrews 12:1 says. But when we are in Christ, the victory is already won. We do not have to let sin rule, because it no longer has power over us. How can we "throw off" sin? By keeping our eyes fixed on Jesus (verse 2), the author and the perfecter of our faith. Our "feeble arms" and "weak knees" (verse 12) receive strength when our time and attention are kept on knowing and loving Christ.

That is why spiritual disciplines such as Bible reading, prayer, meditation, simplicity, service, worship, etc. are so basic to the Christian life. These are means God has given us to stay "tuned into" the real truth about God and about ourselves: God loves us, we are his beloved children, he has saved us and he has freed us from the power of sin. Through such means, we remain "close to" God and have the courage to stand in the power of Christ's resurrection — power he has given to all his children (Romans 8:10-11).

God's grace and power are wonderful beyond description, brothers and sisters. May we continually grow in our faithful walk with our Lord, Savior and Teacher, Jesus Christ.

Joseph Tkach

The End Is a New Beginning

If there is no future, Paul writes, then it would be foolish to have faith in Christ (1 Cor. 15:19). Prophecy is an essential and very encouraging part of the Christian faith. Bible prophecy announces tremendously good news for us. We will find it most encouraging if we focus on the core message, not debatable details.

The purpose of prophecy

Prophecy is not an end in itself—it declares a more important truth. God is reconciling humanity to himself, forgiving our sins and restoring us to friendship with him. Prophecy proclaims this reality.

Prophecy exists not just to predict events, but to point us toward God. It tells us who God is, what he is like, what he is doing, and what he wants us to do. Prophecy urges people to receive reconciliation to God through faith in Jesus Christ.

Many specific prophecies were fulfilled in Old Testament times, and we still await the fulfillment of others. But the sharp focus of all prophecy is redemption—the forgiveness of sins and eternal life that comes through Jesus Christ. Prophecy assures us that God is in control of history (Dan. 4:17); it strengthens our faith in Christ (John 14:29) and gives us hope for the future (1 Thess. 4:13-18).

Moses and the prophets wrote about Christ, including the fact that he would be killed and resurrected (Luke 24:27, 46). They also foretold events after Jesus' resurrection, such as the preaching of the gospel (v. 47).

Prophecy points us to salvation in Jesus Christ. If we don't get salvation, prophecy will do us no good. It is only through Christ that we can be part of the kingdom that will last forever (Dan. 7:13-14, 27).

The Bible proclaims the return of Christ, the last judgment and eternal punishment and rewards. With these predictions, prophecy warns humanity of the *need* for salvation as well as announces the guarantee of that salvation. Prophecy tells us that God calls us to account (Jude 14-15), that he wants us saved (2 Pet. 3:9) and that he has in fact saved us (1 John 2:1-2). It assures us that all evil will be defeated and that all injustice and suffering will end (1 Cor. 15:25; Rev. 21:4).

Prophecy encourages believers that our labors are not in vain. We will be rescued from persecutions, vindicated and rewarded. Prophecy reminds us of God's love and faithfulness, and helps us be faithful to him (2 Pet. 3:10-15; 1 John 3:2-3). By reminding us that all physical treasures are temporary, prophecy encourages us to treasure the as-yet-unseen things of God and our eternal relationship with him.

Zechariah points to prophecy as a call to repentance (Zech. 1:3-4). God warns of punishment, but looks for repentance. As shown in the story of Jonah, God is willing to reverse his predictions, if only the people will turn to him. The goal of prophecy is to turn us to God, who has a wonderful future for us; the goal is not to satisfy our itch to know "secret" things.

A need for caution

How can we understand Bible prophecy? Only with great caution. Well-meaning prophecy buffs have brought disrepute on the gospel with erroneous predictions and misguided dogmatism. Because of such misuse of prophecy, some people ridicule the Bible and scoff at Christ himself. The list of failed predictions should be a sober warning that personal conviction is no guarantee of truth. Since failed predictions can weaken faith, we must be cautious.

We should not need exciting predictions to make us serious about spiritual growth and Christian living. A knowledge of dates and other details (even if they turn out to be correct) is no guarantee of salvation. Our focus should be on Christ, not on assessing the credentials of potential Beast powers.

An obsession on prophecy means that we are not giving enough emphasis to the gospel. People need to repent and trust Christ whether or not his return is near, whether or not there will be a millennium, whether or not America is identified in Bible prophecy.

Why is prophecy so difficult to interpret? Perhaps the biggest reason is that it is often given in figurative language. The original readers may have known what the symbols meant, but since we live in a different culture and time, we cannot always be sure.

Psalm 18 is an example of figurative language. Its poetry describes the way that God delivered David from his enemies (v. 1). David uses several images for this: escape from a grave (vv. 4-6), earthquake (v. 7), heavenly signs (vv. 8-14), even a rescue at sea (vv. 15-18). These things did not literally happen, but biblical poetry uses such imaginative figures of speech. This is true of prophecy, too.

Isaiah 40:3-4 tells us that mountains will be brought low and a road made straight—but this is not intended to be taken literally. Luke 3:4-6 indicates that this prophecy was fulfilled by John the Baptist. The prophecy was not about mountains and roads at all.

Joel 2:28-29 predicted that God's Spirit would be poured out on "all flesh," but Peter said it was fulfilled with several dozen on Pentecost (Acts 2:16-17). The dreams and visions that Joel predicted may not have been literal, but Peter did not press the prophesied details that far—and neither should we. When we are dealing with figurative language, the fulfillment is not intended to match the prophecy literally.

These factors affect the way people interpret biblical prophecy. One reader may prefer a literal meaning, another may prefer a figurative meaning, and it may be impossible to prove which is correct.

This forces us to focus on the big picture, not the details. We are looking through frosted glass, not a magnifying glass.

In several major areas of prophecy, there is no Christian consensus. Ideas about the rapture, the tribulation, the millennium, the intermediate state and hell are widely debated. (See our website for articles on some of these subjects.) These details are not essential.

Although they are part of God's plan, and important to him, it is not essential that we get all the right answers—especially if we think less of people who have different answers. Our attitude is more important than having all the right answers.

Perhaps we can compare prophecy to a journey. We do not need to know exactly where our destination is, what path we will take, or how fast we will go. What we need most of all is to trust in our trailblazer, Jesus Christ. He is the only one who knows the way, and we won't make it without him. Just stick with him—he will take care of the details.

With these cautions in mind, let's look at some basic Christian beliefs about the future.

The return of Christ

The benchmark event for our beliefs about the future is the second coming of Christ. There is tremendous consensus on the fact that Jesus will return.

Jesus told his disciples he would "come again" (John 14:3). He also warned his disciples not to waste their time trying to figure out when that will be (Matt. 24:36). He criticized people who thought that time was short (Matt. 25:1-13) and those who thought there would be a long delay (Matt. 24:45-51). No matter what, our responsibility is the same: to be ready.

Angels told the disciples that just as surely as Jesus had gone into heaven he would also return (Acts 1:11). He will be "revealed from heaven in blazing fire with his powerful angels" (2 Thess. 1:7). Paul called it "the glorious appearing of our great God and Savior, Jesus Christ" (Titus 2:13). Peter said that Jesus would be "revealed" (1 Pet. 1:7, 13). John also said he would appear (1 John 2:28), and Heb. 9:28 says that "he will appear a second time ... to bring salvation to those who are waiting for him."

There will be "a loud command, with the voice of the archangel and with the trumpet call of God" (1 Thess. 4:16). There will be no mistake about it.

Two other events will occur when Christ returns: the resurrection and the judgment. Paul writes that the dead in Christ will rise when the Lord comes, and believers still alive then will also rise to meet the Lord as he comes to earth (1 Thess. 4:16-17). "At the last trumpet," Paul writes, "the dead will be raised imperishable, and we will be changed" (1 Cor. 15:52). We will be transformed—made glorious, powerful, imperishable, immortal and spiritual (vv. 42-44).

Matt. 24:31 seems to describe this event from another perspective: Christ "will send his angels with a loud trumpet call, and they will gather his elect from the four winds, from one end of the heavens to the other." In the parable of the weeds, Jesus said that he will send out his angels at the end of the age, "and they will weed out of his kingdom everything that causes sin and all who do evil" (Matt. 13:40-41).

"The Son of Man is going to come in his Father's glory with his angels, and then he will reward each person according to what he has done" (Matt. 16:27). Judgment is also part of the master's return in the parable of the faithful servant (Matt. 24:45-51) and the parable of the talents (Matt. 25:14-30).

Paul says that when the Lord comes, "he will bring to light what is hidden in darkness and will expose the motives of men's hearts. At that time each will receive his praise from God" (1 Cor. 4:5). Of course, God already knows each person, and in that sense, judgment occurs long before Christ's return. But it will be then that judgment is made public for everyone.

The fact that we will live again, and that we will be rewarded, is tremendous encouragement. After discussing the resurrection, Paul exclaims: "Thanks be to God! He gives us the victory through our Lord Jesus Christ. Therefore, my dear brothers, stand firm. Let nothing move you. Always give yourselves fully to the work of the Lord, because you know that your labor in the Lord is not in vain" (1 Cor. 15:57-58).

The last days

To arouse interest, some prophecy teachers ask, "Are we living in the last days?" The correct answer is "yes"—and it has been correct for 2,000 years. Peter quoted a prophecy about the last days and said it applied to his own day (Acts 2:16-17). So did the author of Hebrews (Heb. 1:2). The last days are a lot longer than some people think. Jesus triumphed over the enemy and began a new age.

Wars and troubles have plagued humanity for thousands of years. Will it get worse? Probably. Then it might get better, and then worse again. Or it will get better for some people while growing worse for others. The misery index goes up and down throughout history, and this will probably continue.

But through the ages, it seems that some Christians want it to get worse. They almost hope for a Great Tribulation, described as the worst time of trouble the world will ever see (Matt. 24:21). They have a fascination with the Antichrist, the Beast, the man of sin, and other enemies of God. They often believe that any given terrible event indicates that Christ will soon return.

It is true that Jesus predicted a time of terrible tribulation (Matt. 24:21), but most of what he predicted in Matthew 24 was fulfilled in the siege of Jerusalem, A.D. 70. Jesus was warning his disciples about events that they would live to see, and that people in Judea would need to flee to the mountains (v. 16).

Jesus predicted constant tribulation until his return. "In this world you will have trouble," Jesus said (John 16:33). Many of his disciples gave their lives for their belief in Jesus. Trials are part of the Christian life; God does not protect us from all our problems (Acts 14:22; 2 Tim. 3:12; 1 Pet. 4:12). Even in the apostolic age, antichrists were at work (1 John 2:18,22; 2 John 7).

Is a Great Tribulation predicted for the future? Many Christians believe so, and perhaps they are right. But millions of Christians throughout the world face persecution today. Many are killed. For each of them, the tribulation cannot get any worse than it already is. Terrible times have afflicted Christians for two millennia. Perhaps the Great Tribulation is a lot longer than many people think.

Our Christian responsibilities are the same whether the Tribulation is near or far — or whether it has already begun. Speculation about the future does not help us become more like Christ, and when it is used to pressure people into repentance, it is sadly misused. Speculation about the Tribulation is not a good use of our time.

The millennium

Revelation 20 speaks of a 1,000-year reign of Christ and the saints. Some Christians interpret this literally as a 1,000-year kingdom that Christ will set up when he returns. Other Christians view the 1,000-year period figuratively, symbolizing the rule of Christ in the church before his return.

For example, the number 1,000 may be used figuratively (Deut. 7:9; Ps. 50:10), and there is no way to prove that it must be taken literally in Revelation. Revelation is written in a highly figurative style. No other scriptures speak of a temporary kingdom to be set up when Christ returns. Indeed, verses such as Daniel 2:44 suggest that the kingdom will be eternal, without any crisis 1,000 years later.

If there is a millennial kingdom after Christ returns, then the wicked will be resurrected and judged 1,000 years after the righteous are (Rev. 20:5). But Jesus' parables do not suggest any such interval (Matt. 25:31-46; John 5:28-29). The millennium was not part of Jesus' gospel. Paul wrote that the righteous and the wicked will be resurrected on the same day (2 Thess. 1:6-10).

Many more details could be discussed on this topic, but it is not necessary here. Scriptures can be gathered in support of each view. But no matter what a person thinks about the millennium, this much is clear: The time period described in Revelation 20 will eventually end, and will be followed by an eternal and glorious new heavens and new earth, which are greater, better and longer than the millennium. So, when we think about the wonderful world tomorrow, we might want to focus on the eternal, perfect kingdom, not a temporary phase. We have an eternity to look forward to!

An eternity of joy

What will eternity be like? We know only in part (1 Cor. 13:9; 1 John 3:2), because all our words and ideas are based on the world today. Jesus described our eternal reward in several ways: It will be like finding a treasure, or inheriting many possessions, or ruling a kingdom, or attending a wedding banquet. It is like all these things, but so much better that it could also be said that it is nothing like them. Our eternity with God will be better than our words can describe.

David put it this way: "You will fill me with joy in your presence, with eternal pleasures at your right hand" (Ps. 16:11). The best part of eternity will be living with God, being like him, seeing him as he really is, knowing him more fully (1 John 3:2). This is the purpose for which God made us, and this will satisfy us and give us joy forevermore.

And in 10,000 years, with zillions yet to come, we will look back on our lives today, smiling at the troubles we had, marveling at how quickly God did his work when we were mortal. It was only the beginning, and there will be no end.

Michael Morrison

The Resurrection: Our Hope for the Future

The apostle Paul tells us, "If there is no resurrection of the dead, then not even Christ has been raised. And if Christ has not been raised, our preaching is useless and so is your faith" (1 Corinthians 15:13-14). In other words, if there isn't any resurrection, our faith is pointless. If Christianity is simply about this physical life and then we die to never exist again, then it really doesn't matter what we do or how we live or what we believe.

Paul said in verse 19, "If only for this life we have hope in Christ, we are to be pitied more than all people." If there is no future for us, then our lives would more sensibly focus on having a good time while we can (verse 32). If there is no resurrection, then it would not be helpful for us to believe in Christ, because that might mean sacrifice and persecution.

If there is no resurrection, then the crucifixion of Christ didn't achieve anything for us, and we are still in our sins (verse 17). But there is a resurrection, not only for Christ but also for us, and this is an important part of the Christian faith. Let's look at the significance of this doctrine—not just for the future, but for day-to-day living, as well. It is relevant every day of our lives.

Biblical evidence

The Old Testament doesn't say much about the resurrection. Ezekiel says a little bit, and Daniel says a little bit, but our belief is based mostly on the New Testament. Jesus talked about the resurrection in several parables. He even called himself the resurrection and the life (John 11:25). The resurrection is mentioned several times in the book of Acts, and in the book of Hebrews, but in most passages we don't learn much except that there will be a resurrection.

There are two passages that describe the resurrection in a little more detail—Paul's first letter to the church in Thessalonica, and his first letter to the Corinthians.

In 1 Thessalonians 4:13-18, Paul writes,

> Brothers and sisters, we do not want you to be uninformed about those who sleep in death, so that you do not grieve like the rest of mankind, who have no hope. For we believe that Jesus died and rose again, and so we believe that God will bring with Jesus those who have fallen asleep in him. According to the Lord's word, we tell you that we who are still alive, who are left until the coming of the Lord, will certainly not precede those who have fallen asleep. For the Lord himself will come down from heaven, with a loud command, with the voice of the archangel and with the trumpet call of God, and the dead in Christ will rise first. After that, we who are still alive and are left will be caught up together with them in the clouds to meet the Lord in the air. And so we will be with the Lord forever. Therefore encourage one another with these words.

Paul isn't saying much here about the resurrection except its timing. There will be a resurrection, and the reason we know that is because Jesus, the example of true humanity, was raised from the dead. We believe in his resurrection, so we believe that he will also bring back to life all who believe in him, and this will happen when Jesus returns to earth. Christians who have died will rise, and Christians who are alive will be changed and rise into the clouds to meet the Lord as he returns, and we will be with him forever.

In 1 Corinthians Paul goes into more detail, explaining not only that there will be a resurrection, but he also comments briefly on what we will be like in the resurrected state. First, he compares the resurrection to the planting of a seed. The seed looks like a seed, but the plant that grows from it looks quite different, depending on what kind of seed it is (verses 37-38).

> So will it be with the resurrection of the dead. The body that is sown is perishable, it is raised imperishable; it is sown in dishonor, it is raised in glory; it is sown in weakness, it is raised in power; it is sown a natural body, it is raised a spiritual body. (verses 42-44)

After we are resurrected, we will be different, perhaps as different as a leaf is from a seed. The important differences are that we will be imperishable, glorious, powerful, and spiritual—and we will look like Christ:

> And just as we have borne the image of the earthly man, so shall we bear the image of the heavenly man. I declare to you, brothers and sisters, that flesh and blood cannot inherit the kingdom of God, nor does the perishable inherit the imperishable. Listen, I tell you a mystery: We will not all sleep, but we will all be changed—in a flash, in the twinkling of an eye, at the last trumpet. For the trumpet will sound, the dead will be raised imperishable, and we will be changed. For the perishable must clothe itself with the imperishable, and the mortal with immortality. (verses 49-53)

Here Paul is using a different figure of speech, that of putting on new clothes. The point that he stresses the most, the point that he mentions the most, is that we will be imperishable—our bodies will not deteriorate, and we will never die. We will have new, glorious bodies, transformed by the Holy Spirit to be like Christ.

Eternal significance

What significance does this doctrine have for us? The significance is that we will live forever—and not just live forever, but we will live forever with Christ—and not just that, but we will have glorious bodies that are like his, with power and glory and life that's far better than what we know now. There is a great reward waiting for us, a reward that far overshadows the difficulties we sometimes have in Christianity. The eternal reward is important. As Paul said, if faith is good for this life only, then it isn't good enough. But there is an afterlife, there is a resurrection, and there are wonderful rewards waiting for us. No matter what kind of sacrifices we make in this life, they are well worth making, because we will be given 100 times and more in the world to come. The resurrection is an important part of this picture.

Day-to-day significance

Our belief in the resurrection has important consequences for our day-to-day lives, too, as noted above. For example, knowing about the resurrection helps us deal with the difficulties and persecutions of believing in Christ when most people around us do not. When our life and ministry runs into problems, we do not just quit. We do not say, Let's eat and drink and be merry, because nothing really matters much. No, there is a future, and life does matter, and we want to live with our future in mind.

The doctrine of the resurrection goes hand in hand with the doctrine of the judgment. As Jesus said, some will rise to a resurrection of life, and others to a resurrection of judgment. God cares about the way we live. He has something to say about the way we live, and he will call us into account for the way we live. The gospel tells us that we will be accepted on the day of judgment—we will be found righteous through faith in Christ. The gospel is built on the reality of the resurrection and the judgment. The existence of the resurrection explains why the gospel is necessary, and why it is good news.

The gospel is good news not only for people

who believe, but also for people who do not yet believe. There is an infinite significance to the gospel. We are not talking about a few years of better feelings, or even 70 years of good things—we are talking about eternal life, an eternity that is infinitely better than anything this life has to offer. Whatever we do in serving Christ, whatever we do in supporting the gospel, is worth doing. It is important for all who need to hear the gospel.

The fact of the resurrection emphasizes the importance of sharing the good news with other people. This is the way Paul ends the resurrection chapter: "Therefore [because there is a resurrection], my dear brothers and sisters, stand firm. Let nothing move you. Always give yourselves fully to the work of the Lord, because you know that your labor in the Lord is not in vain" (verse 58). The resurrection is not just an interesting bit of trivia about the future—it has practical consequences for our lives today. It gives us reason to work, and reason to persevere through whatever difficulties we might face.

The resurrection is also relevant for day-to-day Christian conduct. We see this in Romans 6: "We were therefore buried with him through baptism into death in order that, just as Christ was raised from the dead through the glory of the Father, we too may live a new life" (verse 4). The resurrection to come means that we have a new life now, a new way of life. Paul explains in verse 6 that "our old self was crucified with him so that the body ruled by sin might be done away with, that we should no longer be slaves to sin"

Paul is talking about a change in behavior. When we identify ourselves with Christ, we put to death the deeds of sin. We put them out of our lives, and we walk and live in a new way, just as Christ was raised from the dead into a new life. So our behavior reflects the death and resurrection of Christ. Out with the old, and in with the new. In verses 11-13, Paul tells us,

In the same way, count yourselves dead to sin but alive to God in Christ Jesus. Therefore do not let sin reign in your mortal body so that you obey its evil desires. Do not offer any part of yourself to sin as an instrument of wickedness, but rather offer yourselves to God as those who have been brought from death to life; and offer every part of yourself to him as an instrument of righteousness.

Because there is a resurrection, we are to live in a new and different way. Instead of serving the desires of the flesh, we want to serve the Lord, because we will be with him forever. God's grace doesn't mean that he does not care about the way we live. He does care, he still makes commands, and understanding the resurrection helps us walk in newness of life.

As 1 John 3:2-3 says, "Dear friends, now we are children of God, and what we will be has not yet been made known. But we know that when Christ appears, we shall be like him, for we shall see him as he is. All who have this hope in him purify themselves, just as he is pure."

John goes on to say in verses 4-6 that when we live in Christ, we do not go on sinning. We quit. But if we do sin (as we all do), then we have a defense attorney standing by, Jesus Christ, and the atoning sacrifice has already been given for us. So there is no condemnation for us, but there is still the fact that people who believe in the resurrection also change the way they live. Knowing that we will live with Christ forever changes the way we live with him right now.

Last, knowing about the resurrection gives a new perspective to death. We know that death does not end it all; we know that we will see our loved ones again; we know that life will go on forever. Hebrews 2:14-15 tells us that Jesus shared in our humanity "so that by his death he might break the power of him who holds the power of death—that is, the devil—and free those who all their lives were held in slavery by their fear of death."

By knowing about the resurrection, we are freed from the fear of death. That enemy has been conquered, and we share in the victory that Christ has won! He has triumphed over death, and we share in his life, freed from the fear of death. As we read in 1 Thessalonians, we do not grieve like other people do. We still have grief (and that's OK, because death is still an enemy, even though a defeated enemy), but we have a hope that others do not have.

Knowledge of the resurrection helps us die faithfully, in hope and confidence for the future. We know that the best is yet to come. As 1 Thessalonians 4:18 says, "Therefore encourage each other with these words."

Joseph Tkach

We Are Living in 'The Last Days'

Do we see "the signs of the times"?

"Mark this," Paul wrote. "There will be terrible times in the last days" (2 Timothy 3:1). What do we see now? America at war. Shootings in our schools. Disasters in the weather. Is it all coming to a climax? Will World War III soon be upon us?

We are living in the last days! — and we have been for almost 2,000 years. The last days, said Peter, were already here in the first century (Acts 2:16-17). "In these last days," we are told in Hebrews 1:2, "God has spoken to us by his Son." "The last days" began with Jesus Christ! When Paul told Timothy about the last days, he was not so much predicting the future as describing his own day. He was telling Timothy what kind of world he lived in.

Wars and rumors of wars

Wars have always been with us. Natural disasters have plagued humanity for millennia. Societies have been breaking down, and violence has been erupting, for centuries.

"You will hear of wars and rumors of wars," Jesus said, "but see to it that you are not alarmed. Such things must happen, but the end is still to come" (Matthew 24:6). There will be famines and disasters, but those are only the beginning of problems. There will be persecutions, and there will be predictions. People will say, It is just around the corner, but do not believe it. Do not be alarmed. Just persevere. Just do the job set before you.

Someday, the end will indeed come. But the world has had many disasters since the last days began nearly 2000 years ago, and I am sure that there will be many more. God can end the world whenever he wants to, and I will be happy for the great day to come, but I do not see any biblical proof that it will be very soon.

Frankly, we need faith and hope whether or not there is a war, whether or not the end is near. We need faith and zeal no matter how evil the days are, no matter how many disasters strike near us. Our responsibility before God does not change with the times: Our job is to preach the gospel, to preach repentance and forgiveness, to teach those who believe, and to worship God.

When we survey the world scene, we may see disasters in Africa, Asia, Europe, and America. Or, if we look again, we may see fields white and ready for harvest. There is work to be done, as long as it is day. We must do the best we can with what we have. Where are we now in prophecy? We are now in the time in which the church should preach the gospel.

What should we do?

Jesus calls us to perseverance, to running with patience the race set before us. Paul likewise speaks of the end, when the children of God will be revealed, when all creation will be liberated from bondage (Romans 8:19-21). How then do we live? "We groan inwardly as we wait eagerly for...the redemption of our bodies" (verse 23). We are eager for the troubles of this world to be over, but we are also patient (verse 25).

Peter gives the same outlook. He also waited for the day of the Lord (2 Peter 3:10). What advice does he give us? "You ought to live holy and godly lives as you look forward to the day of God" (verses 11-12). That is our responsibility day in and day out. We are called to live holy lives, not to make predictions the Bible does not authorize us to make. We are to be faithful in our daily lives.

Nevertheless, in the last days there will be people with a veneer of godliness but denying the power of Jesus Christ. There will be people who deceive and are deceived, people who proclaim the end is near. Do not be alarmed; do not be deceived. Simply do what God has been telling his church to do for nearly 2,000 years: worship, teach and preach.

God will take care of the timetable — our job is to be found faithfully working, whenever the end happens to come. Correct predictions don't count for anything on the day of judgment — only faithfulness will be rewarded.

National and physical blessings

Nevertheless, some people seem anxious for the end to come. They would do well to heed the words of Isaiah:

> Woe to those…who say, "Let God hurry, let him hasten his work so we may see it. Let it approach, let the plan of the Holy One of Israel come, so we may know it."… Woe to those who are wise in their own eyes and clever in their own sight. (Isaiah 5:18-21)

The prophecy speculators often mix nationalism in with their prophecies. They are interested in the welfare of America specifically, as if Americans are in greater need of repentance than the Chinese are. They want national repentance so that God will "heal this land" and they can live in peace and safety. Many of them assume that if America obeys God, then we will reap the blessings God promised to ancient Israel.

Repentance is a good thing. It is good to have peace and safety, and I would enjoy such blessings just as much as anybody else. But I wonder how appropriate it is that we would want other people to repent so that *we* can enjoy physical blessings. Does not repentance begin at home, beginning with our self-centeredness? Shouldn't spiritual blessings for others be a greater incentive for us to want them to turn to God? Didn't Jesus tell us to be concerned about all nations, not just our own?

In this fallen world, God allows natural disasters, sins and evils. He also causes the sun to shine and the rain to fall on the bad as well as the good. As Job and Jesus show, he also allows evil to fall upon the righteous. This is the way God allows the world to function.

For the ancient nation of Israel, under a special covenant, God promised that if the nation was obedient, he would prevent the natural disasters that normally fall upon both the wicked and the righteous. He did not give that guarantee to other nations, nor did he say that other nations could elect themselves to a position of most-favored nation in his sight. Modern nations cannot claim as promises the blessings God offered specifically to Israel in a special covenant that is now obsolete.

The Bible makes no guarantees that even if all of America repents, that we will no longer have any troubles. The new covenant, the better covenant, offers spiritual life rather than guaranteeing physical blessings. By faith, we are to focus on the spiritual, not the physical.

Physical things are not wrong, and God does sometimes intervene in physical affairs to help us. But the new covenant does not make guarantees as to when and where he will do it. The new covenant calls us to faith despite the circumstances, to faithfulness despite persecution, to patience despite an eager longing for the better world that Jesus will bring.

Here is one more thought that may put prophecy into better perspective: Prophecy's greatest purpose is not to get us to focus on dates — it is so that we will "know the Lord." Prophecy is to point us to Jesus, the best of all possible blessings. Once we have arrived at our destination, we no longer need to focus on the path that brought us to him.

Joseph Tkach

Heaven

Do Christians go to heaven when they die? Paul said that when he died, he would go to be with the Lord (2 Corinthians 5:8; Philippians 1:23). Since the Lord is in heaven, that is where Paul would go, too. Some people say he's enjoying the presence of God. Others say he is unconscious. Either way, he is in heaven with Christ.

What is this place called heaven—or is it a place? Solomon recognized that heaven cannot contain God, and yet paradoxically it is his dwelling place (1 Kings 8:27-30). Although God is omnipresent, he is not present everywhere in the same way. He lives in believers, for example, in a way that he does not live in unbelievers. We "come into his presence" by becoming more aware of his presence.

Scripture shows that God, although he is everywhere, has chosen to dwell especially in heaven—or perhaps we should say that humans have used the word heaven to refer to the divine realm. Humans knew that God did not dwell on earth, nor in the underworld. They could not see God in the sky, either, but they often used the word for sky to refer to the location of God.

Many people had a simplistic understanding of God's location, and others would have been more sophisticated. Despite the misunderstandings and the limitations of human words, God inspired the writers of the Bible to use the words in Hebrew and Greek that are translated into English as "heaven" for the divine realm. Sometimes it refers to God himself, sometimes it refers to his glory, or his power, or his holiness. He is bigger than heaven, but "heaven" refers to his full presence.

Limits of language

Since God is spirit, words that suggest distance and space can be used only metaphorically. Heaven is neither up nor down, neither east nor west. It cannot be located on a three-dimensional map of the galaxies. So when people are worried about place, about whether Christians "go" to heaven when they die, they are struggling with terminology that isn't adequate to the task.

Our words can't do justice to spiritual realities. Take the trio of love, joy and peace, for example. The love of Christ surpasses knowledge (Ephesians 3:19). God gives us an inexpressible joy (1 Peter 1:8). And his peace transcends all understanding (Philippians 4:7). Words fail us when it comes to discussing these spiritual realities. If we can't even discuss love, joy and peace completely, how much more will we be limited when it comes to discussing the presence of God?

The Greek philosopher Plato created a parable that illustrates our limitations: There was a race of people who lived their entire lives in a cave. Their only contact with the outside world was shadows on the wall. They had only a monochrome, two-dimensional understanding of reality. Now suppose that one of the cave-dwellers was brave enough to venture out of the cave to discover the world of color, texture, smell, depth and density. How could the explorer explain these concepts to a people who had no experience with them? It would be impossible to describe the aroma of coffee, the concept of iridescence, or the warmth of sunshine. The sun would sound like bizarre fiction. An ocean tide pool would be weird beyond belief.

In the same way, we live in a limited world. We see only a fraction of reality. Though we may hear that a spiritual world exists, we cannot see it or investigate it. Those who leave this world to explore the afterlife never come back. Only Jesus has crossed the divide.

Only a few people have seen the glories of God.

"No eye has seen, no ear has heard, no mind has conceived what God has prepared for those who love him—but God has revealed it to us by his Spirit" (1 Corinthians 2:9-10). So we must acknowledge our inabilities when it comes to discussing our eternal future with God.

Spiritual reality

Heaven is in the realm of the spirit. When Paul says that God "has blessed us in the heavenly realms" (Ephesians 1:3), he is not talking about a place, nor about the future. He is talking about a spiritual reality—spiritual blessings right here and right now (same verse). When he says that we are seated with Christ in heavenly realms (Ephesians 2:6), he is not talking about a place. He is talking about spiritual realities: that our life and existence is now with Christ.

With Christ, we are able to enter heaven even before we die. "We have confidence to enter the Most Holy Place by the blood of Jesus" (Hebrews 10:19). We enter his presence not through physical transport, but in the innermost person, in heart and soul. It is a movement of the spirit, not of the body. It is a change in attitude, not in altitude.

Our citizenship is now in heaven (Philippians 3:20). We belong in the spiritual world. God is calling us heavenward, toward this reality (verse 14). Since that is where we belong, we need to focus on heavenly realities. It is our future, and it is our calling even today. We share in a heavenly calling; we have tasted a heavenly gift (Hebrews 3:1; 6:4). We have already come to a heavenly Jerusalem (Hebrews 12:22). These are spiritual realities.

A wonderful future

But there is much more to come. Although we have tasted the good things of God, we long for much more. Though we have glimpsed the goodness of God, we want to see it more clearly and more abundantly. We want to be saturated with his love and glory. Like Abraham, we long for a heavenly homeland (Hebrews 11:16).

We yearn to be with God, for him to satisfy our deepest desires. In 10,000 years, we will have only begun to learn his infinite wisdom and compassion. We have an eternity of joy in front of us. "You will fill me with joy in your presence, with eternal pleasures at your right hand" (Psalm 16:11). Words cannot describe how good it is. It is everlasting joy, blessed peace, and the righteousness of God (2 Peter 3:13).

Our inheritance is being kept for us in heaven (1 Peter 1:4). There are spiritual rewards waiting for us. There is an eternal "house" reserved for us in heaven (2 Corinthians 5:1; John 14:2-3). This will be our home, and that is why the word heaven is used for the eternal destiny of all God's redeemed children. To be in heaven is to remain in Christ in the presence of God. No matter where that is, it is called heaven, and we will be there.

"Meanwhile we groan, longing to be clothed with our heavenly dwelling" (verse 2). We are tired of the pains and sorrows and sufferings of this world. We "groan inwardly as we wait eagerly for our adoption as sons, the redemption of our bodies" (Romans 8:23). We wait eagerly, but patiently (verse 25), knowing that soon enough, there will be no more death, mourning, crying or pain (Revelation 21:3-4; 22:1-5).

In the resurrection, we will have a spiritual body (1 Corinthians 15:44). We will be like Christ in his resurrection (1 John 3:2). It will be heavenly. "Just as we have borne the likeness of the earthly man, so shall we bear the likeness of the man from heaven" (1 Corinthians 15:49). We will be people "of heaven" (verse 48).

The rewards of heaven will be ours to enjoy forever. Exactly when we start experiencing that glory is not very important. Our exact location is not very important. The important thing is that we will be with the Lord forever (1 Thessalonians 4:17). Even more important, it is through the Lord, and only through the Lord, that we can be there at all. It is only by grace that we can enter the kingdom of heaven.

But thanks be to God, for he has given us the victory. With Christ, our future is secure: "The Lord will rescue me from every evil attack and will bring me safely to his heavenly kingdom. To him be glory for ever and ever. Amen" (2 Timothy 4:18).

Joseph Tkach

No One Knows When Christ Will Return

The Bible nowhere tells us, directly or indirectly, when Jesus Christ will return. When Jesus returns is not as important as whether we are ready when he does. Yet people for nearly 2,000 years have constructed elaborate prophetic outlines that can distract people away from the gospel and crush believers' faith.

The early Christians' view

The earliest Christians apparently expected Jesus to return almost immediately. Just before his ascension to heaven, his disciples asked, "Lord, are you at this time going to restore the kingdom to Israel?" (Acts 1:6). They grossly underestimated how much time would pass before Jesus' return. As the disciples stood looking upward, two angels asked: "Men of Galilee…why do you stand here looking into the sky? This same Jesus, who has been taken from you into heaven, will come back in the same way you have seen him go into heaven" (verse 11).

Jesus' return was sure. The disciples didn't need to worry about when it would occur. God wanted them to stop gazing into the sky and get on with preaching the gospel.

The disciples' early epistles show the belief most of them had: that Jesus' return would be soon. For instance, Paul wrote of how "we who are still alive" would be caught up together with the resurrected saints at Jesus' coming (1 Thessalonians 4:15-17). Paul later softened this view and corrected Christians who, thinking time was short, had become idle busybodies (2 Thessalonians 2:1-2; 3:11).

The book of Revelation laid out a grand drama stretching till the end of time. This book included the thought that Jesus' return might be more remote than previously thought. The saints were to live and rule with Christ for 1,000 years (Revelation 20:4). Grasping the Bible's statement that a day is as 1,000 years (2 Peter 3:8), some saw an analogy between history and the seven days of creation. They concluded that the present age would run 6,000 years before a 1,000-year rest under Christ.

Prompted as well by Zoroastrian (Mandean) cosmology and the emphasis on the Psalmist's thousand-year days in 2 Peter 3:8, Christian theologians of the 2nd century A.D. transformed world history into a world week, and the seventh day thereof into the world sabbath, a jubilee of sweetness, peace, and earthly delight after six thousand-year days of human labor. (Hillel Schwartz, *Century's End* [New York: Doubleday, 1990], page 10)

Looking for a kingdom

For some time, Christians, including Justin Martyr (circa 100-165) and Irenaeus (circa 115-200), continued to look for Christ to set up a literal kingdom of God on earth. In the third century, Origen (185-254) asserted that the kingdom existed not in time or space but in believers' souls. "For a collective, millenarian eschatology Origen substituted an eschatology of the individual soul" (Norman Cohn, *The Pursuit of the Millennium* [New York: Oxford University Press, 1970], page 29).

By the fifth century, Christianity was the Roman Empire's official religion, and the church could no longer be seen as a "little flock" at odds with the world. Now Augustine (354-430) wrote *The City of God,* treating the book of Revelation as a spiritual allegory and saying the millennium was realized in the church. But believers went on embracing ideas like the "last days," the Antichrist and the warrior Christ who would physically return to conquer the world.

Warrior Christ vs. Antichrist

Believers fearfully watched for the evil Antichrist, with whom the returning Christ would war.

People were always on the watch for the "signs" which, according to the prophetic tradition, were to herald and accompany the final "time of troubles"; and since the "signs" included bad rulers, civil discord, war, drought, famine, plague, comets, sudden deaths of prominent persons and an increase in general sinfulness, there was never any difficulty about finding them. Invasion or the threat of invasion by Huns, Magyars, Mongols, Saracens or Turks always stirred memories of those hordes of Antichrist…. Above all, any ruler who could be regarded as a tyrant was apt to take on the features of Antichrist. (Cohn, page 35)

Popes were often associated with the Antichrist. So were the Muslims, who controlled the Holy Land and upon whom Europe's Crusaders descended in the 11th, 12th and 13th centuries. So were the Jews.

As the year 1000 approached, various teachers predicted that the world was about to end and that Jesus Christ would appear. An army of pilgrims sold their belongings and trekked to Jerusalem to await Christ. Terror filled them at every storm, comet and other event of nature. They fell to their knees at every crack of thunder, expecting the earth to open and give up its dead. Every meteor over Jerusalem brought Christians into the streets to cry and pray.

Dates that failed

More concerned with the *date* of Jesus' return than with how Jesus commanded his followers to live, prognosticators went on misreading prophecy:

- During the great plague of Europe (1348-1352), prophets said the end was at hand and that Christ would appear within 10 years.
- The Roman Catholic Church has often figured in end-time scenarios. For example, John Wycliffe, a 14th-century reformer, said the Catholic mass was Daniel's abomination of desolation.
- Martin Luther (1483-1546) believed the church's final conflict with evil would pit it against the Turks and the pope.
- John Knox, in 1547, saw the pope in Daniel 7:24-25.
- In 1806, at Leeds, a hen laid eggs bearing the words, "Christ is coming." Many visited the spot and "got religion." Then someone discovered that the ink-inscribed eggs had been forced up into the chicken's body.
- John Wesley said the end would come in 1836. Others suggested 1830 and 1847.
- Based on the text of Daniel 8:14, a New England farmer named William Miller expected the world to end in 1843 or 1844. His followers pinpointed Oct. 22, 1844. Unwilling to accept the Great Disappointment that resulted when Oct. 22 passed without Christ's return, some explained that Christ began to cleanse the "heavenly sanctuary" on that date. They gave birth to the Adventist movement.
- Charles Taze Russell, whose Bible studies formed the foundation of the Watchtower Bible and Tract Society, said Christ had returned to earth in 1874 and would begin his visible reign in 1914. Jehovah's Witness literature later spoke of "the Creator's promise of a peaceful and secure new world before the generation that saw the events of 1914 passes away."

Other failed speculations include those of Edgar C. Whisenant, who in 1988 listed *88 Reasons Why the Rapture Will Be in 1988* (when Christ failed to return, he predicted the rapture for 1989); a book produced in Georgia that placed the rapture on Oct. 8, 1992; and a Korean prophet's assertion that the rapture was set for midnight, Oct. 20 or 28, 1992. (In South Korea, 20,000 Christians left school or quit jobs to await the end.)

Differing views of the Millennium

For nearly two centuries, many fundamentalist and evangelical Christians have embraced a school of prophetic interpretation known as dispensationalism. Adherents teach that Bible prophecy pinpoints the route world events will take toward the return of Christ. His return will inaugurate his millennial rule on earth. Believers mine the apocalyptic significance of Daniel, Revelation and other Bible prophecies.

Early Christians were premillennialists. But by

the time of Augustine (354-430), the church concluded that the millennial period (which may or may not equal exactly 1,000 years) was not totally in the future. Jesus had already bound Satan, said the new orthodoxy, and the church already existed in an age of grace. Most Christians held this view, known as amillennialism, until after the Reformation. It is still the most common view.

During the 17th century, the Puritans asserted that the New Testament church fulfilled the Old Testament prophecies about Israel. The promises of Israelite (church) prosperity were realized in the Reformation. They looked for a worldwide revival of faith before Jesus returned. Many Protestants held to this postmillennialism for two more centuries.

Around the turn of the 19th century, some Christians saw the political and social chaos of the period as a signal that Christ would return soon. The Old Testament prophecies, many decided, referred to Israel and not the church. Thus some began to expect the Jews to return to Judea before Jesus' second coming.

Onto the scene stepped one of the most important propagators of dispensationalism: John Nelson Darby. He was born in London in 1800. Darby, an Anglican clergyman, became disturbed with apathy among Christians. Scholarship had begun to question the Bible and Christian beliefs. By 1828, Darby came to believe that the whole church was apostate. He believed that God has dealt with humanity through a series of different dispensations, or ages. He read Revelation as a prediction of events to occur at the end time.

Rejecting the optimism of both amillennialism and postmillennialism, he taught that the final cycle of prophetic events would begin with a secret, pretribulation rapture of believers. After this, the world would experience the Great Tribulation for seven years, culminating in the return of Christ.

Darby rejected the day-for-a-year idea. He taught that when the Bible said a day, it meant a day. So when Daniel wrote of the beast's 1,260-day rule, he meant three and a half years. Only after Christ's return would the Millennium unfold.

Satan's final rebellion, the resurrection of the dead and the final judgment would follow.

William Miller's work sank because he set dates and belabored one or two scriptures to the exclusion of others. Darby avoided these traps. Instead, he appealed to "the signs of the times" to insist that the end was near, without setting dates. He incorporated all the Bible prophecies into a large, complex system, reinforced with numerous proof-texts. Then he promoted his teachings through preaching and writing. Darby's teachings attracted thousands of British and U.S. Bible students who feared theological "liberalism" and who took special interest in Bible prophecy, particularly end-time scenarios.

The 20th century's towering figure in premillennialism was Cyrus Scofield. Convinced of Darby's dispensational scheme, Scofield published his *Scofield Reference Bible* in 1909. It combined the biblical text with detailed notes that set forth the dispensational view. Printing the notes on the same page with the biblical text made the notes seem to take on the same authority as the biblical text.

Scofield's teachings included a "gap" between Genesis 1:1 and 1:2, the identification of the "Gog" of Ezekiel 38 with Russia, predictions about the Jews' return to Judea and the teaching that true Christians would vanish at the rapture while deceived, "professed Christians" would follow the Antichrist into the Great Tribulation.

Scofield's Bible was revised in 1917, just when the British mandate over Jerusalem fueled the premillennialist belief that the Jews would return to their promised land. The *Scofield Reference Bible* went on to sell millions of copies throughout the world. Dispensationalism, with its emphasis on "literal" Bible interpretation and detailed end-time prophetic scenarios, remains the focus of millions of Christian evangelicals to this day.

Primary point of prophecy

Today's chaotic world almost begs us to look for cosmic significance in its developments. We yearn for Jesus to come and straighten out the mess. But prophetic speculation is still ill-advised in any year.

Prophetic misfires destroy faith. Timothy P. Weber wrote:

Many loyalists will be bothered to see how many times their teachers' minds have changed and how easily they have substituted one sure fulfillment for another... Many of the popular Bible teachers have missed the mark on numerous predictions, especially on the date for Christ's return. Yet they rarely explain or apologize; they just move along with newer, updated editions or different projections. ("If the Rapture Occurs, This Magazine Will Be Blank," *Christianity Today,* Jan. 11, 1993, pages 60ff.)

"The Lord is at hand"

If Christians of the first generation assumed that theirs was the generation that would witness the second coming, those of later generations have learned to be more cautious.... Each Christian generation...should live as though it might be the last one, while bearing in mind that Christians in the remote future may look back on the first 2000 years AD as the early period of church history. The second coming of Christ remains the hope of his people, as it is also the hope of the world (without the world's necessarily being aware of this); but its timing is not of the essence of the hope.

If one asks what, in that case, is to be made of the [New Testament] assurance that the Lord is at hand, an answer may be found in a sermon entitled "Waiting for Christ" by the 19th-century English preacher John Henry Newman. He pointed out that, before Christ's first coming, the course of time ran straight toward that event, but that since then the course of time runs alongside his second coming, on its brink. If it ran straight toward it, it would immediately run into it; but as it is, the great event is always at hand throughout the present era. The course of time will one day merge in the presence or parousia of Christ. If reckoned in terms of the succession of years, final salvation is nearer now than when Christians first believed; but personally, Christ is not nearer now than he was in NT times, and he is as near now as he will be when he returns.

There are times when the partition between his presence now and his coming parousia becomes paper thin; one day it will disappear completely and this mortal life will be swallowed up in the eternal order.... For each believer the partition disappears in the moment of death; at the last advent it will disappear on a universal scale. ("Second Coming of Christ," *Baker Encyclopedia of the Bible*).

Glossary

Millennialism. The belief in a period of the rule of Christ on earth. The most literal view understands this time as being 1,000 years.

Amillennialism. The belief that Christ is already ruling on the earth.

Premillennialism. The belief that Christ will return before his earthly reign.

Postmillennialism. The belief that Christ will return after an earthly reign that does not require his physical presence.

Norman L. Shoaf

About the Publisher

Grace Communion International is a Christian denomination with about 50,000 members, worshiping in about 900 congregations in almost 100 nations and territories. We began in 1934 and our main office is in North Carolina. In the United States, we are members of the National Association of Evangelicals and similar organizations in other nations. We welcome you to visit our website at www.gci.org.

If you want to know more about the gospel of Jesus Christ, we offer help. First, we offer weekly worship services in hundreds of congregations worldwide. Perhaps you'd like to visit us. A typical worship service includes songs of praise, a message based on the Bible, and opportunity to meet people who have found Jesus Christ to be the answer to their spiritual quest. We try to be friendly, but without putting you on the spot. Come and see why we believe the gospel is the best news there could be!

To find a congregation, phone us or visit our website. If we do not have a congregation near you, we encourage you to find another Christian church that teaches the gospel of grace.

We also offer personal counsel. If you have questions about the Bible, salvation or Christian living, we are happy to talk. If you want to discuss faith, baptism or other matters, a pastor near you can discuss these on the phone or set up an appointment for a longer discussion. We are convinced that Jesus offers what people need most, and we are happy to share the good news of what he has done for all humanity. We like to help people find new life in Christ, and to grow in that life.

Our work is funded by members of the church who donate part of their income to support the gospel. Jesus told his disciples to share the good news, and that is what we strive to do in our literature, in our worship services, and in our day-to-day lives.

If this book has helped you and you want to pay some expenses, all donations are gratefully welcomed, and in several nations, are tax-deductible. To make a donation online, go to https://www.gci.org/online-giving/. Thank you for letting us share what we value most — Jesus Christ. The good news is too good to keep it to ourselves.

See our website for hundreds of articles, locations of our churches, addresses in various nations, audio and video messages, and much more.

www.gci.org
Grace Communion International
3120 Whitehall Park Dr.
Charlotte, NC 28273
800-423-4444

You're Included...

We talk with leading Trinitarian theologians about the good news that God loves you, wants you, and includes you in Jesus Christ. Most programs are about 28 minutes long. Our guests have included:

Douglas A. Campbell, Duke Divinity School
Elmer Colyer, Dubuque Theological Seminary
Cathy Deddo, Trinity Study Center
Gordon Fee, Regent College
Trevor Hart, University of St. Andrews
George Hunsinger, Princeton Seminary
C. Baxter Kruger, Perichoresis
Paul Louis Metzger, Multnomah University
Paul Molnar, St. John's University
Cherith Fee Nordling, Northern Seminary
Andrew Root, Luther Seminary
Alan Torrance, University of St. Andrews
Robert T. Walker, Edinburgh University
N.T. Wright, University of St. Andrews
William P. Young, author of *The Shack*

Programs are available free for viewing and downloading at www.youreincluded.org.

Grace Communion Seminary

Ministry based on the life and love of the Father, Son, and Spirit.

Grace Communion Seminary serves the needs of people engaged in Christian service who want to grow deeper in relationship with our Triune God and to be able to more effectively serve in the church.

Why study at Grace Communion Seminary?

- Worship: to love God with all your mind.
- Service: to help others apply truth to life.
- Practical: a balanced range of useful topics for ministry.
- Trinitarian theology: a survey of theology with the merits of a Trinitarian perspective. We begin with the question, "Who is God?" Then, "Who are we in relationship to God?" In this context, "How then do we serve?"

- Part-time study: designed to help people who are already serving in local congregations. There is no need to leave your current ministry. Full-time students are also welcome.
- Flexibility: your choice of master's level continuing education courses or pursuit of a degree: Master of Pastoral Studies or Master of Theological Studies.
- Affordable, accredited study: Everything can be done online.

For more information, go to www.gcs.edu. Grace Communion Seminary is accredited by the Distance Education Accrediting Commission, www.deac.org. The Accrediting Commission is listed by the U.S. Department of Education as a nationally recognized accrediting agency.

Ambassador College of Christian Ministry

Want to better understand God's Word? Want to know the Triune God more deeply? Want to share more joyously in the life of the Father, Son and Spirit? Want to be better equipped to serve others?

Among the many resources that Grace Communion International offers are the training and learning opportunities provided by ACCM. This quality, well-structured Christian Ministry curriculum has the advantage of being very practical and flexible. Students may study at their own pace, without having to leave home to undertake full-time study.

This denominationally recognized program is available for both credit and audit study. At minimum cost, this online Diploma program will help students gain important insights and training in effective ministry service. Students will also enjoy a rich resource for personal study that will enhance their understanding and relationship with the Triune God.

Diploma of Christian Ministry classes provide an excellent introductory course for new and lay pastors. Pastor General Dr. Joseph Tkach said, "We believe we have achieved the goal of designing Christian ministry training that is practical, accessible, interesting, and doctrinally and theologically mature and sound. This program provides an ideal foundation for effective Christian ministry."

For more information, go to www.ambascol.org